Examining Education, Media, and Dialogue under Occupation

CRITICAL LANGUAGE AND LITERACY STUDIES
Series Editors: Professor Alastair Pennycook (*University of Technology, Sydney, Australia*) and Professor Brian Morgan (*York University, Toronto, Canada*)

Critical Language and Literacy Studies is an international series that encourages monographs directly addressing issues of power (its flows, inequities, distributions, trajectories) in a variety of language- and literacy-related realms. The aim with this series is twofold: (1) to cultivate scholarship that openly engages with social, political, and historical dimensions in language and literacy studies, and (2) to widen disciplinary horizons by encouraging new work on topics that have received little focus (see below for partial list of subject areas) and that use innovative theoretical frameworks.

Full details of all the books in this series and of all our other publications can be found on http://www.multilingual-matters.com, or by writing to Multilingual Matters, St Nicholas House, 31–34 High Street, Bristol BS1 2AW, UK.

CRITICAL LANGUAGE AND LITERACY STUDIES
Series Editors: Alastair Pennycook (*University of Technology, Sydney, Australia*) and Brian Morgan (*York University, Toronto, Canada*)

Examining Education, Media, and Dialogue under Occupation
The Case of Palestine and Israel

Edited by
Ilham Nasser, Lawrence N. Berlin and Shelley Wong

MULTILINGUAL MATTERS
Bristol • Buffalo • Toronto

This book is dedicated to Gail Weinstein. Your voice for peace is ever with us. May you finally find true peace knowing that those who stood beside you and learned from your example are carrying on your work.

Library of Congress Cataloging in Publication Data
A catalog record for this book is available from the Library of Congress.
Examining Education, Media, and Dialogue under Occupation: The Case of Palestine and Israel
Edited by Ilham Nasser, Lawrence N. Berlin and Shelley Wong.
Critical Language and Literacy Studies: 11
Includes bibliographical references and index.
1. Mass media and education--West Bank. 2. Mass media and education--Gaza Strip. 3. Education and state--West Bank. 4. Education and state--Gaza Strip. 5. West Bank--Relations--Israel. 6. Israel--Relations--West Bank. 7. Gaza Strip--Relations--Israel. 8. Israel--Relations--Gaza Strip. I. Nasser, Ilham, 1963- II. Berlin, Lawrence N. III. Wong, Shelley.
P96.E292W464 2011
306.43–dc22 2011015614

British Library Cataloguing in Publication Data
A catalogue entry for this book is available from the British Library.

ISBN-13: 978-1-84769-427-0 (hbk)
ISBN-13: 978-1-84769-426-3 (pbk)

Multilingual Matters
UK: St Nicholas House, 31–34 High Street, Bristol BS1 2AW, UK.
USA: UTP, 2250 Military Road, Tonawanda, NY 14150, USA.
Canada: UTP, 5201 Dufferin Street, North York, Ontario M3H 5T8, Canada.

The policy of Multilingual Matters/Channel View Publications is to use papers that are natural, renewable and recyclable products, made from wood grown in sustainable forests. In the manufacturing process of our books, and to further support our policy, preference is given to printers that have FSC and PEFC Chain of Custody certification. The FSC and/or PEFC logos will appear on those books where full certification has been granted to the printer concerned.

Typeset by Techset Composition Ltd., Salisbury, UK.

Contents

I. Nasser, L.N. Berlin and S. Wong

Part 1: Education

Part 2: Media

Contributors

Ahmad Atawneh has been teaching English at Hebron University since 1983. He obtained his MA in applied linguistics from the University of Wales, Bangor in 1983 as a British Council Scholar. He obtained his PhD from the State University of New York at Stony Brook in applied linguistics in 1991 as an Amideast Scholar. He held the positions of chair of the English Department at Hebron University, Dean of Arts and Academic Vice President for about 20 years. He published several papers in phonology, writing, sociolinguistics, culture and discourse analysis. Now he is leading the Masters program in Applied Linguistics, teaching and supervising Masters'dissertations.

Nader Ayish earned a BA in English from The Ohio State University, an MA in educational leadership from the University of Houston and a PhD in multilingual/multicultural education from George Mason University (GMU). An educator with over 21 years of experience, he has taught at the graduate school at GMU, American University (AU) and George Washington University as well as at an inner-city middle school in Houston. He has extensive international experience and has conducted cross-cultural training sessions for K–12 and university educators and international exchange students from the Middle East and Central and Southeast Asia. Nader currently teaches at GMU and AU as well as at a diverse middle school located outside of Washington, DC.

Zvi Bekerman teaches anthropology of education at the School of Education and the Melton Center, at the Hebrew University of Jerusalem. From 2003 to 2007 he was a Research Fellow at the Truman Institute for the Advancement of Peace, Hebrew University. His main interests are in the study of cultural, ethnic and national identity, including identity processes and negotiation during intercultural encounters and in formal/informal learning contexts. Since 1999 he has been conducting, a long-term ethnographic research project on the integrated/bilingual Palestinian-Jewish schools in Israel. He has also recently become involved in the study of identity construction and development in educational computer-mediated environments.

Lawrence N. Berlin is Professor of Teaching English as a Second/Foreign Language and Chair of Anthropology, Philosophy and TESL/TEFL at Northeastern Illinois University in Chicago. Having completed an MA in Teaching English to Speakers of Other Languages in the Foreign Languages Department at West Virginia University and an interdisciplinary PhD in Second Language Acquisition and Teaching at the University of Arizona, he is the author of several publications, including *Contextualizing College ESL Classroom Praxis* (2005, Routledge) and *Theoretical Approaches to Dialogue Analysis* (Ed., 2007, Max Niemeyer Verlag), as well as the founder of the organization 'Dialogue Under Occupation'.

Inas Deeb is the General Director of the Educational Department in the Hand in Hand Center for Jewish and Arab Education in Israel. She is in charge of the educational and pedagogical programs in the four Jewish and Arab Integrated schools. She also is a doctoral candidate at the School of Education in Bar-Ilan University. Her doctoral research is on Arab and Jewish children's conception of ethnic categories. Her areas of interest and research include the development of children's language, early literacy, cultural aspects of development and education and empowerment of educational professionals and organizations.

Nora H. El-Bilawi is a PhD student at George Mason University in Virginia. She has worked for several years as an instructor at GMU in the field of multicultural and multilingual education. Her main interest is developing teachers' awareness of intentional international mindedness in daily classroom instructions especially in the Middle Eastern context. The *War on Gaza* is her first academic publication. Additional research interests include the study of English for Speakers of Other Languages (ESOL) teachers' perspective on the use of multiple intelligences theory in diverse classroom settings. Her dissertation's focus is on teachers perspectives about the application of multiple intelligences in Middle Eastern context especially in Egypt.

Rabah Halabi obtained his PhD from the Department of Education at the Hebrew University. He conducted research on the development of the identity of the Druze minority in Israel. Later he worked as a lecturer in the same University at the Department of Education, and at Tel-Hai

Academic College. Dr Halabi was the head of the School for Peace Research Center for the last five years. He was the School for Peace Director at Neve-Shaloom/Wahat Alsalam for many years. He is the editor of a book on the School for Peace approach, *Israeli and Palestinian Identities in Dialogue* (2004), and the author of the book, *Druze Identity and the Jewish State: Citizens of Equal Duties* (2006).

Stephanie J. Kent, MEd, CI, received a Fulbright Grant in 2008–2009 for her doctoral research on the system of simultaneous interpretation at the European Parliament. She has published two chapters on the intercultural communication practice of simultaneous interpretation in the John Benjamins Translation Library (2007, 2009), several articles for professional sign language interpreting journals in the United States, United Kingdom and Germany, and a conference paper on Bakhtinian dialogism (2009). She is the lead author of an article on problematic moments in group dynamics and discourses appearing in *Radical Pedagogy* (2008). Stephanie has maintained a weblog, www.reflexivity.us, since 2003.

Anna Rita Napoleone holds a BA in Media-Communication from Hunter College, City University of New York and an MA in English from Long Island University-Brooklyn Campus. She is currently a PhD student in Rhetoric and Composition at the University of Massachusetts Amherst where she is working on her dissertation. Her research is focused on exploring intersections between affectivity and social class. She has an article in *Pedagogy*, in press.

Ilham Nasser is an Associate Professor in Early Childhood Education at George Mason University. She has spent over 25 years in teaching and research in different educational settings in the United States and the Middle East. She completed a PhD in Human Development and Child Study at the University of Maryland-College Park and worked for several years as a classroom teacher. She has researched and published on the topic of teacher development, including teachers' motivation, teacher preparation and professional development and teaching for peace with focus on foreign language teaching and bilingual education as a means to promote peace education in early childhood settings.

Nurit Peled-Elhanan teaches Language Education at the Hebrew University and at David Yellin Teachers College in Jerusalem. Her ongoing research since 1995 has been the discourse of education and especially racist discourse in the multicultural classroom and in Israeli textbooks.

Her latest study is The Representation of Palestinians in Israeli school-books. This study has produced five articles in refereed journals and a book (forthcoming: *Palestine in Israeli Schoolbooks: Ideology and Indoctrination*. TAURIS Publishers, London). She is the co-recipient of the 2001 Sakharov Prize for human rights and the freedom of speech, awarded by the European Parliament, which she shared with the late Professor Izzat Gazawi from Birzeit University. She is the founding member of the Russell Tribunal on Palestine (2009–to present) and a member of the Parents Circle – Palestinians and Israeli Bereaved Parents for Peace and Reconciliation.

Khawla Shakhshir is Professor of Education and served as Dean of Graduate Studies at Birzeit University, Palestine. She has also served as a consultant and academic evaluator in various missions with: United Nations Conference on Trade and Development (UNCTAD-Geneva), United Nations Development Program (UNDP), United Nations Children's Fund (UNICEF), American Near East Refugee Aid (ANERA), Associates in Rural Development Inc. (ARD), Save the Children, Palestinian Ministry of Education and UNICEF. Professor Shakhshir is the author of 15 research studies published in academic journals including: *Chemistry Teaching Journal, British Journal of In-Service Education, Research in Post-Compulsory Education Journal* and *Mediterranean Journal of Educational Studies*.

Julia Schlam-Salman is a PhD candidate at the School of Education and the Melton Center at the Hebrew University of Jerusalem. Her dissertation and research interests include English language education, English as a global language, second language acquisition and sociolinguistics. She currently teaches didactics and English as a foreign language at the David Yellin Academic College of Education. She is also an English teacher and English language coordinator at the Hand in Hand School for Arab Jewish Education in Jerusalem.

Razvan Sibii holds a BA in Journalism from the American University in Bulgaria. He has received an MA in Communication from University of Massachusetts Amherst in 2007, and he is currently working on his PhD dissertation in the same department, as well as teaching journalism courses as a full-time faculty member. His research focuses on issues of language and identity construction. His latest academic publication dealt with the student–professor relationship (2010, *Teaching in Higher Education*). He is also currently freelancing for a Romanian newspaper.

Sandra Silberstein is Professor and Director of the Master of Arts in Teaching English to Speakers of Other Languages (MATESOL) Program in the Department of English at the University of Washington. She earned her PhD in Linguistics from the University of Michigan and has served as editor of the *TESOL Quarterly*. Her books include *War of Words: Language, Politics, and 9/11* (2002/4), *Techniques and Resources in Teaching Reading* (1994) and the ESL readings texts *Reader's Choice* (2008) and *Choice Readings* (2nd edn in press) (with Clarke and Dobson), along with numerous articles on critical discourse analysis. She is interested in public rhetoric in times of national crisis and is working on a book on the languaging of war and occupation.

Gail Weinstein was a Professor in the English Department at San Francisco State University (SFSU) since 1992. Her field was the training of ESOL teachers, and her passion was the building of communities of learners around the world. She had recently launched CIRCLE (the Center for Immigrant and Refugee Community Literacy Education), whose mission is to strengthen immigrant families and communities. Gail's research and publications have focused on a range of issues in the ethnography of language and literacy, adult and family literacy in multilingual communities, and learner-centered education for community building. Her professional books include a guest-edited volume of *TESOL Quarterly* on adult literacies (1984); *Learners' Lives as Curriculum: Six Journeys to Immigrant Literacy* (1999) and *Immigrant Learners and Their Families: Literacy to Connect the Generations* (1993). Her adult ESL textbooks include *Collaboration and Stories to Tell Our Children* (1992).

Gail Weinstein died peacefully on December 9, 2010 at home after surviving ovarian cancer for five productive and happy years.

Shelley Wong is an Associate Professor at George Mason University in Multicultural/ESL/Bilingual Education. She received her BA at the University of California at Santa Cruz, an MA in Teaching English as a Second Language from University of California-Los Angeles (UCLA), and an EdD in Applied Linguistics from Columbia Teachers College. Shelley was President of Teachers of English to Speakers of Other Languages (TESOL, Inc.) and served on the Executive Committee of TESOL from 2007 to 2010. She is the author of *Dialogic Approaches to TESOL: Where the Ginkgo Tree Grows* published by Routledge/Taylor & Francis (formerly Lawrence Erlbaum).

Michal Zak has been working in political education since 1986. She is a member of the Arab-Jewish community Wahat Al-Salam-Neve Shalom and has been on the management team of its School for Peace for 22 years. She holds a bachelor's degree in Jewish philosophy and a master's degree from the Hebrew University. Her thesis was on the role and influence of language in encounters between groups in conflict. At the moment she is teaching a course on media and the conflict, at two teachers colleges in Israel, volunteers at the Center for African Asylum seekers in Israel, organizing vocational training courses for the community, and is a staff member of the Regional Council for the Bedouin Unrecognized villages.

Acknowledgements

We would like to acknowledge with gratitude the contributions of many friends and colleagues to this book. First we would like to thank the Al-Quds University, especially the Public Relations Director Rulla Jadallah-Afandi and her team for their generous spirit in hosting the Dialogue under Occupation Conference held November 2007 on the Al-Quds campus in Abu Dis, East Jerusalem. Many of the chapter authors for this volume first met at Al-Quds and we thank each of them for a fruitful collaboration. We would also like to thank the faculty, students and staff at Birzeit University and the teachers and principal in East Jerusalem at Dar Alawlad School (The House of Boys School) and the English and Linguistics professors and teachers in Nazareth, East Jerusalem and Ramallah for sharing their insights and experiences in teaching English. We would like to thank our series editors Alastair Pennycook and Brian Morgan and the anonymous reviewers for their insightful and supportive critical comments. Anna Roderick, Editorial Director from Multilingual Matters, who supported us with prompt answers to all our queries throughout the preparation of the manuscript. Shelley Wong and Ilham Nasser would like to acknowledge support of a grant from the George Mason University Office of the Provost. We would also like to thank our capable research assistants Nora Elbilawi and Maryam Saroughi. Lawrence Berlin would like to thank Northeastern Illinois University Provost, Lawrence P. Frank, for support of DUO I and DUO II. Last but not least we would like to thank our families; especially Mohammed, Carlos and Tyrone, for endless patience, good humor, intellectual and logistical support and love.

Preface

The Israel-Palestine conflict sits at the heart of many current global tensions. As Noam Chomsky (2011) has recently pointed out, one of the most obvious questions is why this has not been resolved. For some of the world's problems, it is hard to see a reasonable solution, yet many find hope for an end to this conflict, which continues to fuel immense resentment across the region, through the recognition of a two-state-solution and the creation of a viable and autonomous Palestinian state, as supported by the Arab League, most of Europe, the United Nations and international law. Every so often, that tantalising alternative of the one-state solution is discussed, a state in which Palestinians and Israelis (and others), Jews and Muslims (and others), Hebrew speakers and Arab speakers (and others) live and work together in a new version of the promised land, but this, we know, is probably the least likely of options. It has the support of many Israeli Arabs, who fear that the two-state option would further disenfranchise them (a one-state option renders them part of a potential Arab majority, a two-state option renders them a minority in a state which would likely acknowledge their rights even less than it does now), and very little support among Jewish Israelis, who quite rightly see such a proposal as potentially threatening the Israeli state as Jewish. Meanwhile, for many Palestinians, life is led under conditions of occupation: walls, checkpoints, harassment and humiliation are daily realities; it can take hours to get through the checkpoints between Ramallah and Bethlehem, or the old city of Jerusalem and Al-Quds University. Why has the two-state option not been finally realized?

To unravel that question is much harder. While the continued lack of resolution to this conflict, the occupation of Palestinian territory, the unrelenting construction of settlements, the lack of rights for Palestinians, represents a continuing injustice not just for Palestinians, but for Arabs and Muslims more generally, other Arab states have all too often overlooked the Palestinian struggle. At the time of writing, the region is going through a new period of turmoil, with Mubarak recently overthrown in Egypt. The longstanding deal between the USA and Egypt, which guaranteed support for that regime and stability in Israel-Egypt relations, has become less certain, but again it is unclear how the Palestinians may emerge from any new deal. And meanwhile, resolutions brought before the UN aimed at resolving the crisis and allowing for the creation of a Palestinian state have been vetoed by the USA. As recently as February 2011, the USA vetoed a UN resolution sponsored by 130 countries branding Israeli settlements illegal. The resolution reaffirmed 'that all Israeli settlement activities in the Occupied Palestinian Territory, including East Jerusalem, are illegal and constitute a major obstacle to the achievement of peace on the basis of the two-State solution' and condemned 'the continuation of settlement activities by Israel, the occupying Power, in the Occupied Palestinian Territory, including East Jerusalem, and of all other measures aimed at altering the demographic composition, character and status of the Territory, in violation of international humanitarian law and relevant resolutions' (United Nations Resolution 18 February 2011).

It is into this space that the authors in this book wish to bring the idea of dialogue. As the Norwegian Foreign Minister Jonas Gahr Støre (2011: 51) suggests, remarking on his own experiences of being in a Kabul hotel when two Taliban suicide bombers blew themselves and others up, or deciding to sit through Iranian President Mahmoud Ahmadinejad's 'vitriol-laden speech attacking the West and Israel' at the UN World Congress against Racism in 2009, 'I find it difficult not to conclude that strategies based on dialogue are indispensable and must be defended, and further strengthened.' As he goes on to argue, this does not mean dialogue with anyone on any topic, nor does it mean that dialogue can replace military force, economic sanctions and so forth, but it is nevertheless important 'to resist the temptation to disavow on moral grounds dialogue with any group or state whose ideology and aims we view as dubious or dangerous.' A group that has been named as a 'terrorist' group by some states should not necessarily be excluded simply on this basis. Should Western powers talk to Hamas? Although the Norwegian government is opposed to many of Hamas' actions and beliefs, and insists it must renounce the use of violence and recognize Israel's right to exist, they still also believe in the importance of dialogue since Hamas is 'a social, political, religious, and also a military reality that will not simply go away as a result of Western politics of isolation'. And with constituencies within Hamas potentially open to dialogue and possibly willing to support a two-state solution and recognize Israel's right to exist, dialogue may be the most important way to proceed.

When we talk of dialogue around the Israel-Palestine conflict, it is worth noting, of course, that is not just Palestinians and Israelis, Jews and

Muslims, who need to be involved in this dialogue: Secular and orthodox Jews need to be talking to each other; Zionists and non-Zionist diasporic Jews; settlers on Palestinian land and long-term occupiers of that land; Hamas and Fatah (who have indeed started to talk again in May, 2011), Likud and Kadima; Israeli human rights groups such as B'tselem and the Israeli military, peace activists and ex-soldiers (see Breaking the Silence, 2010); the Jewish and Palestinian diasporas, who as Said (1992) pointed out, could learn from each other's experiences of exile; the new Egyptian government and Jordan; the UN and the US; Christian Zionists (with their belief in Israel as the site of the *second coming* or the *end time*) and Coptic and Palestinian Christians. There are so many dialogues that need to happen in and beyond the region that it would be dangerous to suggest it is simply Israelis and Palestinians, especially if such labels are used to describe cohesive entities without many differences and divides within them. And there are many forces ranged against such dialogue, not least of which is the accusation of anti-Semitism when taking a pro-Palestinian stance (see Cockburn & St Clair, 2003) as well as the equal problem that a pro-Palestinian stance may indeed draw on the deeply anti-Semitic writing that spills across the internet and elsewhere in all its ugliness.

In making his case for dialogue in international relations, Støre is talking, of course, of diplomacy, of high level peace talks, of negotiations over military options, blockades and people's rights. But what, we might want to ask, could dialogue and pedagogy at a much more local level of social action possibly do that UN Resolutions and diplomatic discourse cannot? And here we enter one of those crucial ways of understanding the role of applied linguistics in the world. As with Higgins and Norton's (2009) book in this Critical Language and Literacy Studies series, work around HIV/AIDS cannot be left only to governments, health organizations and medical workers. Rather than those top-down medical, technical and scientific interventions, the authors in that book show how we need to be immersed in the lives of those with experience of HIV/AIDS, and why intervention therefore needs to operate through language, literacy and education. This is why applied linguistics, at least at its more critical boundaries, matters not just as a pursuit of knowledge about language in context but rather as a form of political action. Reviewing the Higgins and Norton book, Gael Fonken (2010: 126) suggests that 'Applied Linguistics doesn't get better than this'. The editors and authors of *Examining Education, Media and Dialogue: The Case of Palestine and Israel* are likewise attempting to intervene into this political space. Behind this book, lies the idea of activist conferences held in regions deemed under occupation in order to foster dialogue between different parties. A number of years ago, a group of us discussed a similar idea of activist language rights confer-ences around the world, and started to sketch out plans for a language rights conference in Turkey with a special focus on Kurdish rights. Neither that conference, nor those rights, unfortunately, came to fruition, and these editors are to be applauded for doing the hard work of getting conferences together in difficult conditions for political purposes. The next one (in 2011) is to be held in Okinawa, Japan, where the US military maintains a massive and obtrusive occupying presence.

Of course, as the authors acknowledge, dialogue is only one possible strand amongst many that might lead to the 'undoing of occupation,' but they make a good case here that dialogue can lead to change, new ways of thinking and peaceful resolution. Part of this focus is on the roles that education and various media play in the maintenance of oppression and occupation, and their potential, if used differently, to become a tool and a site for change. Dialogue itself as a tool of critical educational practice is also an idea that requires care. As Roger Simon pointed out a number of years ago, both the notion of voice and the notion of dialogue (the engage-ment with voice) are often treated trivially:

> the concept of a dialogic pedagogy is perhaps one of the most con-fused and misdeveloped ideas in the literature on critical teaching. At a simplistic level it has been taken as a process within which a student 'voice' is 'taken seriously' and in this respect is counterposed to a transmission pedagogy. But this is both a vague and trivial statement. (Simon, 1992: 96)

The editors and authors of this book, however, have bravely tried here to set out some of the ways in which dialogue can happen, in which change can occur through education or critical examination of the media.

The book leaves us, unsurprisingly, with many further questions: what role can and should English play amid all this? Can a language that is neither Hebrew nor Arabic play a mediating role, or do its deeper connec-tions to other global hegemonies always compromise such mediating possibilities? How can we start to get beyond the insidious Arab/Jewish binary? How can all those other discourses, by peace activists, grassroots activists, and others be heard amid the discourses that dominate this con-flict? What kinds of dialogue are possible when the relations of power that constitute the discourses are so uneven? What can be learned from other struggles and dialogues elsewhere in the world? Many of these questions are, as they should be, left hanging in the air. In the writing of this book, the authors and editors have been dialoguing extensively with each other. There has also been considerable dialogue with us as series editors. Finally, it is time to see what kinds of dialogue emerge between this book and its readers. We invite people to read and engage with the ideas here.

Alastair Pennycook
Brian Morgan

References

Breaking the Silence (2010) *Occupation of the Territories: Israeli Soldier Testimonies 2000–2010.* Jerusalem.

Chomsky, N. (2011) *Power and Terror: Conflict, Hegemony and the Rule of Force.* London: Pluto Press.

Cockburn, A. and St Clair, J. (eds) (2003) *The Politics of Anti-Semitism.* California: CounterPunch.

Fonken, G. (2010) Review of Higgins, C. and Norton, B. (eds) Language and HIV/AIDS. *Applied Linguistics* 32, 122–126.

Higgins, C. and Norton, B. (eds) (2009) *Language and HIV/AIDS.* Bristol: Multilingual Matters.

Said, E. (1994) *The Politics of Disposession.* London: Chatto and Windus.

Simon, R. (1992) *Teaching Against the Grain: Essays Towards a Pedagogy of Possibility.* Boston: Bergin & Garvey.

Støre, J.G. (2011) Why we must talk. *The New York Review of Books.* LVIII, 6 April 7–27, 51–54.

United Nations (2011) On WWW at http://unispal.un.org/UNISPAL.NSF/0/9397A59AD7BFA70B8525783F004F194A.

Maps

Map of Occupation of Palestinian Lands

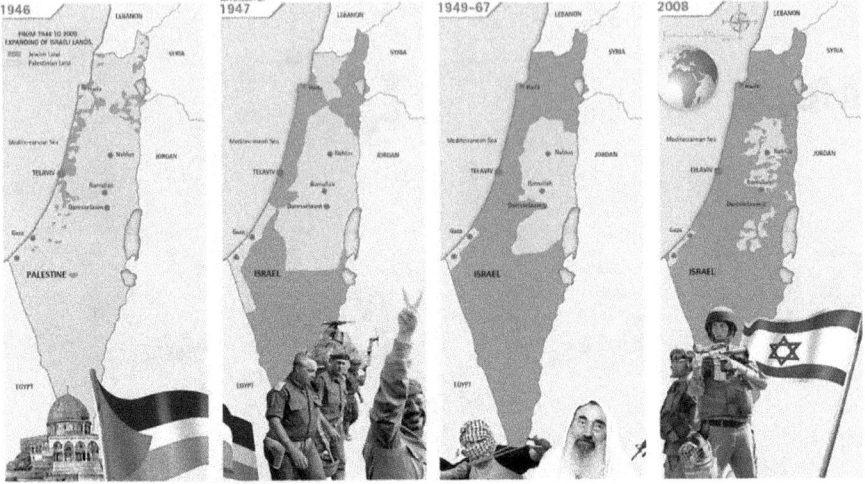

Introduction

I. NASSER, L.N. BERLIN and S. WONG

The purpose of *Examining Education, Media and Dialogue: The Case of Palestine and Israel* is to address the reality of occupation through the domains of *education* and the *media*, while focusing on and problematizing the *dialogues* expressed within and emerging from those domains. In order to undertake the examination, the editors have established a framework for analysis consisting of four strands, identified as enactment, transaction, reaction and resolution. Enactment is the strand where policies regarding occupation are initiated – typically the governing bodies that control and regulate societies and utilize whatever means available to them, education as one of its systems and media as an ostensible partner to exploit and disseminate its policies. Transaction looks to the core of education – the classroom – where ideologies are transmitted, either directly or indirectly (e.g. through declared and hidden curricula and teacher beliefs and practices); and media, its transaction with the public is located in the scripted and shared word, a version of a story that can corroborate a governing body's perspective or refute it. Reaction is the immediate response by the public living under occupation; in the case of this book, the reaction addressed is that of teachers and students to the educational system and that of the recipient public to the broadcast or print media.

Ultimately, *Examining Education, Media and Dialogue: The Case of Palestine and Israel* addresses all three components in the Palestinian-Israeli context and looks at dialogue as a way to take steps toward the final strand: resolution. By presenting difficult issues and being reflective about them, the authors of the chapters in this book have also engaged in dialogue in the sense of Habermas (1971) where 'what raises us out of nature is the only thing whose nature we can know: language' (Habermas, 1971: 314). To that extent, the authors have read and commented on each other's chapters in the preparation of this manuscript, seeking to reveal sources of occupation and/or its reinforcement, and ultimately suggesting that the development of an awareness of where occupation is rooted can provide support to its undoing. We are aware that undoing occupation happens on multiple levels and requires different types of interventions, but we believe that dialogue can promote change and mobilize new thinking and analysis of roots of occupation and ways to peacefully overcome it. To accomplish this, the authors attempt to address the strands and identify how education and media can maintain the status quo of oppression and occupation when used and utilized to do so by policy makers and governments and can also be utilized as mechanisms for change and peace-making. These contradictory roles are highlighted throughout this book by multiple voices from multiple countries and backgrounds.

The Context

The Israeli-Palestinian conflict has occupied the public arena and defined the discourse of the Middle East for over a century. It is one of those conflicts where the lines between the oppressed and oppressor are confused and easily manipulated. In 1917, when the British Foreign Minister promised the land of Israel for the Jews, a new era started and was marked by critical events and wars, resulting in a whole population of Palestinians living on that land being displaced either by becoming refugees in neighboring Arab countries or in other villages and towns. Those who remained witnessed the start of the Israeli occupation of greater Palestine which followed years of occupation under the Ottoman Empire and the British Mandate (Bennis, 2007).

Israel was established as the homeland for the Jewish people who had been persecuted for generations, culminating with their imprisonment and virtual annihilation by the Nazis in World War II. After World War II, the United Nations stepped in as the British gave up their League of Nations' Mandate over Palestine (Bennis, 2007). The UN Special Commission on Palestine, or UNSCOP recommended the partition of Palestine. The United Nations Resolution of 1947 partitioned Palestine, providing 55% of the former British Mandate to the new State of Israel, leaving 45% for a future Palestinian state. But the Palestinian state never came into existence and the new Israeli Jewish state by the end of the 1948 war had already taken over 78% of the land, far more than the 55% allocated by the United Nations (see maps above of Israel and Palestinian loss of land). Thus, while the creation of the state of Israel resulted in creating a long awaited home for the Jewish people, it simultaneously resulted in the displacement and subsequent subjugation of a whole population of natives of the same land.

Several attempts were made by the Palestinians to resist the occupation utilizing all means available, including engaging in nonviolent as well as violent means of resistance ever since the establishment of Israel.[1] The ongoing conflict between the Palestinians and Israelis has changed the politics of the region and the reality of the people in that part of the world. Through the enactment of Israel as a new state and the transacting of identities, settlement begat resettlement and placement produced displacement (e.g. confiscation of land, mass killing and destruction of 400 villages in 1948 alone). Today, the hostility has continued and escalated with no definitive resolution on the horizon. Many books have been written on the political reality of the conflict, but few focus on education, media and dialogue, especially as means to address contradictions in the conflict while attempting to negotiate peace and justice in occupied contexts.

A number of chapters in this book analyze education, media and dialogue from theoretical frameworks of postcolonialism (see e.g. Wong & Nasser, and Halabi). Of importance in the historical context is to identify the ways that the former colonized are divided against one another by the colonial masters who leave a legacy of divide and rule as a feature of the postcolonial condition. In dealing with the contested geography of Palestine and the history of why with the establishment of Israel, the land was partitioned in 1948, the renowned Columbia University professor of literature, Edward Said pointed out:

> How for instance, do you deal with more than one people who say that this is our land? The habitual, imperial legacy has been what they call 'divide and quit.' You leave a place, but then you divide it, as the English did in India, as they did in Palestine, as they did in Ireland as they did in Cyprus, and as NATO and the United States is now doing in the Balkans.[2] (Said, 2000: 437)

This is true in the example of understanding the historical context of the various Palestinian communities and the narratives of the authors. We cannot truncate what is going on today without understanding the colonial past from the end of the Ottoman Empire to the British Mandate.

The current volume has attempted to address some of these contradictions head on. In one example, *naming* was a central topic of discussion between different authors of this book who used different ways of describing the populations they address in their chapters. A question that emerged from the dialogue was '*What should go first, 'Israel' or 'Palestine'?*' A few of the chapter contributors posed whether the order was a trivial question or whether it mattered, but the majority agreed that naming *is* important. However, in contrast to formal structural approaches to language which analyze language as an abstract system, Bakhtin (1981) stresses the *social* and the *ideological* nature of language:

> Linguistics and the philosophy of language acknowledge only a passive understanding of discourse ... it is an understanding of an utterance's *neutral signification* and not its *actual meaning*. (Bakhtin, 1981: 281)

Bakhtin's (1981, 1986) conception of language, then, provided a way to address the question when there is a power differential between the parties, in this case between the positioning of the two names signifying the powerful and the powerless. For Bakhtin, all actual meaning is active. The speaker's meaning is always in relation to the listener; all utterances are dialogic:

> In the actual life of speech, every concrete act of understanding is active: it assimilates the word to be understood into its own conceptual system filled with specific objects and emotional expressions, and is indissolubly merged with the response, with a motivated agreement or disagreement. To some extent, primacy belongs to the response, as the activating principle: it creates the ground for understanding; it prepares the ground for an active and engaged understanding. Understanding comes to fruition only in the response. Understanding and response are dialectically merged and mutually condition each other; one is impossible without the other. (Bakhtin, 1981: 282)

Ultimately, it was decided that it was important and symbolic to mention Palestine before Israel to highlight the legitimate quest for Palestinian self-determination, a right that Israelis have already attained.

The role of education in creating change and transforming students is another important aspect to consider when addressing issues of language, language policy and power and how they all shape the curriculum and kind of schooling children receive in Israel and Palestine. Contributors to Part 1 share their experiences around bilingual education, teaching English as a foreign language and the influence curriculum has on shaping students' opinions and knowledge about the conflict. The influence of the media and mostly mainstream media in shaping opinions about the Middle East has been documented in the United States and abroad. Contributors to Part 2 address the reporting on the Middle East by US, Israeli and Arab-Palestinians media sources. Lastly, dialogue (Part 3) has been a major mechanism in people's attempts to transform others and share their narratives. Contributors to this part examine the role dialogue plays in promoting understanding and removing barriers for communication among different sides of conflict.

The Education Domain

Part 1 of the book includes original work on educational initiatives. It is well documented that education has always been identified as a mechanism for change and betterment of people's lives in developing regions of the world. In Palestine and Israel, education plays a role in the indoctrination of the masses and shaping up their views about the conflict. Education also plays a role in shifting these views related to the conflict between Palestinians and Israelis, its roots, sources and major players. Education is as influential in doing so as the roles that media and dialogue play. One can detect the state of affairs between both people based on what is happening in the educational arena. In the short periods of peace between both, schools and students were invested in and improved, but in times of hostility schools in Palestine were closed, destroyed and abandoned and schools in Israel were distancing themselves from the political happenings and being impacted by the hostility between both people.[3]

The Palestinian as well as the Israeli curricula went through massive revisions right after the Oslo accords. The establishment of the Palestinian Ministry of Education in 1994 was a step toward revising and constructing a new Palestinian curriculum of study in different content areas. Both sides aimed at educating for democracy, human rights and respect for others. For years both sides, especially the Palestinian with large financial support from the European Union, Israel, and the United States, attempted to reeducate the population to live in peace, to respect and tolerate and to prepare for new generations of children and teachers. Unfortunately this process was cut off by the eruption of the second Intifada in the year 2000 which was evoked *not only* by the famous visit of Sharon (former Israeli Prime Minister) to the holy site of the Dome of the Rock in the city of Jerusalem (in the year 2000), but also by the failure of the peace treaties to deliver change for the Palestinians.

Education is critical for civic development for populations under occupation, especially in Palestine where high motivation for learning already exists. A UNESCO report states that educational development in Palestine is 'unique because it is one of the very few places in the world, if not the only one, where a Ministry of Education is being built from scratch,[but] rich because of the eagerness and motivation of the Palestinians to learn from others [and]challenging because Palestine is not yet an independent country and is witnessing conflict on a daily basis' (http://www.unesco.

org/education/news_en/131101_palestine.shtml). This same report states that Palestinians are highly motivated to learn and about a third of the Palestinian population is comprised of students at various levels of education. The Ministry of Education in the Palestinian Authority is one of the few functional ministries in Palestine to date.

Part 1 also addresses several matters related to education and provides multiple perspectives on those from theoretical inquiries to practitioners' reflections and analysis of the field. It introduces an examination of the role of bilingual education and other innovative models to use education as a change mechanism and to have an impact on people's thoughts and ideas. It also provides general information on the status of education under occupation, and a close examination of textbooks and curricula and ways in which they shape students' opinions about the conflict.

The uniqueness of Part 1 is in its detailing of educational issues related to separated communities of Palestinians, those inside Israel who carry Israeli passports and are legal citizens of Israel (about 20% of the population of Israel); those in East Jerusalem who have residency rights, but are not citizens (they are under Israeli occupation as far as the Palestinians are concerned); and those in the West bank and Gaza who are under Israeli occupation.

Part 1 begins with an informative chapter on the state of education and the impact the conflict has on the challenging development of an educational system in Palestine. Shakhshir provides the reader with an insider perspective on the challenges facing Palestinian students in higher education, as well as young children in K–12 education. Shakhshir examines the impact of school closures, the separation wall and withheld taxes on students' lives. Perhaps more importantly, though, she highlights the aspiration of Palestinians and the importance of education for them. She also describes gains made in the education of women and girls despite the occupation. Shakhshir shares the results of her study among Palestinians in the occupied West Bank and East Jerusalem.

Deeb and Weinstein share the experiences teachers had telling their stories in two locations across the globe. The model, 'learners' lives as curriculum', created by Weinstein in the United States and implemented with immigrant children in the United States and then tried in Israel amongst a group of Israelis and then followed 10 years later by a Palestinian teachers' group from Hebron (in the West Bank) posed too many challenges when it was implemented in East Jerusalem, especially those issues related to the realities of students and teachers in the divided city. This chapter reveals the importance of the context and adjusting curricula to fit the local realities of teachers and their students. It is a product of multiple dialogues between the authors in an effort to analyze what worked and what did not, and the potential reasons for that. It is also a dialogue between a Palestinian and a Jewish American author looking for ways to collaborate.

Wong and Nasser take a closer look at teacher training and the lens in which they both attempted to learn about this issue of teaching English as a foreign language in Palestine. In 'Positionalities and Personal Perspective on Educational Research under Occupation' the authors testify to the creation of an apartheid regime and what they saw to support that. They discuss the application of Said's concept of 'Orientalism' in their own attempt to conduct research in the context of conflict. They saw firsthand the separation policies of Palestinians that Israel has imposed since 1948 and how they are applied in the four distinct regions they visited during their study in Palestine: (1) the Palestinian community within Israel; (2) the Palestinians in East Jerusalem; (3) the Palestinians under occupation in the West Bank and (4) the Palestinians in Gaza whom they were unable to reach because of the physical closure of the area.

In 'Emancipatory Discourse? An Ethnographic Case Study of English Language Teaching in Arabic-Hebrew Bilingual School,' Schlam-Salman and Bekerman provide many vivid examples of exchanges between Jewish-Israeli and Palestinian Israeli students learning English as a foreign language. The authors state that an 'in-depth study of linguistic behavior can enrich our understanding of identity negotiation processes and minimize the often politically delineated categorizations'. In fact, the exchanges and negotiation of who is who illustrate the identity formation going on and provide a rich context for the formation of political identities and students' own understanding of that. The process is heightened in Arabic-Hebrew bilingual schools where issues are brought up and students are exposed to curriculum addressing both people's cultures and society. The exploration is unique to schools operating to promote respect and understanding through the teaching of language and bilingual education. Adding English as the language of dominance and power in this mix provides a complex reality in which English might function as an empowering and emancipatory language.

'The Presentation of Palestinians in Israeli Textbooks' provides an in-depth analysis of how Palestinians are introduced to Jewish Israeli students in textbooks used in K–12 schools. Nurit Peled-Elhanan provides a critical view of the information provided to students in Israel about the events leading to Israel's independence and the conflict between the two people. She builds the argument that Israeli education promotes racism toward Palestinian Israelis, as well as all other groups of Palestinians.

Peled-Elhanan takes the reader through her provocative and challenging analysis of history and geography schoolbooks used to educate generations of Israeli students. The verbal and visual representations of Palestinians are examined closely by the author to support the argument for the power of textbooks in shaping people's views, perceptions and memories of the other. The author also takes a closer look at how maps and language are used to address Israel or 'the land of Israel', which usually refers to the biblical reference to the land that includes all areas of Palestine and greater Syria. She also provides an illustration of the exclusion of Palestinians from the Israeli narrative. In addition she uncovers evidence about how Israel relates to Palestinians under occupation as 'the Palestinian problem' with the intention to exclude. Textbooks, Peled-Elhanan concludes, are political tools 'to persuade readers and listeners to accept interpretation as fact or truth, thereby putting the disciplinary politics of truth at stake' (Peled-Elhanan, this volume: 90).

The Media Domain

The chapters in Part 2 examine media in the case of Palestine under occupation from various perspectives. The last chapter of Part 1 (Peled-Elhanan, this volume) presents a *bridge* from the field of education to the field of media in at least three ways: (1) the *medium* of Israeli history and geography schoolbooks are analyzed with respect to the construction of a Jewish-Israeli national identity in which Palestinians are presented as 'Other' (Said, 1997) and the indigenous Palestinian narrative is erased; (2) critical discourse analysis tools present a multimodal analysis (Halliday, 1978; Kress & van Leeuwen, 1996; Reisigl & Wodak, 2001) and of oral, written and visual schoolbooks (and more broadly curriculum) in which identity is constructed through 'everyday racist discourse' and the 'Palestinian problem' is naturalized; (3) media serves to legitimize Israeli military occupation, killing and expelling of the indigenous population. In Chapter 6, Nader Ayish challenges us to consider the effect of stereotypes in the media on Palestinian Americans and more broadly in the US context, Arab American and Muslim American students. As a Palestinian American educator based in US public schools, Ayish asks how it is possible 'for a place, Palestine, and a people, the Palestinians, to be so highly visible in popular culture, yet at the same time remain so seemingly invisible to the typical American' (Ayish, this volume: 97). Ayish offers three areas as an explanation for the level of miss-information concerning Palestinians: (1) a psychological explanation; (2) the conflation of Palestinians, Arabs and Muslims into one 'other' in popular culture and (3) an absence of accurate and comprehensive information about Palestinians and the Israeli-Palestinian conflict in Kindergarten through Grade 12 (K–12) curriculum. In analyzing the complex reasons why dehumanizing Palestinian stereotypes persist, Ayish sees curriculum and dialogue as a way to critique media stereotypes for a comprehensive shift in thinking that is necessary for meaningful and sustained change in people's thinking about Palestinians.

Ahmad Atawneh utilizes Critical Discourse Analysis to compare a corpus of statements to the press by Israeli and Palestinian political leaders in 'The Language of Occupation in Palestine.' Atawneh utilized Vaughan's (1995) model developed to analyze media during the war in Lebanon in 1982. Vaughan used newspaper editorials to analyze key words to support arguments, and imagery and metaphors concerning war and peace. Like Vaughan, Atawneh utilizes critical discourse analysis to show the asymmetry in power relations between the Israelis and Palestinians which enables the Israelis to make threats, insult and justify killing.

'The War on Gaza: American and Egyptian Media Coverage' by Nora H. El-Bilawi also employs Critical Discourse Analysis to compare mainstream US and Egyptian Media coverage and adds a new dimension which is to situate the analysis within the contemporary historical context. El-Bilawi draws from those in communication and media studies (Schwartz, 2008) who have identified a dynamic metamorphosis of media in the contemporary global economy or what James Gee and others call 'fast-track' capitalism. El-Bilawi frames her analysis within the context of the transformation of the media itself in the 21st century in which the 'new global media bring images from around the world into our living rooms to make the world smaller' (El-Bilawi, this volume: 129). She also draws our attention to significant trends such as (1) privatization of television, (2) deregulation of media ownership, and (3) the rise in new media giants who have control over networks of information (Schwartz, 2008). El-Bilawi utilizes media framing, narrative theory, news de-contextualization and dramatization to explain how US public opinion is shaped and altered.

In 'Language and the Art of Spin: Commendation and Condemnation in Media Discourse' Lawrence N. Berlin also uses critical discourse analysis tools to analyze transcripts from live news broadcasts of Al-Manar, the news source of Hezbollah, located in Lebanon, and CNN World Middle East edition. Perspectives toward the Israeli-Palestinian conflict (in the second Intifada) are compared to reveal a multimodal analysis. Intifada refers to resistance, ostensibly justified to aggressors or in the case of the Palestinian territories, more generally to occupiers. Berlin's multimodal analysis differentiates at multiple levels, not only in the texts themselves, but in the interactions between broadcasters and their respective listening and viewing audiences, who tend to present the dominant ideologies of their respective regimes. The theme of the 'other' is a major difference in the two news sources, with Al-Manar tending to identify the individuals responsible for making statements and personalizing them in the account. In contrast, CNN referring to 'factions' generally refer to the Palestinians as 'terrorists', justifying the use of this term with a disclaimer that the groups themselves have claimed responsibility for the attacks on Israelis. Berlin's critique of bias in journalism, and his analysis that media is largely responsible for creating ideologies, or at the very least, 'spinning' and in turn, influencing public opinion, challenges us to consider the implications of media for the two other parts of our book, education and dialogue. As educators, how can applied linguists and language teachers encourage students to critically view the media? How can news sources be utilized to present multiple perspectives, particularly those that the mainstream media excludes: the human faces, names and voices of Palestinians under occupation?

Focus on Dialogue Domain

The concept of dialogue has taken on expanded use in contemporary society to the extent that the original meaning of the word becomes less and less clear as speakers use it to stand for an ever-widening range of ideas. Consider, for example, the functional shift that has occurred wherein *dialogue* has come to be used as a verb which simply signifies *to converse*. In modern use, then, it is both a noun and a verb, a basic conversation (spoken or scripted), and an attempt to engage others through spoken language. It can be synonymous with the most mundane discussion between two people about the weather and as purposeful as a means employed between polities to resolve conflict and negotiate peace. Thus, through generalized use, the intent of dialogue is often misunderstood. It therefore becomes incumbent on us, the contributors to this volume, to explain how we understand dialogue and even more specifically how we intend dialogue under occupation.

The original Greek (διαλοζος) breaks down into two components – 'dia-' and 'logos' – which together can be roughly translated to mean 'through words' (Berlin, 2007). Such a straightforward translation appears to coincide with Habermas' (1971) notion surrounding the use of language to raise us out of the basest of human nature, but his theory of communicative competence (1970; Hymes, 1966, 1971) also recognizes 'an unlimited interchangeability of dialogue roles demands that no side be privileged in the performance of these roles' (Habermas, 1971: 367). The *Merriam-Webster Dictionary of American English* defines *dialogue* (when used in the sense of spontaneous spoken discourse) as follows '2a: a conversation between two or more persons; b: an exchange of ideas and opinions; c: a discussion between representatives of parties to a conflict that is aimed at resolution'. It is this essential, yet gradually more and more complex understanding that we will use for our purposes herein. In Part 3, dialogue is presented as a complex concept, requiring certain elements. Those elements roughly parallel Webster's definition and are broadly defined according to (1) the participants, (2) the conditions for dialogue to commence, (3) the goal(s) of the dialogue – preestablished or arrived at through the dialogue itself. First and foremost, a minimum of two parties (i.e. individuals or groups of individuals representing a side or perspective) must be present. Second, conditions may include preconditions necessary to bring the parties together, procedures for engaging in dialogue (i.e. who gets to say what, how the exchange will proceed, etc.), and – minimally – a certain degree of mutual respect, without which the dialogue could not proceed and will not lead to any resolutions. Lastly, the dialogue must have a goal or purpose. Purposeful dialogue has the potential to lead somewhere, albeit a compromise, an outcome that recognizes and respects the needs of the various participants while emerging as an agreement which all parties can abide. Without an agreement which emerges through a process of negotiation, distinct perspectives on what was actually accomplished can undermine any outcome and digress to a worse state of affairs than had previously existed.

While the three components mentioned above provide a framework for our definition of dialogue, they must be considered against the backdrop of occupation. Occupation is a complicating factor which brings in issues related to power and the difference in power between the occupied and the occupiers. If dialogue, then, typically requires participants to enter into an exchange in which everyone is on relatively equal footing, the existence of occupation seems to impede the successful initiation of dialogue, let alone a successful outcome.

> Only in an emancipated society, whose members' autonomy and responsibility had been realized, would communication have developed into the non-authoritarian and universally practiced dialogue from which both our model of reciprocally constituted ego identity and our idea of true consensus are always implicitly derived. To this extent the truth of statements is based on anticipating the realization of the good life. (Habermas, 1971: 314)

It is therefore necessary to make one of the conditions for dialogue the realization that a power differential exists; it is also necessary that the powerful be willing to concede their preconceived, often hegemonic, notions of their position in order for the less powerful or powerless to have more leverage. It must also be understood that by engaging in dialogue under the reality of an occupation can never mean that the less powerful or powerless are accepting the occupation in any form, but that they are willing to confront their occupiers in an effort to be recognized as having equal human rights, including the ability to make autonomous decisions about how they should live and pursue their own definition of 'the good life'.

Vološinov also stressed social interaction and the ideological dimension of the utterance, that 'meaning belongs to a word according to its position between speakers' (Vološinov, 1973: 102). For Vološinov, the utterance must be understood as a social phenomenon. One cannot understand the philosophy of language without understanding the ideological dimension:

> Since signs are socio-ideological constructions and a word is a sign, Vološinov argues that utterance can be only understood as a social phenomenon. That is language is not an isolated phenomenon but a phenomenon that has its roots, creation, and existence within social relations. (Moraes, 1996: 26)

As such, language:

> can't be interpreted without consideration of the relationship of the interlocutors and the broader situation in which the language is being used (i.e. the context). It is situated within the broader culture and behavior occurs relative to the situation. [...] rather than taking us *beyond words*, it leads to a deeper understanding of their meaning. (Berlin, 2007: 4)

In the ensuing chapters, the authors in Part 3 approach our definition from different angles, sometimes focusing more prevalently on one of the necessary components, but always looking to increase the efficacy of dialogue under occupation. The first chapter, 'Dis-covering Peace: Dominant and Counter-Discourses of the Middle East' by Sandra Silberstein, provides an excellent bridge from Part 2. By examining an interaction that took place in the news media between representatives from two states (US and Iraq), she focuses her attention on the participants and demonstrates how the unwillingness to agree to any preconditions for dialogue, especially on the part of the more powerful participant – the United States – ultimately led to war. Switching then to this second component, the conditions for dialogue to commence, Silberstein shifts the discussion to the Palestinian-Israeli context where the Parents Circle–Families Forum emerges as a joint effort for seeking some degree of reconciliation between the two sides, adding a cautionary note for all those wishing to enter into dialogue, however, that 'organizations that promote dialogue do not necessarily suggest specific solutions' (Silberstein, this volume: 178). The chapter underscores the earlier point, though, that one of the preconditions for any dialogue under occupation is the recognition of the power differential between the occupied and the occupiers.

Taking the power differential as a point of departure, Michal Zak undertakes an in-depth study of another joint venture in 'An Israeli-Palestinian Partnership: Can We Find a Joint Language and Should We?' Bringing personal insight to the participants and how they entered the dialogue through her own work with the School for Peace, Zak demonstrates that changes in the context, including bringing in participants from 'the same side' but with a different perspective and reality, requires changing the rules of interaction. Adding to the previous chapter's findings, the study reveals that a precondition for engaging in dialogue is that participants question and self-examine their own positions, motivations and goals in undertaking joint endeavors. Furthermore, Zak suggests that, in order to achieve some degree of success in undertaking a dialogue under occupation, participants should shift away from an individualistic positionality – one that could lead to the pursuit of separate and disparate individual goals based on varied perspectives of the purpose of the dialogue and potentially undermine the process – to more of a group positionality where participants from the same side establish common goals in order to work with the opposing sides to resolve conflicts.

The next chapter, 'Postcolonialism and the Jewish Palestinian Encounter' by Rabah Halabi, takes up the issue of the approach to dialogue discussed by Zak and cites research that advocates for a focus on 'between *two groups* in conflict rather than between individuals [and] looks at the relationship between the groups *in terms of power*' (Halabi, this volume: 207, emphasis added). Halabi expands on the earlier discussion, though, by interjecting the theoretical framework of postcolonialism as a way to frame the encounter. By positioning the Palestinian-Israeli conflict in postcolonial terms, the central disagreement is over land and the purpose of the dialogue is to resolve the land disputes. The participants, already defined, agree to terms of interaction wherein they accept and move beyond a colonialist discourse which 'alienates the natives from their own culture and language, and tries to make them forget their history [thus stripping] them of any power of resistance' (Halabi, this volume: 208). Making concrete suggestions for changing the dynamics of the interaction, Halabi particularizes the Palestinian-Israeli situation in order for dialogue under occupation to be effective. The emphasis on history is significant because according to Halabi the narratives of those who have been colonized have been suppressed or erased from the collective memory as evidenced in the media.

In the final chapter, 'Checkpoint: Turning Discourse into Dialogue' by Stephanie J. Kent, Razvan Sibii and Anna Rita Napoleone, dialogue under occupation is again examined through recourse to the conferences of the same name, particularly one that took place in Palestine. Integrating theory and practice in conflict resolution, the authors trace the development of interactions over time using a group development model to identify potential pitfalls and suggest how to overcome them in order to uncover hidden forms of institutionalized discourse into genuine and effective dialogue. Reiterating the concepts underlying our definition of dialogue, they emphasize that the identification of participants, including well-meaning outsiders, is insufficient without the explication of their positionalities and perspectives. By undertaking an analysis and sharing their interpretation of participants' intentions and motivations in an exchange over e-mail prior to meeting face to face, they uncover strands of institutionalized discourses which could disrupt true engagement and conflict resolution. Thus, both self-reflection on the part of the participants' themselves and the keen eye of the researcher 'can explore the efficacy of role enactments at specific moments to the group's overall progress toward tangible, common goals [making sure that attempts at engaging *through words* are] transformed into levers for dialogue rather than barriers to connection' (Kent *et al.*, this volume: 232).

The three areas presented in this book were placed in different parts despite the fact that the heteroglossia (Bakhtin, 1981) within each part and chapter evokes and illuminates problems and issues addressed in other parts of the book. For example, chapters in Part 1 do not stand alone, but can incorporate dialogues present within the educational context, and chapters from Part 3 may overlap with those from Part 2. At the same time, these sometimes discordant voices are actually between people who are willing to engage in dialogue on both sides, as opposed to those who remain entrenched in their own positions.

Our attempts to approach this project as a balanced one led to the realization that there is no balance; we come from the standpoints of the oppressor and the oppressed, occupier and occupied. There are multiple narratives and different points of view that we cannot hope to re-present, nor should we want to. They are already well documented in other narratives and in the mainstream media and government in the United States. Our goal is to present the voices that are not heard and those who are critical of the issues under investigation (i.e. we want to know how and why these other narratives have become the only story). With all of these years trying to seek balance, we have lost the real stories of people from different camps and political views. The sacred balance, especially in the US media has allowed the Israeli government, for example, to legitimize the transfer of Palestinians across the Jordan River, the demolition of homes, the building of a separation wall and the creation of a new Apartheid in the Middle East (Carter, 2006). The Israeli government needs to be called on to answer for these practices that impact civilians on both sides and this book aims at raising those voices that demand social and political change through dialogue and the influence of the media and education on the public. We aim to raise awareness of the role those three arenas play in shaping students' opinions and knowledge base, as well as the public at large.

Notes

1. The two Intifadas (uprisings) were examples of that. The first Intifada broke in 1987 and was mostly nonviolent, and the second in 2000 had a mixture of violent and nonviolent resistance to occupation.
2. The quotation comes from an interview with Edward Said conducted by two of his former Columbia University students, Moustafa Bayoumi and Andrew Rubin, when Said, during summer of 1999, was battling with leukemia.
3. The two major uprisings impacted the political environments on both sides for a long time. The first uprising (Intifada) in 1987 resulted in the Oslo agreements, and the second Intifada in 2000 increased violence and hostility between both peoples.

Part 1

Education

Chapter 1

Palestinian Education under Occupation: Successes and Challenges

K. Shakhshir

Introduction

It is a common belief among Palestinians that education is extremely important for social mobility. This motivation stems from the fact that education is considered a necessity for survival because of the harsh and adverse political and economic conditions under which the Palestinians live. Accordingly, education plays a significant role in the lives of Palestinians for cultural, political and economic reasons, irrespective of whether the Palestinians are living on their soil (historic Palestine) or in the Diaspora. It is considered by most Palestinians as the only available alternative to survive (Hallaj, 1980; Yusuf, 1979; Shaath, 1972; Tahir, 1985). The advanced levels of education acquired by the Palestinian people afforded them protection in many Arab and non-Arab countries (Hallaj, 1980). Others attribute the high motivational level of the Palestinians to the versatility education provided them to seek professions that enabled them to acquire and hold gainful employment for themselves and their large families in the camps (Shaath, 1972). Yusuf (1979), however, suggested that the high enrollment of Palestinian children in schools is attributed to the fact that education provided them with financial and psychological security. Accordingly, it may be stated that Palestinian education has unique merits, which are related to being under occupation for more than 40 years, the struggle for independence and for educating females beyond the levels observed in the Arab world.

Historical Background

Official public education in Palestine started in 1869 when the Ottoman education system was introduced (Palestine was under the Ottoman ruling from 1516 to 1917). This system stipulated that education should be free and compulsory at the elementary level. Furthermore, towns with populations of at least 500 residents were entitled to have their own elementary schools, whereas those with 1000 residents were entitled to have preparatory schools. Only district centers were allowed to have secondary schools. General examinations were held at the end of the school year and the school curriculum covered subjects such as reading, history, the Koran, mathematics and Turkish language (Tibawi, 1961). Teaching during this stage was restricted to academic subjects and excluded vocational teaching.

During the British mandate over Palestine (1917–1948), the educational system was divided into four phases from age six years to 14 years: kindergarten, lower elementary school, upper-elementary school and lower-secondary school, (Tibawi, 1956). Vocational education was first introduced to Palestine in 1932, Al-Khudori Agricultural College was established, which admitted students aged 14 years (8th and 9th grade). The Arab Commercial Public School was established in Haifa in 1937; it catered to students aged 12 years, for a three-year term. The total number of Palestinian students enrolled in school in (1945–1946) reached 82, 775, of which 20% were female (Statistical Abstract of Palestine, 1943; Tibawi, 1956).

Following the first Arab-Israeli War in 1948 and the subsequent dismantling of historic Palestine as the result of the creation of the State of Israel, the remaining segments of Palestine (West Bank and Gaza Strip) were subjected to Jordanian (West Bank) and Egyptian (Gaza Strip) educational systems. During the period 1964–1965, the total number of students in the West Bank was 195,000, of which 37% were females enrolled in the elementary and preparatory stages (Hashemite Kingdom of Jordan, 1951–1965). In the Gaza Strip, the number of students enrolled in public and United Nations Welfare Agency (UNRWA) schools was on the rise. In 1950, there were 19,114 students enrolled in UNRWA schools, which increased to 47,258 in 1958, and finally reached 67,189 students in 1967. The ratio of female students to the total student population equaled 40% in the year 1965 (UNRWA Yearbook, 1989). In 1967, shortly before Israel occupied all of historic Palestine in addition to the Syrian Golan Heights, the educational ladder was completed and articulated to span 12 years of free and compulsory preuniversity education. The education system remained intact during the occupation period (1967–1994). The occupation did not end in 1994 but the Palestinians gained control of their educational system for the first time after the Oslo Accords were signed with Israel in 1993. The continuation of occupation, however, did not ease the obstacles that hindered the educational system such as collective punishment, incarceration of students and teachers and frequent closures of educational institutions, especially public schools (Shakhshir, 1994).

Palestinian Education System

Following the establishment of the Palestinian Ministry of Education in 1994, the educational system in Palestine witnessed significant positive developments. The first was the development of the Palestinian school curriculum, school textbooks, and teacher training programs. Among the features in the new curriculum is that it includes the outlines of the objectives, content, extracurricular activities and notes particular to every unit in the textbook. The second area of improvement in the Palestinian educational system was in the rapid growth in the number of teachers, classrooms and schools that were rented or constructed. Indeed, the total number of public schools increased from 1084 in 1994/1995 to 1725 in 2005/2006. Likewise, the number of public school teachers increased from 14,938 in 1994 to 35,013 in 2006, and the number of classrooms almost doubled from 11,817 to 22,082 during the same period. Table 1.1 shows the number of students, teachers, classrooms and schools in the Palestinian educational system in 2005–2006.

For higher education, the Palestinian educational system includes 11 universities, 13 colleges (four-year programs) and 18 community colleges (two-year programs). They include about 138,000 students in 2005–2006 (PNA, Ministry of Education, 2006a). Of the total, about 90% are enrolled in universities, while only 10% are enrolled in community colleges and university

Table 1.1 Number of Palestinian schools, students, teachers and classrooms in 2005/2006

Types of schools	Number of schools	Number of students	Number of teachers	Number of classrooms
Male	802	536,752	22,700	5655
Female	786	541,736	25,974	12,736
Mixed	688	–	–	12,610
Total	2276	1,078,488	48,674	31,001

Source: PNA, 2006a, Ministry of Education Statistics, Ramallah, Palestine

colleges. The Palestinian universities offer almost all disciplines at the undergraduate level, including medicine, pharmacy, engineering, the arts, the humanities and law. However, most of the programs are related to the humanities, teaching and the sciences, while advanced professional programs are limited to 12% as presented in Table 1.2.

Enrollments by university degree show that 88% of the students in higher education are in bachelor (BA) degree programs, but only 2% of the total are in graduate (master degree) programs. Meanwhile, 10% are enrolled in community college diploma (comparable to Associate Degree) programs. There are more than 30 different programs of study at the master's level in Palestinian universities. The Palestinian universities system is a credit hour with semester system with small classes and lectures taught in both Arabic and English with mainly American textbooks. The funding of higher education institutions comes from students' fees, the Palestinian Authority budget and Arab and European sources.

The educational system in Palestine can be divided according to the following three segments, but with identical curricula. Schools within the Ministry of Education system comprises approximately 70% of the total number of students and offers free education at the basic cycle (Grades 1–10), and for a nominal cost for secondary students. These schools are by the government's budget. UNRWA schools offer free education to refugee students at the basic cycle (Grades 1–9). Private and NGO schools, which comprise 6% of the total number of students, offer education at the kindergarten, basic and secondary cycle levels at a high cost to the student. Finally, the community colleges and universities account for 24% of the total Palestinian student population. Most of the Palestinian universities operate as NGOs and charge moderate fees.

Table 1.2 Percentages of students enrolled in Palestinian higher-education institutions distributed according to specialization and degree

Indicators	*Percentage*
Enrollment in teaching specializations	28
Enrollment in medicine, engineering & health	12
Enrollment in other specializations	60
Community college students	10
Bachelors and higher-diploma students	88
Masters students	2

Source: Ministry of Education Statistics, Ramallah, Palestine 2003–2006

There exists only one private university (Arab American University) and two governmental universities.

Women and Education

The Palestinian educational system has its own set of successes and challenges concerning the gender issue. First, there is equal opportunity for both genders to access education at all levels of education, plus an equal opportunity for employment in the educational system. In addition, gender awareness has been incorporated within curriculum materials, textbooks and extracurricular activities. Nondiscrimination according to gender has been incorporated in the laws, regulations, schools practices and the public consciousness as reported by Shakhshir (2003). Second, females view the teaching profession in Palestine positively. A study indicated that female teachers, who make up the majority of teachers in Palestine, were generally satisfied with their students' behavior in school, reporting no cases of violence between students and most students adhering to school regulations. According to the study (Shakhshir, 2003) whenever a problem arises, they said it was resolved quickly.

When asked, some female students see teaching as one of the best professions in Palestinian society due to teaching's main attractions, as it allows for interaction with others. Other females see it as an opportunity to acquire new skills and a chance to apply what they have learnt to real life. Through teaching, female students see a chance to restore the positive image of educators (Shakhshir *et al.*, 2006). The study suggests that there were negative attitudes existing toward the teaching profession by Palestinian male teachers. Unlike the females' perception, male teachers considered teachers' salaries to be too low and not sufficient to cover daily necessities. They also claim that teachers have lost their good image as well as the respect and admiration of their students in recent times. They feel that the teaching profession is exhausting because teachers are subject to confrontations, stress and anger (Shakhshir *et al.*, 2006).

Third, the share of female students enrolled in the different levels of education is equal to or better than that of the males at all levels. For example, 51% of enrolled students in basic and secondary education are female, and 52% of the enrolled students in higher education are females. In addition, 53% of teachers working in the educational system are female and 98% are employed in kindergartens. Fourth, there are a significant number of women in the informal educational system including kindergartens and social committees to eliminate illiteracy. Kindergarten (preschool age children 3–5) is still not part of the educational system. The official educational system starts at the age of six for first grade through 12th grade, while children under the age of six are enrolled in private and NGO schools, which are completely dominated by females.

There are some negative aspects pertaining to the gender issue in Palestine. For example, the enrollment of female students in vocational secondary schools is limited to 13% of students enrolled in vocational schools. Furthermore, females constitute no more than 20% of the faculty and staff employed in higher education institutions (Shakhshir, 1996). Considering the females faculty members holding doctoral degrees and working in the Palestinian universities, this percentage drops to only 10% of the total faculty members. This is due to the fact that doctoral degrees are not offered in Palestine and students have to leave the country that is not common for single women and come up with financial means to support travel, tuition and accommodation in foreign countries.

Another disadvantage is related to the specialization of females. The majority of females enrolled in higher education are majoring in educational and arts disciplines compared to males who prefer medicine, engineering, pharmacology and the sciences. For example, while females make up about 50% of teachers, they only account for 20% of professions such as dentists, journalists, lawyers, chemists and civil engineers, as shown in Table 1.3.

In a study conducted by the author, there are still some traditional obstacles to the equality of women. Parents encouraged their sons to study professional majors but urged their daughters to become teachers despite of the daughter's dislike of the profession or her superior academic performance. Teaching is considered as the most suitable profession for a girl, especially after marriage when working hours allow for taking care of her family and home. In addition, the majority of the girls themselves view teaching as a respectable profession and they prefer it to other professions (Shakhshir *et al.*, 2006).

Education under Siege and Occupation

Serious problems have been created by the Israeli occupation of Palestine from 1967 until today. They escalated during the first Intifada (civilian uprising) from 1988 to 1993, and resumed after the second Intifada (from 2000 till now). These include collective and partial closures of educational institutions at all levels, frequencies and durations (up to three years). This section highlights issues created by the Israeli occupation during different periods.

Table 1.3 Gender indicators in the Palestinian educational system

Indicators for female	*Percentage*
Female students enrolled in basic and Secondary Education	51
Female students enrolled in higher education institutions	52
Female students enrolled in vocational secondary schools	13
Female teachers working in basic and secondary education	53
Female teachers working in kindergartens (two to five years)	98
Female teachers working in all levels of education	50
Female teachers working in higher education	20
Females holding doctoral degrees and working in universities	10
Females in advanced professions	20

Source: Compiled by the author based on Palestinian Ministry of Education Statistics

The first Intifada (1988–1993) witnessed numerous violations perpe-trated by the Israeli occupation authorities that included deportation and detention of students, teachers and other employees working in the edu-cational sector, including arbitrary dismissal, restrictions on freedom of movement for teachers and students within and outside the Occupied Palestinian Territories and prohibition of resorting to the use of alterna-tive educational models (e.g. using homes, mosques and churches as venues to instruct students). In addition, school premises were turned into military installations.

The most ominous measure taken by the Israelis during this period is the extensive use of repeated individual mass closures of educational institutions. For example, the Israeli authorities shut down Birzeit University on 15 different occasions between 1967 and 1992. The most pro-longed closure of BZU lasted for four years. These disruptions impacted negatively the entire educational system in Palestine, including the Palestinian schools in East Jerusalem. Not only the academic calendar's start and end dates, but also the closures and disruptions led to the fragmentation of the curricula and the learning process. Teachers found it difficult to tie materials together, and often had to repeat what was presented before the closure. Furthermore, student and teacher morale was severely affected.

The closure policy led to the shortening of the school year and affected greatly the academic years during the uprising and beyond (1987 and 1993). Schools were closed for about four months every academic year (Al-Haq, 1990). The closure of the educational institutions included also East Jerusalem's Arab schools despite the fact that Israel deals with Jerusalem as part of Israel. Many orders (by the Israeli authority) have been issued to close many of the Arab schools of Jerusalem including the closing of all government schools (Jerusalem Media, 1989). The picture in Figure 1.1 illustrates some of the difficulties faced by students going to school. Very often, Israeli soldiers guarding checkpoints disrupt and delay students' daily arrival to schools. The figure shows an Israeli soldier preventing a group of Palestinian girls from going to school.

Teachers were also affected by the occupation during the Intifada, about 8000 government teachers were forced to get leave without pay during 1987–1988 and 1988–1989 academic years. Many were dismissed (1200 teachers at the end of 1987–1988 year), forced to retire and others were detained (Al-Czar, 1989). The occupied authority used the schools as make shift detention centers as well as temporary military bases during the periods of closures, and the evidence of army vandalism was found in more than 31 schools when the schools reopened in May 1988 (Al-Haq, 1989).

Figure 1.1 Israeli soldier disrupting a Palestinian school
Source: Education and chronic crisis in Palestine (FMR, Education Supplement).

During this period, the Palestinian people resorted to educational alternatives to provide their children at least with a semblance of instruction in lieu of their regular schools. The alternatives took several forms of teaching off campus. First, universities set up off-campus classes to offer a limited number of subjects to a limited number of students. This attempt was only partially successful because many of the science and engineering courses could not be offered since the instructors lacked the labs needed. However, it did achieve significant success in many of the theoretical disciplines that relied on the lecture and discussion methods. Second, Palestinians set up 'popular' or neighborhood schools in which children met in their homes and were taught by teachers within their geographic areas. Third, private and UNRWA schools augmented the instruction and education conducted in the neighborhoods by distributing special educational materials and handouts as remote education. Of the three forms of alternative education, the university off-campus experience was the most successful one due primarily to universities functioning independently in regulations and curricula. The universities implemented many semesters of teaching during the period of the first Intifada, and many students fulfilled the requirements for graduation within the closure period (Shakhshir, 1994).

The second instrument of education was what became known as 'popular' education that was conducted by the popular and neighborhood committees. These committees aimed to carry out the basic activities of the Palestinian people including the education process. The committees were comprised of teachers from private schools and universities, and parents who tried to organize classes in mosques, churches and private homes to teach students most of the school subjects using integrated classes while giving priority to the first and twelve grades. However, this experience faced serious challenges, including the strong opposition of the Israelis to the process and the punishment of the organizers, participating teachers and students. The popular model did not extend to all geographical areas or levels of education. However, it was more successful in some places such as big cites, but it was very limited in the villages and in refugee camps. Over time, it dwindled since the Israeli occupation banned such educational activities (Johnson & Tailor, 1990).

The third educational experience was using auxiliary educational materials. The private and UNRWA schools tried to implement a remote education program during the period of school closures by delivery to the students' weekly educational materials and assignments. However, few of the private schools managed to distribute many of the educational materials or meet the students outside of their schools. The reaction of the Israeli occupation authorities to the alternative methods of education was extremely irrational. They used all possible means to stop it, including the detention and incarceration of teachers who participated, raiding venues for holding classes and the repeated announcements that the popular committees were illegal and their members could face imprisonment and prosecution. One military officer stated, 'Under no circumstances can you teach in houses or anywhere else. If we find anyone teaching or students carrying books, we will take appropriate measures against them' (BZU, 1989: 2–3). The reaction of the Israeli authorities was condemned by all parties including some liberal Israelis. A professor at Hebrew University wrote: 'Police said yesterday that they had uncovered a network of illegal classes held by two West Bank universities at private schools in East Jerusalem' (*The Jerusalem Post*, April 19, 1989). The Israeli authorities decided that education was so dangerous that it must be prohibited and police must organize raids to uncover secret teaching networks. It is worth noting that this measure violates the Fourth Geneva convention as well as Universal Declaration of Human Rights (Cohen, 1989).

During the second Al-Aqsa (Dome of the Rock) Intifada (2000–2006) the measures taken by the Israelis were more brutal and bloody. These measures led to greater loss in human life and damage to the infrastructure, including the educational sector. The statistics reflecting the losses incurred by the educational sector are staggering: 844 killed, 1594 detained and 4780 injured among teachers, students and employees as shown in Table 1.4 (Palestinian National Authority Information Center, 2006). However, it should be noted that these figures represent losses within the educational sector; the overall losses were much higher. For example, of the 3500 killed during this period, 676 were children. Furthermore, 10,000 were imprisoned, 38,000 were injured, and 2852 homes were demolished (HDR, 2005).

Schooling was also disrupted due to tight curfews, closures, sieges and raids on schools. For example, between 2000 and 2003, 367 curfew days were imposed in various cities, 548 schools were under shelling and breaking either by raids, tight siege or by closures (PNA, 2006b, Ministry of Education). In addition, missiles and tank shells in various occasions shelled many schools in The Gaza Strip. In addition, hundreds of checkpoints and barriers imposed by the Israeli military prevented movement between cities and villages. Many of these barriers were created by placing large boulders on the main roads or by digging deep trenches in them to prevent cars or pedestrians from crossing. In July 2006, a UN report stated that there are about 540 checkpoints and barriers still existing in the Occupied Territories to paralyze and hamper Palestinian movement, as presented in Figure 1.2 (UN, July 2006). These obstacles and barriers were

Table 1.4 Human losses in the Palestinian education sector, 28/9/2000 to 12/4/2006

The case		*Total*
Killed	Teachers	32
	Students	599
	University students	200
	University staff	13
	TOTAL	844
Imprisoned	Staff	29
	Teachers	176
	Primary and secondary Students	669
	University students	720
	TOTAL	1594
Injured	Teachers	54
	Students	3471
	University students	1245
	Staff	10
	TOTAL	4780

Source: Palestinian National Authority, National Information Center, 2006

located not only on the main roads connecting cities, towns and villages, but also on streets within the towns and cities. Such measures often disrupt the entire educational process (UN declaration November 10, 2006).

The extent of the physical damage to the assets belonging to educational institutions such as school and university buildings, vehicles, furniture and equipment was great. It included government schools, UNRWA and private schools, universities, community colleges and educational headquarters. The estimated damages for the first year of the Intifada (2000/2001) were valued at approximately 3 million US dollars (PNA, Ministry of Education, 2006b).

Impact of the Apartheid Wall

In 2002, the Israeli occupation authorities began erecting a concrete wall inside Palestinian areas that resulted in the confiscation of huge tracts of Palestinian land and created serious problems by isolating many

Figure 1.2 Palestinian student trying to go to school
Source: PNA, Ministry of Education, 2004 'Expansion & Annexation Wall' (International & Public Relations Palestine).

schools from their respective students and teachers. The International Court of Justice in the Netherlands ruled in July 2004 that the erected separation wall in the West Bank was illegal under international, humanitarian and Human Rights laws. Nevertheless, Israel continued to build the wall. The UN reports showed that, about 51% of the Wall has been completed (362 km) by that time. Of the completed sections, 42 km were concrete segment slabs and 320 km of fences, tracking sands and an electronic observation system. Thus, Palestinians who live in areas behind the wall face an uncertain future in terms of their personal and land status as reported by UN reports (UN, April 2006). According to the UN report, when the Wall is completed, 60,500 West Bank Palestinians living in 42 villages and towns will reside in enclosed areas and will need to obtain a permit to pass through a gate to access health and educational services, jobs and markets in the West Bank. In addition, about 500,000 Palestinians living within a one-kilometer strip of the barrier will suffer from this aggressive project (UN, April 2006).

For example, one-third of the students of Al-Quds University, located in the Jerusalem district are unable to reach the University and are cut off from it physically. In addition, many localities and villages are *cut off from their schools because their homes or* residences are behind the walls as shown in Figure 1.2. International pressure on the Israeli government to allow mobility mounted in opening small gates to permit students to go and come back to their schools everyday at specific times as illustrated in Figure 1.3. As seen small children wait in the morning for an armed Israeli soldier to open the gates.

Figure 1.3 Students waiting for the gate to open
Source: PNA, Ministry of Education, 2004 'Expansion & Annexation Wall' (International & Public Relations Palestine).

Impact of Siege Imposed on Arab Jerusalem

Following the war in 1967, Israel annexed about 70 km^2 of East Jerusalem (where most Palestinians reside) to the municipal boundaries of West Jerusalem. These annexed areas included 28 Palestinian villages. The United Nations Security Council declared several times that the Israeli annexation of East Jerusalem is illegal (SC Resolutions number 252, 298 and 478; UN, February 2006). The annexation made it more difficult for Palestinians move around and for children in West Bank to attend schools in Jerusalem. Furthermore, today there are about a quarter million Palestinians holding East Jerusalem residency cards and live in the West Bank and outside the boundaries of the Wall. They are required to obtain permits to enter Jerusalem and have to go through checkpoints on daily bases.

One should mention here that economic and financial challenges have been an obstacle of promoting change in educational system. One reason for that is Israel withholding taxes collected on behalf of the Palestinian Authority (World Bank, 2006). According to the economic Paris agreement between the PA and Israel the Palestinians should pay taxes imposed on customs and VAT initially to Israel and the collected funds are then transferred to the PA. Israel used the agreement to withhold taxes illegally in the amount of 500 million USD for several years. This past year and after four years, Israel released the funds to the PA.

Educational Accomplishments under Siege

In spite of the adverse conditions and limited financial sources in Palestine, the Palestinian educational system was able to achieve many successes. The challenge of the occupation and willingness to receive education under adverse conditions was critical in ensuring that teaching continues even when formal schools were shut down. The motivation for learning increased during the period of both Intifadas. In addition, teachers and students managed to resume the educational process despite the damage caused by the closures. In addition, the universities became a model for resistance and a mark in the educational record of the Palestinian people.

A study conducted by the author (Shakhshir, 1990) during the first Intifada indicated (as Table 1.5 presents) that 95% of the Palestinian children of age 11 to 14 recognized the following concepts: name of their home (Palestine), village, the colors of the Palestine flag, a name of a holy city in Palestine, the language spoken in Palestine, name of an Arab state and city, name of capital of Palestine (Jerusalem) and name of the closet Arab state. The study suggested that the Intifada increased the national awareness among Palestinian children as shown Table 1.5. For example, most Palestinian children were able to recognize their country as Palestine, knew its geographic features, cities and towns irrespective of their ages.

The Palestinian National Authority just completed the process of introducing a new curriculum that replaced the Jordanian and Egyptian curricula and textbooks used up to 1995. The process of producing school

Table 1.5 Responses of two age groups of Palestinian children

	Age 4 to 7 (%)	*Age 7 to 14 (%)*
Name of home	45	94
Name of their city or village	90	100
Name of Language	80	100
Colors of Palestinian Flags	63	98
Capital of Palestine – Jerusalem	13	82
Name of Arab city	48	90
Name of Arab state	30	90
Name of a holy city in Palestine	35	88
Draw a map for Palestine	3	50
Name of another village of city in Palestine	43	94

books for Grades 1 to 12 took about 10 years and ended this year. The primary aim of this process was to create a Palestinian national curriculum and unify it across the West Bank and Gaza Strip. The new curriculum also introduces English language in the first grade instead of the fifth grade as used to be, and introduced courses in Information Technology (IT), electives and civic education (Shakhshir, 2003). To accomplish this, the Palestinian Ministry of Education established a special institution to implement a series of in-service training programs to prepare teachers for the newly adopted curricula and textbooks.

There is a high (91%) adult literacy rate; thus, the Palestinians are the most educated population in the Middle East and North Africa (MENA) region. Based on a recent World Bank report (September 2006) showed that the total enrollment ratio for Palestinian secondary education is above 80% distributed proportionately according to gender, domicile, refugee status and household income. It is considered in the lead among the MENA region. This also applies to the high enrollment rate in higher education, which is above 40% for the 18–24 age group. Furthermore, for the first time Palestinian eighth graders participated in international tests and scored above average in International Mathematics & Science Study (TIMSS) within the MENA countries.

Conclusion

It should be noted here that there have been significant improvements in various aspects of the Palestinian educational system in general, and in the postsecondary institutions in particular. Many improvements were made during the last decade since the emergence of the Palestinian National Authority, with the exception of vocational education. In addition, the number of schools, classes and enrolled students at the basic and university levels increased dramatically. The average number of students per class in primary and secondary classes is about 35 students, while the average number of students per teacher is 24.

In spite of the educational situation in Palestine, repressions of the Israeli occupation authorities and the limited allocated financial sources, various positive outcomes may be seen as stated by a recent World Bank report (September 2006). The report stated that the gross enrollment ratio for Palestinian secondary education is above 80%, which is distributed equitably with respect to gender, rural, urban, refugee status and household income. This figure is considered in the lead within the Middle East and North Africa region. This also applies to the high enrollment rate in higher education, which is above 40% for the 18–24 age group.

Finally, there is a lot of work ahead to improve the educational experiences of Palestinian children and there are various issues that need to be addressed to improve the present Palestinian educational system. For example, early-childhood education for at least four and five years should be integrated into the official educational system. More attention should be given to the students' social and emotional aspects by providing counseling services, psychologist and special education teachers. Finally, there is a need to provide continuing training programs to educators through professional development opportunities and to increase the qualifications of teachers in general and train them on the use of the newly adopted Palestinian curriculum in particular.

Chapter 2

The Healing Power of Stories: Dialogue through English Language Learning

I. DEEB and G. WEINSTEIN

Learner Stories and Teaching English to American Immigrants and Refugees

> My parents named me after my grandfather. He died before I was born. My mother told me that my grandfather was good to everybody – so the people in the town told her to name me after him. My grandfather's name was Abu Bamba so my mother said okay, now my son's name is Abu Bamba.
>
> I like my name so bad. I wish I was the only one on earth called Abu. I will never change my name! If my first child is a boy, I'll name him Abu.
>
> Abu means somebody who never tells a lie. But I can't tell the truth all the time! If I like a girl so bad, sometimes I lie a little bit, sometimes I tell the truth a little bit. So grandfather I'm sorry I can't be like you!

This story is one that started many conversations among American immigrant teens about their names, their roots, where they have come from and where they belong. Abu's story is one of several that informed a teacher-written unit about the theme of names, in which children learn language while talking about the issues that matter most deeply to them. In this unit, middle- and high school children read extensively about others like themselves, they listen for the gist as well as for details of additional narratives; speak up using new vocabulary and word forms; and write extensively in service of expressing themselves in English. In this teacher-written unit, children develop research skills by investigating the origin of their school's name and the surrounding neighborhood streets; teach their teacher about kinds of names used by friends on their computer social networks; write 'cinquain' poems which are highly structured poems about their names, and create a collage to post in their classrooms.

In this chapter we explore the potential for using learners' stories in the English language classroom to improve English language teaching, and to lay the groundwork for dialogue. Specifically, *Weinstein* describes the model and its evolution in the United States, and then describes her experience using it with teachers and students throughout Israel and in Hebron. Next, *Deeb* shares her first impressions of the model, and her experience in trying to weave the principles into her teacher training activities in al-Quds, exploring the context and conditions there. Together, we will explore the possibilities for learner-centered education for the region, in which learners develop autonomy, self-efficacy and community – with the ultimate aim of creating an English language curriculum in which stories humanize the other, and lay the groundwork for dialogue.

'Learners' Lives as Curriculum' (Weinstein, 1999) is a model for developing language lessons and thematic units that grow from learners' lived experiences. A lesson using this model begins with an authentic story as a way to start the conversation. It then leads learners with their teachers as facilitator through a series of activities including nuts and bolts of the anatomy of the language to support the meaning-making work. Specifically, an LLC lesson begins with a theme or hot topic of high interest to learners that provides language development through listening, speaking, reading, writing, grammar, vocabulary and functions; invites investigation of a problem and collective discussion of solutions; and provides learners with an opportunity to monitor their own progress.

With this model, outside 'experts' do not write the curriculum. Rather, teachers are invited to engage in developing materials as part of their own professional development, following a step-by-step collaborative process with clear models for the product they are creating. This encourages teachers to listen deeply to learners, an approach consistent with the growing field of practitioner inquiry (Cochran-Smith & Lytle, 2009). It also keeps materials current, because lived experiences of learners continues to update and inform the evolving curriculum. The model is a challenging one, because it acknowledges the teacher as an expert on how the English language works, but also assumes that learners are the experts on their own lives, their strengths and resources, as well as their goals and desires. The approach combines a 'transmission model' in which the teacher 'transmits' information to the learners about how English works, with a 'constructivist approach' in which learners build knowledge by investigating and documenting issues, as well as planning and creating products and events in which they have a true stake.

Process and Tools: Conversations with Teachers in Israel and Palestine

Teacher stories, learner stories

My name, David, is the name my mother's father carried. I never met him. He died more than 30 years before I was born. I always liked the name – and when I learned about King David in school, I thought about my name. Here, I am known mostly as Daveed, the Hebrew pronunciation. Some people, when they hear me speak with an American accent, think they are being nice by pronouncing my name Day Ved. I feel best about my name when I am called up to the Torah with the name I was given at my brit- the 8th day of my life. Daveed Shimon Ben Eliyahi – I like it best because it connects me to those I am named for – my mother's father and my father's eldest brother and the title ben – son of – Eliyehi – my father, who I think of fondly very often, especially when I am called up to the Torah.

During the speaking tour I took in Israel in 1998, teachers in Jerusalem, Tel Aviv, Ramat Aviv, Beersheba and Haifa shared their own stories before collecting learner stories for developing lessons. It was a time of great excitement, with Jewish, Christian and Muslim teachers imagining together an English language textbook written by teachers for use in Hebrew and Arabic language settings. The teachers' narratives revealed some universal themes – longing for safety, belonging and connection to their past. As the teachers imagined lessons for children, they explored potential collaborations that would illuminate diverse learners' common ground.

One proposal that grew from participants in the workshops was to create an electronic forum where readers could respond to the learner-storyteller with reactions as well as with stories of their own. English was considered as the 'lingua franca' that would facilitate communication in a neutral language that was not 'home turf' for any of the interlocutors.

Teachers as learners and change agents

'This could never happen in Hebron!' was the initial reaction of one English teacher among the group that would study with me at the University of

Hebron in the winter of 2007. Under the leadership of Ahmad Atawneh (this volume), these teacher-learners began their work with me by reacting to a list of principles for learner-centered instruction. Their task was to reflect on a personal experience as a learner, in which the principle was honored or violated. This is the list they considered:

Some principles of learner-centered instruction

(1) Learner-centered approaches: Require ongoing inquiry (listening to/ learning about learners):
- Identify learners' interests and needs.
- Identify learning styles and preferences.
- Address learners' contexts: issues and challenges.
- Address learners' contexts: resources and possibilities.

(2) Build on what learners know:
- Identify learners' current knowledge and skills.
- Honor and celebrate language and culture.
- Provide opportunities to integrate the past with the present.
- Nurture intergenerational transmission of culture and values.

(3) Balance skills and structures with meaning making and knowledge creation:
- Provide information about how the language works.
- Develop skills for addressing learners' purposes.
- Provide opportunities to address those purposes.
- Provide learners with opportunities to create and transmit knowledge.

(4) Strive for authenticity:
- Provide access to authentic texts, authentic tasks.
- Move beyond 'rehearsal' to authentic interactions in pursuit of real purposes.
- Employ project-based learning.
- Aim for measurable linguistic and nonlinguistic outcomes.

(5) Entail shared responsibility for learning among students and teachers:
- Build in learner choice over *what* to learn and *how*.
- Create mentoring opportunities in which more proficient learners to help less proficient learners.
- Foster learner initiative in setting goals and monitoring progress.
- Provide opportunities to apply new knowledge outside the classroom, and to report/document results.

(6) Build communities of learners and practitioners:
- Create opportunities for sharing stories and experiences.
- Provide support for analysis of situations.

- Create opportunities to collectively develop strategies for action.
- Provide opportunities for reflection and planning for further action.
- Engage teachers as learners in ongoing discovery.

In addition to skepticism, particular individual principles also sparked rays of recognition: 'I had a teacher who did this, and it made me so excited to learn!' This laid the groundwork for conversations that were difficult, challenging and also exhilarating as participants thought about teachers who really brought learning to life for them – within and despite the constraints.

In our work together to explore 'Learners' Lives as Curriculum' 10 years after my initial tour, the teachers in Hebron began by writing their own stories, and creating a community of writers with techniques that would mirror what they would be asked to do for their own English students.

After my return to the United States, the group was divided into three teacher teams according to themes they selected: Ways of Teaching and Learning; Belonging; and Meanings of Names. They were provided with several tools as well as a step-by step process to:

- collect narratives from the children they teach among others;
- collectively decide on how to use those stories to invite learners to discuss their lives;
- design a project to engage learners in creating a product or an event; and
- develop language activities for practicing skills and functions of language in service of discussing the themes or creating the project.

Working face-to-face with one another in teams, and with me and the larger group online, each teacher team wrote a unit, provided peer review to another team and continually reflected on their experiences. This mirrors the kind of experiences that they are being trained to provide to learners in their own English classes. The frustration and excitement that is evident in their reflections is consistent with the kinds of feedback English learners also express when their lives become central to the work. Despite their initial suspicions and the inevitable frustrations, for many the rewards were also great:

> There is no doubt that taking part in composing this thematic unit is one of the most creative and unique works I have ever done … Although it is not my own production alone, I feel that I have my own impression on it. In fact, accomplishing this unit is something unforgettable and makes me proud of for years to come. (Ayyoub Al Ayyoubi, English teacher)

this reminds me of a question that my students always used to raise: 'Why do we study this stupid topic?' I used to defend it by fabricating the reasons to justify presenting such irrelevant topics. [By using their stories and photos], I was surprised how the kids were actively involved and so enthusiastic. They really 'felt' it! (Muna Al-Nammoura)

Working on the 'Names' unit was a very interesting and beneficial job. It is an experience I practiced and worked hard which makes me feel proud and full of love and energy to create such things in order to develop our Palestinian syllabus ... I believe that the most important things for me as a teacher is to be self-confident, not giving up, and learning by doing and then we will be successful and creative. (Sameeha Eideh)

If these teachers can bring their own learning experiences and blossoming confidence into the kinds of experiences they provide for children, it is my belief that they can begin to create fertile ground to plant the seeds for change and dialogue. Before teachers and learners can engage with the 'Other', they must first have the tools and the confidence to engage with each other, trust their own experiences and develop their own voice. Reflections throughout the course also revealed, as Deeb discusses further below, some of the cultural and institutional barriers to engaging teachers and learners as experts on their own lives, and their purposes for using language.

In the section below, Inas Deeb talks about the applications of this model in her work with Palestinian English teachers from al-Quds. It reflects a different experience that leads Deeb and her teachers to discover challenging areas of their work and how they perceive their roles as English teachers and as mediators in making change. The experience explores how the proposed model, Learners' Lives as Curriculum, could be implemented in a restricted and controlled educational system as opposed to a more flexible setting as described in Weinstein's work in the United States.

Learner-Centered Education with Palestinian Teachers and Learners from East Jerusalem

First exposure to the model

The implementation of the 'Learners' Lives' model seemed to be very interesting and promising. We both were quite enthusiastic and assumed that it would certainly capture the teacher and learner to discover new opportunities and create different learning experience. A learning experience that allows both the learner and the teacher to build up closer relationships, to open up to each other's worlds, to learn English in a meaningful way and above all to become independent learners. Weinstein shared an outline for a course she taught in the US, for Deeb to adapt for using at the Pedagogical center in East Jerusalem for Palestinian English teachers. The course plan was approved by the Ministry of Education and 20 teachers registered for the course. The plan was that we both start teaching the same course; Weinstein with teachers of immigrant students at San Francisco State University, and Deeb with her Palestinian English teachers from East Jerusalem who are taking this course as an in-service training course.

In this section I will relate to the status of East Jerusalem to Palestinians as manifested historically and politically. We cannot discuss the educational practices in schools in East Jerusalem without giving a glimpse into the political and social context. I will focus on the English teachers in East Jerusalem and their struggle with the curriculum, their identity and hope for a promising future. I will reflect on the experience with English teachers in making change, and developing learning units based on learners' lives. The evaluation of this experience will provide some important insights into how this model, which reflects an innovative western line of thinking, can also be applicable in schools where teachers unfortunately lack the autonomy and flexibility.

The status of East Jerusalem

Straining links between the Palestinian towns and Jerusalem

The spiritual, cultural and economic lifeline of any Palestinian town has traditionally been tied to Jerusalem, located just a few kilometers away, allowing residents to freely visit their holy sites. Today this centuries-old link is being undermined. A number of Israeli settlements have been built around the cities. Additionally, building the separation wall on Palestinian lands with the aim of protecting Israeli civilians from suicide attacks and other violence has significantly restricted the Palestinian movement, and their daily life became impossible. Today, Palestinian youngsters who live in the West Bank or Gaza read about Jerusalem in books but never had the chance to visit Jerusalem, one of the most visited cities in the world. Needless to say, Palestinians cannot move from one place to the other without a military permission that is hardly given to anyone. This situation exceeds the gap and the distance between Palestinians from the occupied territories and other friends and family members who live in the East of Jerusalem.

A striking destiny that all Palestinians share is the daily suffering when crossing the checkpoints, whenever they wish to move from one neighboring area to another. They have to go through constant humiliation when they pass Israeli military checkpoints. Becoming dependent on these daily obstacles easily interrupts their daily lives and threatens their freedom and autonomy! They become obedient residents and are expected to follow rules and orders. Is it possible in these conditions to become a free person and think critically of the future? Has the fact that Palestinians are considered residents of Jerusalem but not citizens put their identity and future under continuous threat? How will these conditions facilitate or interfere in the attempt of making change and challenging the present situation?

The way to English

English as a foreign language is taught in schools starting from the first grade. They learn Arabic as their mother tongue and most schools urge that English be taught even from the first grade. For Palestinians, English is considered a second language because it is their window to the outside world and it could offer a better future and hopefully reach further professional advancement.

The desired practiced approach is the communicative teaching approach, but it is yet prevailed with a small number of teachers. In other words, the teacher is yet perceived as the main focus and center of the teaching situation, and pupils are perceived as recipients. In fact, Wong and Nasser (this volume) have identified one of the major gaps between theories learned about best practices and what is actually seen and perceived in actual classrooms.

The challenge

The plan was to have high school teachers take a training course to help them develop learning units based on learner's stories as an additional material to the curriculum. The conflict started when 11 teachers dropped out of the course after three sessions, and we ended up with nine participants only. Great effort was invested to save this course and keep more teachers as possible, but unfortunately we had to close the course after five sessions. At this stage, the LLC model was mainly introduced to teachers, the course objectives and expectations were set. Teachers succeeded to write stories about their names and were excited to find out that each had a real story behind their names. Teachers introduced the same activity to their students who were excited to ask parents and grandparents about the meaning of their names. This simple activity became a start of a conversation with the other. Teachers collected the stories and allowed students to share the stories. It became a shared meaningful learning experience. However, this good beginning did not advance the introduction phase because only nine teachers remained and the Ministry of education stopped funding the course with this small number of participants. Many questions were asked to understand the reasons behind the sudden withdrawal. Was it the timing or the location of the course? Was it caused by the requirements of the course? As a result of our own dilemmas and confusion, we decided to go back to the teachers and interview them. We insisted that the learning experience can be further investigated and there is more to learn.

The interviews

Nine English teachers attending at least three sessions were interviewed, and then given a questionnaire inquiring about the classes they teach, the English level of their students, their attitudes to English learning and teaching, the books they use and their level of satisfaction from the curriculum in use. The other part of the questionnaire checked the specific reasons behind the sudden withdrawal and teachers' feedback regarding the course objective (see Appendix 1).

The Feedback received from teachers, regardless of the different points of view, was that 'Learner's Lives Curriculum' project could improve the English level of their students, and make learning more meaningful. Yet, from teacher's responses we could classify specific conditions that were necessary for the implementation phase that focused on teachers, the learner, the administration and the curriculum.

Without the teacher's approval and ownership, a project can be destined to failure. One teacher said: 'this project did not work because it did not come from us, it was kindly imposed on us.' Teacher's explanations for such ambivalence to take part in such projects, was due to the fact that teachers don't like to do extra work. 'We hardly have time to finish the required curriculum.' One teacher added.

A second pre-condition for the success of this model was the proficiency level of the learners in language skills and particularly in writing. One teacher said: 'when the level of English is good, and writing is practiced regularly, then it will become an easy task.' However, when students write English only once a month and their level of English is low even in high school, then this task becomes a burden and their writing is not satisfactory. Therefore, to develop sufficient learning units as this project aims, teachers should make sure that the level of English proficiency is also sufficient, and that the writing products are also adequate.

Third, the school administration should perceive this intervention as valuable, and thus support the ideology to have this project or other projects successfully implemented. Therefore, before getting teachers involved in such projects that aim to make a considerable change in curriculum, the school principal should be fully involved and updated with all the procedures. Without the principal's approval and continuous support to teachers, the project will not be launched.

Last but not least, the lack of flexibility in adapting new and extracurricular materials caused another obstacle in the implementation stage. The heavy curriculum that should be completed at the end of the school year leaves teachers in stressful conditions and prevents them from creativity. They said: 'we cannot use extra materials because we have to finish the books.' They are worried that if they use the new developed learning units, they have no time to finish their own work. In other words, they feel that this project becomes a burden that will be impossible to carry out. In fact, one teacher is not convinced that developing learning units is the teacher's responsibility; rather she suggests that this course should be given to curriculum designers instead.

Reflections of a Palestinian educator

We realize that we should approach teachers differently before we negotiate any change. It is somehow internalized that we are trying to 'sell' something that probably does not fit this target group. We learn that it is not enough to entirely rely on the ideology behind the project, and assume that it will work in the Palestinian context as it did with immigrants from the United States. One should examine the conditions first to guarantee maximum support and necessary conditions for the process to occur.

We do not wish to conclude that the LLC model is terminated or did not work with Palestinian teachers. On the contrary, we are trying to say that unless we consider the social, cultural and political conditions that are characteristic to the Palestinian context, we will face difficulties in the adaptation and implementation part. It is true that Deeb has not reached the stage of real implementation of the model as Weinstein has, but she discovers other issues that are highly important as well. Deeb as a Palestinian teacher trainer herself realizes that teachers need more time and space to make a change. She suggests that educators and teacher trainers in particular should be more attentive to the real voices of others and not solely focused on their line of thinking. The model becomes more feasible when we prepare the ground rules for effective use of the model that will improve language skills and meaningful learning.

Reflections of a Western educator

Bringing learner-centered practice to education is not easy anywhere. In the United States, where adult education in particular is woefully underfunded and many English language teachers work on a part-time basis without benefits, there is little motivation to take on additional responsibilities that are difficult, time-consuming and not always rewarded. We have had to struggle with how to connect materials development with professional development in ways that benefit the teachers and that will be used by the programs where they work. In addition, teachers must have time to reflect collectively on how to adapt the model to their own context, both in terms of the institution, the learners, and their own teaching philosophies. When these conditions have not been met, teachers might get a few good ideas from the initial training for their teaching, but that is the extent of our impact. We have found two settings in particular where 'Learners' Lives as Curriculum' has worked best in programs where the administrator sees the benefit and supports teachers with time (to meet, plan and/or write); as well as in teacher-training programs where pre-service teachers are developing their philosophy as part of a process rewarded with course credit. In one case, an entire state Department of Education adopted the model as a way for teachers to create and share materials throughout the state as part of their paid duties (Pennsylvania Department of Education, 2006).

My colleague Inas Deeb tried to do something that is already difficult in conditions that are even more challenging than the ones we face in the United States. Conditions that she illuminates (not only for teachers, but for learners as well), as well as long-standing educational paradigms, are among the factors that made it a nearly heroic task for her to try to take this on. Despite the frustrations and limitations of the educational institutions in the Palestinian context, it is my wish that forward-looking educators like Deeb will get the support they need to lead the way for changes that made education relevant, exciting and sow the seeds for self-efficacy and dialogue.

In October of 2009, as this chapter was in process, I had the opportunity to revisit the group in Hebron. One teacher, who was very enthused about her experience writing a thematic unit, shared that she loved the model but could not use it in her school with a set curriculum. This supports Deeb's observation of some of the institutional challenges to doing things differently. Another teacher told me with great excitement that she worked in an after school program with more freedom to choose her materials. She continued that her students loved the unit her team had created, and that this experience would fundamentally change the way she taught. It will be up to educators like Deeb as a teacher educator, and other teachers, to see where the possibilities are in the Palestinian context, and to find the 'ways in' so that helping teachers find their own voices will help learners, in turn, find their own. These are a fundamental prerequisite, in my view, for engaging the 'other'.

Conclusion: Our Hope for the Future

Education, self-efficacy and understanding the other as the basis for dialogue

The possibility of developing real dialogue and negotiation of ideas that Weinstein describes with her immigrant students and with other participants, who are exposed to this model, can be also achieved with the Palestinian group of teachers if given the suitable conditions. Deeb is pleased that the introduction of this model allowed her to negotiate and dialogue different issues that seemed to be critical to their professional development and the willingness to make change. The goal is not yet achieved, but at least an initial attempt is put in action to allow for real dialogue to occur.

As Weinstein opens this chapter and says that stories can start many conversations, Deeb thinks that the experience with the Palestinian teachers has been the story that started many conversations and became a unique learning experience to both of us as two teacher educators with different perspectives. We wish to end this chapter with the following two stories that reflect the real emotional world of our learners that are hardly heard or shared. Two affecting stories among many other stories that were shared and could develop meaningful discussions and reflective learning and hope for a better future.

One teacher wrote:

> My name is Harab the Arabic word for war, because I was born during the six-day-war. The name is heavy and difficult. I promise that if

there will be peace in the middle east, I will change my name to Salaam. (From the Peacemakers Camp, California)

And back to Jerusalem, closer to the turmoil, more than 80 Palestinian students from three different East Jerusalem high schools wrote about the meaning of their names. One of these stories is as follows:

My name is Samah. My sister gave me this name. I like it because it means forgiveness. Forgiveness is the best thing between the people, to forget all painful and problems. So when the people forgive each other, the peace will be back and fill the world and the problems will go away!

There is a saying, 'One cannot hate someone whose story you know.' With models for curriculum in which teachers and learners have an opportunity to tell their stories, shifts begin to take place, some of which are subtle, and others that are huge. We believe that the English language classroom can be the linguistically neutral setting where skilled teachers can tell our own stories while creating channels for the stories of our students – through the materials that we create, and through all the ways in which we teach and learn.

Appendix 1

Teacher questionnaire

Your opinion and feedback to the following questions has a significant importance to the general evaluation of the LLC project.

Part 1:

1. Years of teaching experience: _____
2. Classes you teach: _____
3. English classes per week: _____
4. Books you use with the different classes:

    _____

    _____

5. Other materials in use: _____
6. The level of English proficiency of your students is considered:
    (a) very low (b) sufficient (c) average (d) good (e) very good
7. Your students' general attitude to learning English is considered:
    (a) very negative (b) somehow negative (c) neutral (d) very positive

8. Which teaching method do you find most effective? You may choose more than one and explain why.
   (a) Frontal teaching – The teacher is in control most of the time
   (b) Group and pair work – students learn from each other
   (c) The teacher is the facilitator and the learner is responsible for his/ her own learning.
   (d) Learners learn independently using the different resources; the internet, books and each other.
   (e) Other _____

   Explain your choice:
   _____
   _____

9. If your students practice writing in class, what do they write about?
   _____
   _____

10. Are they used to share their work and read each others' stories? Why?
    _____

11. Are you happy and satisfied with the English curriculum? Why?
    _____

12. If you were given the freedom to choose your own materials in addition to the text book, what would you use?
    _____
    _____
    _____

13. Do you think your students learn English in a meaningful way? How?
    _____
    _____

    If you attended at least 5 sessions from the course: 'Learners' Lives as a Curriculum', please proceed to the second part ...
    _____

Part 2:

14. The main goal of the course was to develop learning units based on learner's real stories. Do you believe that this goal would improve

their English level and make learning more relevant to our students? Explain.

_____

_____

15. It seemed to me that teachers did not want to stay in this course because it was too demanding? What do you think?

_____

_____

16. Why do you think teachers might not like to take this course?

_____

_____

17. What would you change in the course structure to make things work in the future?

_____

_____

Thanks for your time and effort

Chapter 3

Positionalities and Personal Perspectives on Educational Research under Occupation: Where is Hope?

S. WONG and I. NASSER

> *Sleeplessness for me is a cherished state, to be desired at almost no cost: there is nothing for me as invigorating as the early-morning shedding of the shadow half-consciousness of a night's loss, reacquainting myself with what I might have lost completely a few hours earlier......*
> *the themes of one's life are borne along during the waking hours and at their best they require no reconciling, nor harmonizing......With so many dissonances in my life I have learned to prefer being not quite right, out of place.*
>
> Said, 2000: 415

Introduction

We are two researchers in teacher education who are engaged in an ongoing study concerning teacher education in the area of Teaching English to Speakers of Other Languages (TESOL). The broader study analyzes professional development from the perspectives of beginning Palestinian teachers (classroom teachers of school aged children) and English language and linguistics university faculty in the Palestinian territories of East Jerusalem and the West Bank which have been under Israeli occupation since June 1967).[1] While both of us share interests in international education, language, literacy and culture, and teacher education, we bring to the research project very different levels of involvement in the lived experiences of students, teachers, families and communities in Palestine. One of us is an 'insider' and the other is an 'outsider'.

The 'insider', Ilham Nasser, is a trilingual (Arabic, English and Hebrew) Palestinian American scholar with expertise in Early Childhood Education and Palestinian education and schools. The 'outsider', Shelley Wong, is an Asian American scholar, a specialist in TESOL and multilingual multi-cultural education who was visiting Israel and occupied Palestine for the first time.

From the vantage point of researchers who work in the United States we had an ethical responsibility to present the voices of the Palestinian teachers whom we interviewed within a context that US-based readers would understand. In this chapter we will step back from our teacher research project to reflect on some of the antimonies or dissonances in conducting research in occupied Palestine. Second, we will discuss 'Orientalism' (Said, 1978) and how postcolonial approaches can contribute to cultural – historical (or sociocultural) activity theory and dialogic research methodology. Third, we describe sites of our field work and pose dilemmas concerning the language of research in providing the context of occupation to diverse audiences and conclude by discussing a question for which there is no easy answer: Where is the hope in conducting research under occupation?

Theoretical Frameworks for Conducting Research under Occupation

Research on Teaching English under volatile social political contexts of war and occupation is a relatively under-researched and under-theorized area. Researching TESOL under conditions of social and political con-flict and violence requires theoretical frameworks that can account for both complexity and chaos (Davies, 2004; Weaver-Hightower, 2008), and historically produced (and contested) social systems, structures and pro-cesses (Giddens, 1979). Sociocultural analytic tools offer theoretical and practical frameworks for teachers in the field of TESOL in that they empha-size the *social* nature of learning (Moll, 1990; Vygotsky, 1978) and situate the development of cognition and language learning within particular cultural and historical contexts (Lantolf, 2000; Lantolf & Appel, 1996). Dialogic approaches to research enable teachers to address the traditional chasm between theory and practice through reflecting on their own emerging work in progress (Wong, 1994). In a dialogic approach to research (Wells, 1999; Wong, 2005), there is a concern to try to avoid placing the subjects of research 'under the microscope'. Dialogic research is also critical of using a medium of inquiry that places subjects at a disadvan-tage. Instead, researchers attempt to engage in reciprocity or 'giving back' to the subjects of research and attempt to foster respectful communities of inquiry.

Gutierrez and Stone (2000: 150) argue for a 'syncretic' cultural – historical framework that combines interdisciplinary theoretical and methodological tools to research on language and literacy development. By 'syncretic' we refer to ecological models of research which view 'The Age of Discovery' from not only the standpoint of the explorers but also from the indigenous people who lived there previously (Zinn, 2001). In a cultural – historical framework conquest and occupation are viewed not only from diffusion of Western culture but look at the indigenous cultural resources and resistance from 'a political commitment to undermining and dismantling coercive and dominating modes of knowledge' (Behdad, 2005: 10). They present and interrogate various perspectives and voices of the colonizers, the colonized and the descendents of slaves, over-seers and slave-owners over time as reflected in education, religion, spirituality and work.

Critical paradigms in English language teaching (ELT) investigate inequality of power within institutional policies and practices. Research through critical paradigms investigates how ELT can be used to support those who have traditionally been oppressed, marginalized and excluded due to race, gender, class and other constructions of difference. Because critical paradigms reveal the reproduction of alienation, exploitation and oppression, they provide multiple tools to conduct research on TESOL under occupation. Examples of critical research include postcolonial frameworks, critical ethnography and critical discourse analysis (Fairclough, 1989; Kress, 1989; Luke, 1995).

When English has been associated with Western culture, empire, military occupation and/or the oppressor (Edge, 2006) English teachers may find that it is not easy to motivate students to learn English. Teaching English under these circumstances requires teachers to develop new and innovative perspectives that are responsive to the sociopolitical realities and needs of their students. Educational research must attend to the broader historical and sociopolitical contexts including 'seismic shifts in political economy and empire affiliated with "fast" and globalizing capital', (Lin & Luke, 2006: 66).

A syncretic approach links synchronic (analysis of activity at one point in time) and diachronic dimensions of social practice (analysis of activity over time). Incorporating in a research study diachronic or *historical* dimensions of the participants and the educational institutions enables educational researchers to identify both stable and emergent characteristics in classrooms and schools, (which are themselves constitutive of multiple activity systems). Within the field of educational research, critical Vygotskian researchers (Lee, 2000) emphasize the importance of history and power in relation to language, literacy and culture. Micro-genetic studies within classrooms must be linked not only to the communities in which the participants reside, but also to the histories of the participants, educational institutions and speech communities, for example, if parents were excluded from schooling due to their race, class background or gender. This is true in the example of conducting educational research under occupation, in understanding the historical context of the various Palestinian communities and the narratives of the participants. We cannot truncate what is going on today without understanding the colonial past from the end of the Ottoman Empire to the British Mandate.

Orientalism: Discourses of the Other

Orientalism (Said, 1978) was a path-breaking book of literary criticism from a Palestinian professor of literature at Columbia University that inspired and generated new critical scholarship in the fields of politics, history, anthropology, sociology and education. Said first had difficulty finding a publisher for the book because of its unorthodox and controversial perspectives, but after its publication in the United States in 1978, it was later translated into 25 languages (Bayoumi & Rubin, 2000).

By 'Orientalism', Said referred to the entire body of 19th-century Western scholarship concerning the Orient, a geographical area extending from the Middle East to South Asia, Southeast Asia and East Asia. He examined the travelogs and writings of the explorers, missionaries, military and colonial governors to look at the total body or ensemble of Western writing – as Foucault did – as a 'discourse'. Western scholarship represented the Orient and the Oriental as exotic, savage, irrational and in need of civilization. This view of the Orient as 'other' served to justify colonial conquest and occupation. Said's construct of Orientalism also drew from the imprisoned Italian Marxist theoretician Antonio Gramsci (1971). Gramsci pointed out that political power was exercised not only through the state and military but also through civil society – through dominant ideologies and cultural hegemony.

Orientalism provided a way to challenge readings of 'the other' by those who were involved in antiracist and anticolonial movements. Orientalism engendered a group of readers who had a 'contrapuntal' reading. They resisted representations that made them 'less than' or 'subordinate to' the Western views of scholarship (Chuh, 2005: 23). Scholars and activists from diverse perspectives in ethnic studies (Yu, 2005), women's studies (Hale, 2005) and queer theory (Gairola, 2005) see in Said's critique of orientalism a powerful weapon of criticism against domination and as a new theoretical tool in the quest for racial justice, self determination and self-definition. Although Said never wrote about feminism, feminists have critiqued images of Arab or Muslim women as 'secluded, inaccessible, mysterious, erotic' (Hale, 2005: 5). They argue that these representations have contributed to the subordination of both Middle Eastern and western women.

Inspired by the Civil Rights Movement and its transformation to Black Power, consciousness and liberation, the French student revolt of 1968 and the Red Guards in China the US student movement took a stand with Third World movements internationally against US racism, colonialism and imperialism. Naming ourselves Black Students, Chicano Students, Asian American and Native American students we forged new identities in the political movements of the 1960s. In using these new names that emerged from the grassroots movements, Third World students saw themselves as living 'in the belly of the beast.' They 'wrote back' in poetry and manifestos that expressed in solidarity with oppressed people and claimed new self-identities (Gates, 1986). Ironically in the United States today (Ayish, this volume: 97) although Arabs and Muslims may experience racial profiling and other forms of racism and racial discrimination, according to the Census they have been categorized as 'white' (Bayoumi, 2001–2002). Ethnic studies of the history of Arab Americans in Detroit, Michigan and examples of Arab Black unity among autoworkers are needed to counter dehumanizing images of Arabs in the media (Shaheen, 1988, 2000).

Understanding the Historical Context

In 1948, when Israel was established, a whole population that defines itself as Palestinian became uprooted from their homeland. Many became refugees who were either driven out or fled to Jordan and other surrounding countries with the hope of coming back to their homes once the war was over. That year of achieving the Zionist national dream for a homeland became the year of the *Nakba* for Palestinians, which is the Arabic word for 'disaster'.[2]

Since 1948, Israel has created four different classes of Palestinians separated from each other and prevented from access to their livelihood: (1) the Palestinians inside Israel who hold Israeli passports and are second-class citizens of the state (18% of population); (2) Palestinians in East Jerusalem who have been given official residency; (3) West Bank Palestinians who are sealed in and have restricted movement within the West Bank and extremely limited access to Jerusalem (special permits are required to enter Jerusalem and men younger than 40 are denied access); and (4) Gazans who are totally sealed off from the outside world.

The Palestinians who remained inside the borders of Israel in 1948 became a minority. As a group, they have been caught between their national identity as Palestinians and their status as Israeli citizens (Rouhana, 1997, 2006). Many members of this community, namely second-generation citizens born in Israel, have internalized certain aspects of Israeli language and civic life in addition to their solidarity with the Palestinian people. Despite the intense Israelization process experienced, such as mastering Hebrew and becoming familiar with Israeli-Jewish culture, the majority of this population continues to experience economic, political and educational policies of discrimination and deprivation (Abu-Nimer, 1999; Jabareen, 2006). Many reunited with the rest of the Palestinian people when Israel occupied the West Bank, East Jerusalem and the Gaza Strip from Jordan and Egypt in 1967. In fact, these areas were occupied only a year after the military ruling was lifted off the Palestinian concentrations inside Israel. Without proper documentation and special permits, Palestinian people in the new state of Israel were not able to visit their relatives in the occupied areas. Palestinians in East Jerusalem who were granted resident status are also caught between their aspirations to remain residents of a unified East and West (Israeli-controlled) Jerusalem and their struggle for an independent Palestinian state with East Jerusalem as its capital.

The West Bank is isolated from Jerusalem by tens of check points and a huge separation wall. Today in 2010, Gaza remains under siege and in isolation from the rest of the Palestinian territories. Gaza became sealed off from the other areas by the Israeli military after Hamas was democratically elected in 2006. It is clear that Israel has successfully created four isolated communities with very limited access among them. Education is affected by lack of freedom of travel, lack of supplies and Israeli restrictions or Israeli requirements for the curriculum that privilege Israeli interests over Palestinian interests (Shakhshir, this volume). Gaza in which 2 million people are restricted from leaving or entering in the most densely populated area in the world is the most extreme example of oppression (El-Bilawi, this volume). A particularly disturbing example of the role of the Israeli Defense Forces in Gaza was provided by the Independent Fact Finding Committee on Gaza presented to the League of Arab States April 30, 2009.

From December 27, 2008 to January 18, 2009, the Israeli military offensive (hereinafter operation Cast Lead) resulted in more than 1400 Palestinians killed, including at least 850 civilians, 300 children and 110 women and over 5000 Palestinians were wounded (Independent Fact Finding Committee, 2009). The Committee did not accept the figures provided by Israel who claimed only 295 civilians were killed as they did not provide the actual names of the dead.

From the Principle of Colonization to the Principle of Separation

Implications for conducting research under occupation

Based on this new reality of separation, the structure of Israeli occupation of Palestinian territories has shifted from the principle of 'colonization' to the principle of 'separation' (Gordon, 2008). The following features of the occupation must be taken into account when conducting research:

- The increase in violence against Israelis and Palestinians.
- The erection of walls and barriers to divide the Palestinians from Israelis; and Palestinians from each other.
- The illegal seizure of Palestinian lands that prevents Palestinians from engaging in agriculture, fishing and industry.
- The barriers preventing Palestinians from having freedom of travel to engage in work, receive medical attention or have commerce with the rest of the world.

Reflections on the separation reality

When we arrived at the airport in Tel Aviv, we saw a collection of travel posters displayed in the jet ramps leading from our airplane to the terminal. In each travel poster there was the text 'The first ...' and a colorful picture of an internationally recognized symbol of a country. Accompanying the text on the poster 'The first Israeli' was a picture of a cactus.

In the Israeli narrative, portraying the cactus as the first Israeli indicates that the Israelis have a legitimate claim to the land because it was desert, devoid of human life. An image of Israel that has been promoted through a Broadway musical is that their collective labor turned a wasteland into a land of 'milk and honey'. In contrast, the cactus has a very different meaning for Palestinians. Previous to the establishment of Israel, there were many Palestinian villages in the area that later became the Tel Aviv airport.

When Israel was established in 1948 about 350 Palestinian villages in the northern and central part of Israel were destroyed. Some villages were destroyed by Haganah (Hebrew for 'the defense' a Jewish paramilitary organization). Other villages were deserted when Palestinians heard about massacres occurring in other villages. Thinking that they would return when it was safe, many left all their possessions and fled from the fighting. Some Palestinians were forced by Haganah and other paramilitary forces to leave their homes and exiled to neighboring countries. Refugees consider themselves to be different and distinct (mostly by virtue of their refugee status and their inability to assimilate in those countries who still treat them as refugees) from Palestinians in West Bank, or Gaza who are addressed as West Bank Palestinians or Gazans.

For Palestinians the cactus represents evidence of previous Palestinian homes and agricultural landscaping. Palestinian children are taught that one of the ways to identify the areas where Palestinian villages were destroyed is to look for cactus because Palestinians plant cactus around their homes to enjoy the cactus fruits that they chill and eat on hot summer nights.

Nazareth[3]

Our drive from the airport to the Galilee, the first stop on our journey, clearly set the tone for the rest of the trip. Used with the dominant language Hebrew, Shelley noticed the signs on the roads and highways and had questions about the language used and naming of certain places and towns. We also got a glimpse of the separation wall right on the borders of West Bank and central Israel, Tel Aviv area.

As a Palestinian who grew up in Israel, Ilham was accustomed as a child to the dominance of Hebrew on street signs and shops. Ilham noted that despite the fact that Arabic is an official language; English was more prevalent and was the language with more prestige.

When we arrived in Nazareth, Ilham's hometown, she knew right away that this journey would have an emotional tone to it that would be more intense than her regular yearly visits to her homeland. As part of the team organizing a conference on dialogue under occupation, Ilham was very excited about the ability to invest in Palestine but also dreaded all the politics involved in organizing academic activities in the midst of the political environment of that period.

An example of conflict in use of words is 'naming' or which term used to address the different Palestinian groups. For Palestinians growing up in Israel after 1948, the term 'Palestinian' was prohibited and people naming themselves Palestinians were harassed and targeted by the Israeli security forces. The ability of this group of Palestinians inside Israel to maintain their identity has been a struggle. They are constantly addressed as 'Arab Israelis' by mainstream Israelis or 'Arab minorities' by others. When Palestinians are referred to as 'Arabs' their claim to the land as being indigenous people prior to the establishment of the state of Israel is erased and the fiction of Israeli settlers working in the wilderness, occupying a land without people is created. Rather than conceding that Palestinians – Christians, Muslims and Druze also have a historic identity to the land as a homeland, the Israeli policies privilege only the Jewish claim to the land of Israel. Israel extends the right of return to Israel for Jewish people around the world. However Palestinians who also called the land home and were driven from their land or left out of fear for their lives do not have the right to return. Many Palestinian refugees who left their homes still hold their keys as a symbol of their hope to return to their homes that they kept as they fled, thinking they will be back in days or weeks.[4] In addition, the use of the name 'Arabs' rather than Palestinians creates an 'us' 'them' mentality in which the Israelis are viewed as the underdog (surrounded by a sea of hostile Arab nations).

In a typical exchange between Ilham and a woman she met at an academic conference in the United States, this issue of what name to call Palestinians came up to the surface quickly when Ilham introduced herself as a Palestinian from Israel. The woman, who self-identified as an Israeli Jew immediately responded by asking: how come you name yourself Palestinian while my students call themselves Arabs? Implied in her tone was that because her students referred to themselves as Arabs, Ilham should also call herself Arab. The tone of her voice was argumentative (my students call themselves Arabs, why aren't you like them?). Ilham explained that those students who are younger than her have been trained and brainwashed to stray away from their identification with Palestinians and that she needed to address them the way they tell her to.

When we took a tour of the city of Nazareth, we noticed about 30 people with red flags and picket signs standing by the famous Mary's well in the center of the city. We approached them and realized that this was a demonstration about the sharp increase in prices of bread and milk and other basic necessities. This is a typical scene in this country and more typical in Palestinian Arab towns and villages where constant discriminatory policies and practices impact the daily lives of Palestinians. This is evident in lack of proper infrastructure, sewage systems, and local services. Still, this was also a scene to illustrate the democratic process and civic engagements to which Palestinian citizens in the West Bank and East Jerusalem are not entitled.

Jerusalem

After spending two days in the Galilee (The northern part of the country inside the borders of 1948), we drove to Al Quds (Jerusalem) where it was clear we were entering a different zone of existence. The Eastern part of Jerusalem has its own unique environment that is clearly historic and central to Palestinian culture and society despite Israel's attempt to move that centrality to nearing Ramallah (many nowadays call Ramallah the capitol of Palestine).

We spent one day visiting in a school, observing and interviewing teachers and the principal. The school had three floors, the first was where the female teachers' and male teachers' lounge rooms and the principals and assistant principal offices. The second floor had the classrooms where about 30–35 boys sat on rows of old wooden disks. We were greeted by a loud chorus of boys standing up out of respect to us. The boys wore simple school uniforms. The third floor of the school was a dorm where children (about nine of them) lived at the school because of the inability of families to drive them back and forth from where they live to the school every morning. The children who slept at the school had to go through check points and a drive that previously took 20 minutes by car often took as much as three hours (on a 'good day' when the check point was not closed).

When we arrived at the primary school, the principal of the school was very welcoming and his warm smile showed his eagerness to show us around. Breakfast was ready for us in a bare teachers' lounge that had clean painted walls, a table and few chairs. Our breakfast was simple and typical of the local cuisine: pita bread, olives and hummus. Space for meeting on the school premises was limited – there was no 'faculty lounge' or conference room. The principal graciously allowed us to use his office to conduct our interviews. The school, an all boys' environment, had three EFL teachers, all females. We wondered how the teacher's felt about meeting 'in the principal's office' and how it might inhibit teachers from expressing themselves freely. We were also concerned about using English as a medium of research in conducting the interviews and whether this could be intimidating to the teachers. We wondered whether because one of us was a foreigner and a native English speaker, that teachers may not feel as comfortable to express themselves with English being the medium of research as if the interviews were conducted in Arabic. Research that draws on participants' funds of knowledge can be tapped through bilingual media (Gonzáles *et al.*, 2005) to obtain multiple voices of the research subjects. One after the other, teachers came in to meet with us. The principal told them that we wanted to talk to them and learn about the program for teaching English as well as challenges and successes they have as teachers of English as a foreign language. How can research with Palestinian women teachers draw from their experiences to 'write back' concerning stereotypical perspectives of Palestinian women? 'Orientalism is about representation, about the "Other," but most especially it is about the ways in which the "other" is transfixed by the gaze, is reduced, exaggerated, exoticized, eroticized, romanticized, truncated and always decontextualized. [...] Said argues that any form of representation is violence' (Hale, 2005: 3).

For Ilham returning to Jerusalem after living there for 10 years in the 1980s has always been painful. In Israel's attempt to create a larger metropolitan Jerusalem that is unified for the Israelis, highways cut through Palestinian neighborhoods separating Palestinians who were formerly neighbors. In order to travel to an area that once was a walk across the street, the separation wall and checkpoints make it impossible for Palestinians to frequent neighborhood stores without a permit and traveling miles by car. For those without vehicle transportation, the separation of Palestinians from Israelis and Palestinians through maze of walls and underground tunnels means that while Israelis can avoid driving through the Palestinian sides of the Old City – many Palestinians are deprived of a way to get to their work or to water their fields.

Jerusalem was no longer a city of spirituality and serenity but of conflict, power and oppression. The old city, once a center for Palestinian trade and social gatherings, is now crowded, dirty and neglected on the Palestinian side and too European and falsely touristic on the Jewish side. Negotiating with shop owners in the old city is an art that even Arabic speakers have a hard time mastering. Every exchange with a shopkeeper, bargaining on behalf of my American colleagues, produced more and more stories and complaints about what the Israelis did to tourism in the old city and the economic hardships that shop owners face on a daily basis. In fact, since access from the West Bank and Gaza to Jerusalem is totally restricted by Israel, Palestinians inside Israel (of all religions and faiths) have been organizing weekly shopping and worship trips to the holy city in support of its existence and economy.

The West Bank

Next, our journey took us from Jerusalem to the West Bank. We were given a ride to the home of one of the faculty from Birzeit University. We had to go through Kalandia checkpoint that separates Jerusalem (the contested capital of Israel after the annexation of East Jerusalem to the West part of the city in 1967), with Ramallah and the rest of the West Bank. The checkpoint looked more like a border crossing and the way into Ramallah, from Jerusalem was a shocking contrast from residential, developed Jerusalem to Ramallah with barbed wire, bombed-out buildings that had not been repaired, rubble in the street. The traffic was incredibly congested and reminded me of crossing the border between the United States and Mexico with the exploitation of Mexican workers, traffic and difference in street lights, roads and 'wild West' kind of lawlessness.

Our hosts from Birzeit lived in a quiet residential area around Birzeit. The house sits and is surrounded by beautiful scenery of hills and many olive trees. The serenity is disturbed each morning by all the traffic resulting from another checkpoint that connects Ramallah with the northern parts of the West Bank. Trucks and taxis line up to pass through the check point to get in and out of Ramallah. These checkpoints are part of the everyday lives of Palestinians in the West Bank. There are about a little more than 500 checkpoints separating villages and towns from other Palestinian populated villages and towns. As of today, Israel has dismantled some of the smaller checkpoints as a gesture after the attack on Gaza (December, 2009).

We entered the campus on a cold morning in November. We arrived an hour prior to the focus group session. We were welcomed by faculty at the education department and received a tour of the campus. On that day, the campus was full of students and activities commemorating the death of Yasser Arafat. We were told that a huge demonstration will begin later that morning. While conducting the focus group we were able to hear the chanting and speeches going on outside the building. One of the education faculty interrupted us and invited us to see 'democracy in action'. It was an extraordinary moment for us since it is not often that we are interrupted by a call for demonstration and activism certainly not in higher education institutions in the United States.

Birzeit University (BZU) is the oldest university in Palestine and is one of the 11 universities and nine colleges offering BA in the Palestinian territories as reported by The Educational Institutions Census of 2005/2006. Among these there are eight universities and six university colleges in the West Bank and three universities and three university colleges in Gaza Strip. The findings also showed that there are 20 community colleges in the Palestinian Territory, among them there are 16 in the West Bank and four in Gaza Strip (Palestinian Central Bureau of Statistics website retrieved on November 27, 2007).

BZU was established in 1924 as a school for girls in the town of Birzeit right outside of Ramallah, West Bank. As the first higher education institution in Palestine, BZU has been a symbol for academic freedom and independence. It has always been in the minds of many Palestinians a symbol for resistance of the occupation and a source of pride for many as an institution that serves students and the community despite hardships and struggles to remain open through repeated closures by the Israeli military. This was illustrated especially when it was closed for four years after the first Palestinian uprising (Intifada) which lasted from 1987–1992. Many students and faculty of BZU have been imprisoned and the latest estimate (December, 2010) based on the University's Public Relations office 420 BZU students were arrested by the Israeli Occupation Forces and 72 students are still in Israeli detention today.

Where is the hope?

In *Orientalism*, Said criticized the travelogs of Western explorers and colonial governors, explorers for representing the 'other' as exotic, strange and in need of western culture, civilization and governance. In our travel to Palestine as we reflected on the research project with an international readership in mind, we saw the responsibility to provide context for discussing teacher education. In engaging in dialogue with the Palestinian teachers and educators we found out more about ourselves than we had initially anticipated and we found that 'the other' was ourselves. 'They' are 'us'.

The various conversations we had in Jerusalem as well as the focus group and interviews we conducted at BZU highlighted for us the role that the political conditions of occupation play in teaching in general and teaching English in particular. We were reminded that educational research cannot be conducted in a vacuum but must be contextualized for audiences in the United States who may have a distorted perspective due to the corporate media misrepresentation of Palestinians and are not aware of the intensity of the injustices that Palestinians face on a daily basis (see Part 2 – Media, in this volume).

Areas for hope include: Research that includes the voices of Palestinian teachers and academicians who have been silenced. We learned through discussion with Palestinian teachers that in many schools, teachers were not allowed to discuss any of the daily events related to occupation. One teacher who taught in a refugee camp stated that they were not allowed to discuss the death of a six-year-old girl at the school the morning of her death. What insights can they share on how to sustain the work of education when a child has been killed? How do they deal with children's fears? How do they address symptoms of distress such as bed-wetting?

A focus group participant commented on forbidding discussion of the death of the young student as a form of dehumanization: 'How can you do this to children? This is not only political but not *human*.' Paulo Freire sees that the process of developing critical consciousness is a process of reclaiming humanization. Hope lies in educational research that records those voices that have been submerged.

How do teachers view the connection between schools and society? As one teacher shared with us, 'Anything that happens on the way to school is left behind once you enter the classroom. This creates false consciousness for the teacher and students.' An area of hope in educational research is to document how teachers define 'false consciousness'. How do they analyze their subjective processes in developing critical consciousness?

Research that uncovers the stories that have been historically suppressed through Orientalist discourses. As Hale pointed out in discussing the contributions of Orientalism to feminist scholarship:

> We feminists read Orientalism by Braille. This process is not unusual for feminist scholars engaged in interventions – a process of feeling the context more than deconstructing the words. Feminist and gender studies scholars have had to read a number of major figures by Braille in order to find ourselves in the text and to give the text meaning to our field – for example, Karen Sacks (Brodkin) re-reading of Engels and Marx; Gail Rubin reading the traffic in women into Freud, Marx, and Levi-Strauss ... and Middle East Women's Studies scholars reading feminism into Gramsci, Foucault and Said. (Hale, 2005: 2)

The focus group conversation at Birziet shed more light on the influence of separation policies installed between Jerusalem and the West Bank. The participants struggled daily at BZU with check points and transportations from and to the school. One participant who came from Jerusalem spent two hours on the road to get to the focus group interview. The daily humiliations at check points and students and teachers' tardiness were brought up by all participants. Having space to critique, the students and faculty at BZU had a huge sense of pride and a critical view of the conflict and occupation including criticizing scholars and professionals in teacher training.

It is difficult to explain the reasons behind these different spirits we have encountered but it seemed to us that the physical occupation in the West Bank and the limited freedom of movement have created more resilience and the ability to survive and continue the learning journey. In addition, the face-to-face contacts with the diverse women we met were amazing within one small society. The women we spoke to ranged from very religious women to very secular, older and young, mothers and single, professionals and housewives and many more roles that women play in the Palestinian society.

Research is a tool but it is not a neutral one. Research can be used to draw attention to the separation policies and structures of oppression or to cut off an examination between the classroom and the broader society.

Collaborative research across north south divisions – between educational researchers in the United States and Palestinian researchers and educators cannot ignore the asymmetries in power. Researchers in privileged regions must collaborate with researchers and educators under occupation to counter the media blockade and talk about the myths. For researchers in the United States there is an ethical responsibility to focus attention on US foreign policy and financial aid that supports illegal military actions by Israel and policies of separation.

The hope lies in creating spaces and projects for Palestinian voices and their allies that previously have been absent from the research agenda and the analysis and determination of curriculum. In the creation of research questions, projects have to emerge from common and specific ground that furthers justice for all – including the most dispossessed – those who have lost their land, their livelihood and their human rights, including the freedom of movement. Unless outsiders follow insiders' voices, the voices and the research will remain colonialized.

Notes

1. After the signing of the Oslo accords, areas in the West Bank and Gaza came under the ruling of the Palestinian authority. After the second Palestinian Uprising (Intifada), in 2000, Israel reoccupied the West bank territory. The Oslo Accords (Declaration of Principles on Interim Self Government Arrangements) was the first direct face-to-face agreement between the government of Israel and the Palestinian Liberation Organization.
2. See map of Palestinian loss of land on p. xx of this book.
3. See map of Israel and Palestinian territories on p. xix of this book.
4. United Nations Resolution 194 states that ' Refugees wishing to return to their homes and live at peace with their neighbors should be permitted to do so at the earliest practicable date, and that compensation should be paid for the property of those choosing not to return' (Bennis, 2007: 21).

Chapter 4

Emancipatory Discourse? An Ethnographic Case Study of English Language Teaching in an Arabic-Hebrew Bilingual School

J. SCHLAM-SALMAN and Z. BEKERMAN

Introduction

> *Language [is] a set of resources which circulate in unequal ways in social networks and discursive spaces, and whose meaning and value are socially constructed within the constraints of social organizational processes, under specific historical conditions.*
> Heller, 2007: 2

There is the closest of links between language and power; between language that assembles and language that disassembles and between language that occupies and language that emancipates. The outcomes of language are not inherently occupying or emancipating but unfold in practice. Language users construct systems of meaning that can both challenge and reinforce the status quo.

This chapter investigates language use and, more specifically, instances of emancipation (and occupation) through language. Using ethnographic observations and discourse produced in one English language classroom in an Arabic-Hebrew Bilingual School, this study investigates learner identity construction and looks at whether participants used English as a means to construct identifications beyond the sociopolitically imposed categorizations of Arab and Jew. Three salient identifications will be addressed: multilingual identifications, cultural identifications and Arab-Jewish identifications. In addition, this chapter will examine the idea of English as an emancipatory language and will consider the postulation that English, as a global language and one that is outside the enduring

Israeli-Palestinian conflict, might serve as a force for emancipation when constructing conceptions of the self and others.

Both authors are deeply involved in the educational initiative that served as the context of this study – one of five bilingual integrated Palestinian[1] – Jewish schools in Israel. The school is part of a national initiative entitled *'The Center for Jewish-Arab Education in Israel'. The Center* is a non-profit organization designed 'to initiate and foster egalitarian Palestinian-Jewish cooperation in education primarily through the development of bilingual and multicultural coeducational institutions' (Bekerman & Horenczyk, 2004: 391). Since 1998 the Center, in conjunction with the Israeli Ministry of Education, has established four schools in Israel.

This chapter attempts to show how the in-depth study of linguistic behavior can enrich our understanding of identity negotiation processes and minimize the often politically delineated categorizations that, at times, constrain – and even flatten – who one is and what one believes. What rises to the surface is a richer, more textured reality.

The Context

We will briefly address the surrounding macro- and microcontexts within which the educational initiative evolves before discussing some of the major findings of the study.

The national context

Israel is a nation, like any other nation-state, and Israel is a nation, unlike any other nation-state. Some view Israel as a western democracy where, just as in any other nation-state, the majority determines the identity and character of the state. At the same time, as the declared homeland of the Jewish people, the State – at least unofficially – privileges Jews over other ethnic/religious minorities residing within its borders (Peled-Elhanan, this volume; Smooha, 2001).

In particular, conflict is sustained within Israel between the Jewish majority and the Palestinian minority – which constituted 19% of the population in 2003 according to the Israel Central Bureau of Statistics. In 1948, Israel became a sovereign state and a war with a number of neighboring Arab countries ensued (Dershowitz, 2003). Referred to as the war of Independence by Israelis and the *Nakba* ('the catastrophe') by Palestinians, this war marked an escalation of open military clashes between Zionist and Palestinian nationalist movements. It symbolized the inauguration of a long and devastating conflict that today remains one of the most palpable clashes in the world.

In addition to an indigenous Palestinian minority, Israel has absorbed over two million Jews from all over the world since 1948. For the most part, the State has discouraged multiethnic, multicultural and multireligious expression in an effort to keep Israel, in the words of Smooha (2001), 'increasingly Jewish in demography, language, culture, institutions, identity and symbols' (Smooha, 2001: 50). This ideology combined with systematic segregation between Palestinian-Israelis and Jewish-Israelis, serves as the basis for a deep and divisive Arab-Jewish binary. This divide, we will subsequently argue, shapes Israeli society, the Israeli educational system and the school and classroom that served as the context of this study.

Language policies and practice

In the State of Israel, the macro context of this ethnographic study, languages have particularly palpable sociopolitical ramifications which, among other things, perpetuate a language hierarchy in which Hebrew emerges as the dominant language and Arabic has little representative power (Amara, 2002; Bekerman, 2005). Although Arabic is the second official language in Israel, according to Spolsky and Shohamy (1999) the country operates as an essentially monolingual society where Hebrew is associated with national identity and other languages are marginalized. Hebrew, as the dominant language, delegates values, norms, beliefs and practices. It is 'the language of the legal system, of statehood, of communication, of education and of the media' (Olshtain & Nissim-Amitai, 2004a: 5). Most Palestinian-Israelis become bilingual in Arabic and Hebrew (Spolsky & Shohamy, 1999) while Israeli-Jews have little need for proficiency in Arabic.

The continued development of English as a global language (Crystal, 2003) has added another dimension to language practice in Israel. As a language of wider communication (LWC), English provides access to business, science and education and facilitates entrance into contexts that extend beyond the borders of Israel (Spolsky & Shohamy, 1999). In addition, given that Arabic and Hebrew are symbolic representations of two peoples involved in a deep-seated sociocultural, political conflict, English potentially offers a more neutral avenue of discourse within a context where ideology and functionality are profoundly intertwined and often in opposition (Olshtain & Nissim-Amitai, 2004b). The predominance of English can be viewed as a double-edged predicament characterized by increased opportunities and social mobility on the one hand and identity loss and westernized assimilation on the other hand.

The educational system in Israel

In order to understand the unique positioning of the school where the research was conducted, a brief explanation of Israel's education system is required. The Israeli educational system can be divided into four subsystems: official state schools operating separately for Arabs and Jews, official state-religious schools, unofficial but recognized schools and unofficial and unrecognized schools. All four systems receive State funds. However, the unofficial and unrecognized schools receive minimal supervision from the Ministry of Education (Shiffer, 1999).

De facto, albeit not legally, schools in Israel are separated along secular–religious lines and along ethnic/linguistic lines. There are two State-funded systems for non-Jewish pupils, one designated for the Arab (Palestinian) and Bedouin sectors and one designated for the Druze sectors (Spolsky & Shohamy, 1999). Both sectors frequently fall under the categorization of the Arab educational system (a term used primarily by the Israeli Ministry of Education as well as other government agencies).

Given this segregation within the Ministry of Education, the concept of a recognized, integrated, bilingual educational system is a radical enterprise. It requires a reconceptualization foreign to many players in the Israeli Educational system.

The school

As previously mentioned, the school is one of four bilingual integrated Palestinian-Jewish schools supervised and funded by both *The Center for Jewish-Arab Education in Israel* and the Israeli Ministry of Education.

The school is situated on the border between a low-income Jewish neighborhood and a relatively affluent Palestinian-Israeli neighborhood. For the most part, pupils attending the school come from educated, upper-middle-class families. The school primarily serves Ashkenazi Jews (Jews of European decent), a high percentage of Christian Arabs (as compared to their representation in the wider society) and Muslim Arabs. In addition, there are a number of students who can be defined as 'other'. These students include Bedouins, Armenians, non-Jewish Russians, non-Arab Christians and, on occasion, a combination of the above delineated categorizations.

Students attending the school are all either residents of Israel or Israeli citizens and must be distinguished from Palestinians living in the West Bank and Gaza strip. The latter live under the auspices of the Palestinian

Authority. The former, are full citizens of the State of Israel although they may encounter institutionalized discrimination and ethnic/linguistic marginalization (Smooha, 2005). This study refers only to Palestinians living in the State of Israel and, in some cases, East Jerusalem. Many identify themselves as Palestinian and identify with Palestinian national expectations. However, in conjunction with such identifications there remains the complicated fact that they are a minority population living in a majority Jewish-Zionist State.

The school is categorized as a nonreligious, state school. For the most part, teachers use standard, nonreligious state curriculum with both Arabic and Hebrew serving as the languages of instruction (Bekerman, 2005). Teachers frequently supplement this curriculum to include the multiple religious and historical narratives present in the school. Each classroom has two homeroom teachers, one Arabic speaking and one Hebrew speaking. In addition, in the third-grade pupils begin learning English as a Foreign Language (EFL). Special classes are formed for native English speakers or pupils exhibiting high proficiency in the English language. The EFL classes also use nonreligious, state curriculum. However, as is evident in the observed, advanced English class, teachers have substantial autonomy to introduce texts and materials they deem relevant.

The classroom context

Observations for this study were gathered in a class of native English speakers and involved nine 4th–6th graders, five girls and four boys. Three of the pupils were in fourth grade, three of the pupils were in fifth grade and three of the pupils were in sixth grade. Four of the participants came from English-speaking homes where one or both parents were native English speakers. Two of the participants used a fourth language at home but were highly proficient in English. The remaining participants were Israeli – one Israeli Palestinian and two Israeli Jewish. The Israeli Jewish students were each proficient in a fourth language. The Israeli Palestinian was the only fluent Arabic speaker. Of the nine participants in this study, four identified as Jewish, three identified as Christian, one identified as part Jewish and as part Christian and one identified himself only as Israeli. An obvious weakness of this study is the lack of Muslim participants but no Muslim students were part of a class of native English speakers. In current research being conducted by the authors, preliminary findings indicate differences between Palestinian Christians and Palestinian Muslims in their attitudes and experiences toward English. Clearly, having a Muslim or Muslim participants as well as additional native Arabic speakers in this study would have enriched the available discourse and potential instances of emancipation and occupation through language.

The teacher conducting the classes was a young, English-as-a-Foreign-Language (EFL) teacher trained in the United States and living in Israel for the year. English was the language of instruction. The participants were all advanced English students and able to express themselves competently in the language.

Methodology

This chapter is based on research conducted during one academic school year in the largest, and most thriving integrated school in Israel. The methodologies that inform this study fall within the qualitative and ethnographic traditions. The study took place in an English language classroom and consisted of four 45-minute classroom observations and two 90-minute classroom observations. The two, 90-minute classroom observations were informed, in part, by a focus group activity on perceptions of others. Although we, as the researchers, designed and wrote the activity, the teacher conducted it and the students were not aware of our role in the activity design.

On completion of the observations, the videotapes were analyzed and much of the classroom discourse transcribed. We looked for patterns of discourse focusing on 'talk' that related to perceptions of self and perceptions of others. This process of 'Record-View-Transcribe-Analyze' within the context of the classroom falls within a methodological tradition known as discourse analysis (Demo, 2001).

Insofar as this study's findings were evidenced through an analysis of recorded and transcribed talk, the study can be seen as discourse analysis (Tracy, 2001). However, given that a portion of the findings were based on observations and the teacher-facilitated focus group activity, this study also falls within the realm of ethnography. In fact, we have attempted to incorporate both of these research traditions producing what Tracy refers to as a 'hybrid discourse analytic/ethnographic study' (Tracy, 2001: 731).

Any consideration of identity construction based on language use by members of a community must always be qualified by and in conjunction with the 'context of situation.' According to Billig, 'individuals, when they speak, do not create their own language, but they use terms which are culturally, historically and ideologically available. Each act of utterance, although in itself novel, carries an ideological history' (Billig, 2001: 217). As such, our analysis of the gathered 'talk' strives to take into account the presented discourse while continuing to bear in mind the multiple historical, political, sociocultural and economic factors at play.

Findings and Discussion

Analyzing salient identifications

The findings from the classroom discourse presented here reveal subtleties and complexities concerning learner identity construction in the EFL classroom. In particular, we will look at how students used English as a means to express three clusters of salient identifications: bilingual/multilingual identifications; cultural identifications and Arab-Jewish identifications.

Bilingual/multilingual identifications

The analyzed classroom discourse suggests that English served as a means for expressing multilingual identifications and for the pupils involved in this study, multilingual proficiency played a meaningful and significant role in their identity construction. The following excerpt exemplifies this saliency of language.

The teacher facilitated an activity in which she asked the students to pretend that they are moving to another country. They could take only four items with them – two in a bag and two in their hearts. In response to this exercise, three out of the five students present declared that the item that goes in their hearts is language. Iris, a Jewish-Israeli, was the first student to share her ideas. She stated the following:

Iris: In my heart, I am taking the languages that I know.

As the classroom discourse proceeds, pupils begin to elaborate on why they identify languages and multilingualism as the most important item they feel they need to take with them. Michael – a German-Israeli – expresses the following:

Michael: In the heart, maybe all the languages I know.
Teacher: And why do you think the languages are something important to take with you?
Michael: Then I can speak with all the people, not all the people but many of the people, in English and Hebrew and Arabic and German.

Students seem to understand language proficiency as an access tool that enables them to express themselves in their language of choice and to communicate with others. As the lesson continued, Nahani, a Jewish-American-Israeli, commented further:

Nahani: While, you know, first of all I have a lot of languages from this school, and I know Arabic so if I want to work [for peace] it will be a lot easier for me, so.

For Nahani, knowing 'a lot of languages' emerges as both a part of her self-perception and a tool that she believes will serve her in the future. Several other students also discuss the usefulness of their multilingual abilities and the power that accompanies language proficiency. The teacher summarizes their discussion nicely:

> So what James and Bader are pointing out here is that language has a lot of power, right? [...] You can use language, almost, as a tool, to get what you want [...] So we're seeing that language is pretty powerful.

The findings related to multilingualism suggest that the pupils perceive themselves as bilingual/multilingual. They expressed pride in knowing several languages and commented on their potential to serve as bridges between peoples and communities. That said, several instances of classroom discourse show the limits of the non-Arabic speakers' multilingualism and their unintentional perpetuation of the Hebrew-Arabic language hierarchy.

In the following example, Bader – the only native Arabic speaker – is struggling to express himself in English or Hebrew. Speaking haltingly and mumbling he says the following:

Bader: (holding his hand over his face) I don't know how to say it in Hebrew or in English
Teacher: The what?
Bader: You will understand if I say it in Arabic?
Teacher: Try to explain to us
Bader: Ahh,
Teacher: Or say it in Arabic and somebody can translate for me.
Bader: Who will translate
Nahani: (all the pupils are giggling) Nahani (raising her own hand), or he will (pointing to James)
Bader: (He says one word in Arabic and says in Hebrew)
                 Keelu, atah mkir milah kzot (like you know a word like that)
James: lo (no)
Bader: (throwing his head back and loudly laughing).

Bader has no expectation that his fellow classmates will understand comments in Arabic. Beyond one word, he does not even try to express himself. Proficiency in Arabic is a 'lovely' addition, but as evident by the pupil's accompanying incessant laughter, achievement of this proficiency by non-Arabic speakers borders on being 'a joke.' In other observations, similar snippets of discourse accompanied by laughter reinforce the perception that learning Arabic to a level of fluency is a farce.

The pupils involved in this study live in a society where one language – namely Hebrew – dominates and one language – namely Arabic – is marginalized. Despite concerted efforts by the school to promote bilingualism, the lingua franca of the school is Hebrew (Amara, 2005). Within the framework of this study, the primary language used was English. However, any instances of code switching/code mixing[2] or translation were always into Hebrew. Moreover, the discourse pertaining to competency in Arabic indicated that most Hebrew-speaking participants had not acquired a high level of proficiency in Arabic.

The language hierarchy constructed in the classroom perfectly mimics what continues to be perpetuated in Israeli society. Despite the students' professed multilingual identity and the fact that they are learning in an environment that strives to achieve bilingualism and to promote a bilingual language policy, they still – albeit unintentionally – maintain a Hebrew-Arabic language hierarchy, only this time they do it in English. In this example, English does not function as an emancipatory tool but rather a portal for the continued perpetuation of the status quo.

In general, the findings elucidate how these students understand and perceive themselves as multilingual persons functioning within a rich and complex sociopolitical/cultural context. They are aware of the power associated with language but seem to be unaware of their reinforcement of the Hebrew-Arabic language hierarchy.

Cultural identifications

The findings that emerged out of classroom discourse also suggest that English served as a means of articulating cultural identifications related to the self and to others.

The context surrounding the school as well as the particular classroom at hand can be defined as a bastion of multiculturalism. Although the predominant discourse espouses one of two identifications – Arab or Jew – a closer look reveals a rich and complex heterogeneity. According to Burr (2003), cultural identifications are negotiated, constructed and produced out of the discourses that are culturally available to us. As such, individuals construct their own cultural identifications based on what they find to be relevant within the sociocultural discourse available to them.

Within the context of this study, participants are both noticeably multicultural and yet limited in the discourses that are made available to them. They bring to the classroom their multilingual capacities and expressed sensitivities toward others who are different. At the same time, they are actors within a particular cultural context that imposes on them a certain multicultural discourse (for further discussion see for example, Al-Haj, 2002; Karayanni, 2007) For the most part, such 'talk' allows/enables and reinforces one of two ethnic – cultural identifications – Arab or Jew. This binary is politically constructed, adopted by participants, reinforced by participants and, in some instances, reconstructed by participants. Despite the saliency of Arab-Jewish identifications (which will be addressed in the following section), the following snippets demonstrate that these students are also linked to other cultures/heritages which they identify as part of their basket of identifications.

Teacher: Do any of you ever feel that you need to choose between different identities or cultures or language. Is that something that you've ever felt?

Nahani: No, but I do have two cultures. I mean I grew up here but I am from, like I was raised by Americans so basically for, on one side I grew up feeling like an Israeli or whatever but I still have a whole American culture that I just, it's pushed into me.

Nahani, whose parents are originally from the United States, describes having two cultures – Israeli and American – where the latter, she states, is pushed into her. On the one hand, 'American culture' is imposed upon her. On the other hand, she states, in a very matter of fact way, that she has two cultures with which she identifies. As the discourse unfolds, it becomes clear that Nahani is not alone in her bicultural identifications.

Teacher: ... Michael what do you think? (the pupils start laughing) Do you ever deal with the idea of two identities?

Michael: I think I deal with it.

Nahani: He's half German.

Michael: I am half German, half Israeli.

Michael, with Nahani's assistance, states that he is half German, half Israeli.

Both Michael and Nahani have at least two salient cultural identifications. However, the wider sociopolitical context, including the milieu of the school, does not foster/favor 'half identities'. Rather, to maintain the status quo – Israel maintains a homogeneous national/cultural identity (Spolsky & Shohamy, 1999; Y. Suleiman, 2004). Such an ideology does not favor low, weak, diffused or multiple cultural/ethnic identifications (Phinney, 1995: 59) and Nahani and Michael are left without a legitimized language with which to express their multiple cultural identifications. This point is further reiterated when the students discuss their perceptions of others.

Based on a focus group activity addressing cultural perceptions of others, the students were all given a piece of paper with six different cultural groups: Chinese, Palestinian, American, Iraqi, Israeli and Mexican. They were asked to write whatever they know about each group of people. In preparation for the focus group activity, the teacher, Miri, asks the students to think about whether different cultural groups have anything in common. The following discourse unfolds:

Teacher:	Ok. 'I', what do you think? What do different cultures have in common?
Iris:	well they all have feelings . . .
Teacher:	Ok, they all have feelings.
Iris:	And um, they all have the same basic human needs.
Teacher:	Ok, like what?
Iris:	Well, I don't know. They all want to have respect and um, they all want to say their opinions and so –
Eric:	Well I think they all also act the same, kind of
Teacher:	That all people act the same?
Eric:	Not all, but quite a lot.

Initially, the students reach an agreement that different cultures have some basic commonalities. However, as the activity evolves, Iris, one of the Jewish-Israeli girls, and Michael, the German-Israeli boy, begin to voice dissent.

Iris:	I'm finished.
Teacher:	You don't know about Israelis?
Iris:	I know a little, I'm one of them, right.
Teacher:	So write what you know. And Mexicans?
Iris:	Well, it's kind of a racism to write what I think about the Chinese. Everyone is another person, it's not like in a group where they are all the same, they're not.
Teacher:	You're absolutely right, you're absolutely right. So if that, if you feel like this is a racist activity, that's totally fine.
Michael:	Ken. Ani lo katavti et haregashot shli oh aich hem margishim. Ani kotev hem nimtzaaim basia, yesh harmon anashim bmdinah shlehem, aochlim aim maklot– ani lo rotze lhikanes lpratim cmo yeish lhem sichsoch oh lamah.

('Yes, I didn't write my feelings or how they feel. I wrote that they are located in Asia, that there are a lot of people in their country, that they eat with chopsticks – I didn't want to get into details like whether they have conflicts or why')

Following their comments about the exercise, Miri asks Iris to further elaborate on what she is thinking/feeling.

Teacher:	I'm interested in knowing what exactly went on in your mind that said, I don't feel comfortable doing this.
Iris:	It's kind of a racist because I can't say, all the Israelis are the same, no, that's what the Shoah (Holocaust), German Nazis said all the Jews are bad and that was the same racism we are doing right here writing that everyone, that all the Americans are the same and all the Chinese are the same.
James:	But there is something that all are the same. All Chinese have eyes like this (and he pulls his eyes to the side).
Eric:	That's what I wrote.
Iris:	That's not so.
Eric:	Oh, look at their eyes.
Michael:	tstakel al kol hasinim (look at all the Chinese)
Iris:	And the Japanese, and the Koreans?
Eric:	They also have it.
James:	All Chinese have eyes like this.
Iris:	NO.

After a lengthy back and forth between the students, Miri begins to initiate closure to the exchange. She asks the students to think about whether different eyes or darker skin constitute meaningful differences between peoples.

Teacher:	... So we can say that there are these differences but how deep do those differences go?
Eric:	Not really deep.
Teacher:	Why?
Eric:	Because all, all people are the same. It doesn't matter how you are outside.
Iris:	Everyone is different ...

The students do not reach an agreement about the pervasiveness of similarity versus difference. However, they continue to express a highly tolerant contradiction whereby they articulate a respect for similarity and a respect for difference. Although students have difficulty articulating diversity within the Arab-Jewish binary (as is evident in the subsequent paragraph), the emphasis on this categorization both within the observed classroom and the wider context of the school, seems to facilitate a respect and a tolerance for cultural identifications that fall outside the single Arab-Jewish binary. One hypothesis that we would contend warrants further investigation is the possibility that out of this binary emerges a discourse that enables students to say 'we are all different and yet we are all the same.' Such language reflects emancipation from dominant adversarial discourses and a multicultural tolerance and sensitivity not readily found in their surrounding society.

In order to bring closure to the focus group activity, Miri asks the students to think about whether there are any groups on the list presented to them that they know nothing about. A number of the students assert that they 'know nothing about Iraqis really'. The three examples below were expressed at different points during the last videotaped lesson:

Eric: I didn't know about the Iraqis really.
[...]
Amanda: I said Iraqi I don't know anything.
[...]
Yael: I know about Palestinians but I don't know anyone that is Iraqi or what are they doing there. When you told me, what do you think about Iraqis and I didn't ever thought about it deeply.

Despite previously expressed cultural nuances and sensitivities, this point brings us back to the pervasiveness of the Arab-Jewish identification and its bearing on participants' cultural perceptions. The saliency of this binary flattens the discourse available to students and limits the scope of what is conceivable or imaginable to them. Their talk suggests that they are unable to articulate any cultural diversity within the categorizations of Jew and Arab. Thus, for example, students have no conception that most Iraqis are Arabs, that some Iraqis are Jews and that many Iraqi-Jews could be legitimately categorized as Arabs (for further discussion on the classification of Arab-Jew, see Chetrit, 2004; Shenhav, 2006). Although Iraqi-Jews live in the neighborhood where the school is located, pupils do not include them as part of the discourse on Iraqis. Iraqi-Jew, Iraqi-Arab and Iraqi-Arab-Jew are phraseologies that are not part of the discourse that is culturally available to these students. Ultimately, pupils communicate no sense of the heterogeneity prevalent on both sides of the binary and each side becomes locked in the limitations of the discourse.

Arab-Jewish Identifications

Classroom discourse from this study has shown that students use English to express numerous identifications and, at times, via English language use, pupils are temporarily emancipated from available hegemonic discourses. Nevertheless, the findings of this study also suggest that pupils make use of a binary discourse and use English to reinforce the already salient Arab-Jewish binary.

Within the wider social context and within the specific context of the school, Arab-Jewish identifications frequently exemplify a broader ideology known as nationalism. Conceptions of national identity involve an intricate interplay between cultural, socioeconomic and political forces. According to Anderson, 'Nationalism has undergone a process of modulation and adaptation, according to different eras, political regimes, economies, and social structures' (Anderson, 1991: 157). Nations are formed and collapse over time and through political, social, economic and cultural negotiations. Wars are fought, treaties are drawn. Identifications are adopted and shed. The face of 'nation-ness' (Anderson, 1991) changes over time and inhabitants imagine themselves in new and varied ways.

In the observed English classroom, the discourse pertaining to Arab-Jewish identifications both reinforces and disassembles this politically perpetuated nation-state binary. The following examples of classroom discourse connect to an ongoing discussion of nation-state nomenclature that preoccupied many of the observed lessons. During the time of the classroom observations, the students were studying a book titled *Habibi*.[3] On multiple occasions, the students discussed the fact that the characters in the book are returning to what the father in the book calls Palestine.

Teacher: One day the father turns to them and says, I want to go home. What do you think that means that he turns to his kids and says, I want to go home? What's he talking about?
Eric: to Israel
Teacher: Ok
Iris: Or maybe to move his family to Palestine

Initially, most of the students comfortably use both the word Israel and the word Palestine to refer to the place that the father in the book calls home. As the discourse continues, the teacher, in an effort to grapple with the Arab-Jewish (Palestine-Israel) national categorization, introduces the phraseology Palestine/Israel. For one pupil in particular, this binational validation is particularly unnerving.

Teacher: (referring to the characters in the book) We have Mami and we have Papi. Mami is from the United States. She was born there, she grew up there, she's American. Papi is from Palestine. He was born, in what he calls Palestine –

James: Israel

Teacher: Palestine, Israel, we're going to talk about that

James: There's nothing to talk about

Teacher: We're going to talk about it.

Miri and the pupils do not talk about the Palestine-Israel terminology in an explicit way. However, as the classroom discourse evolves, some of the pupils begin to adopt the Palestine/Israel phraseology as opposed to saying Palestine or Israel. In the beginning of the third observed lesson, Michael explains the following:

Teacher: ... Michael, at the beginning of the story, tell Bader where do they live? (referring to the family in the story). Where do they start off?

Michael: In the USA

Teacher: In the USA, and then what happens?

Michael: They flew or fly?

Teacher: Fly

Michael: They fly to Palestine/Israel.

Miri's usage of the slash and the students' adoption of this Palestine/Israel phraseology, constructs a new possible perception of the already salient Arab-Jewish (Palestine/Israel) binary. Even James, who previously adamantly declared *'There's no Palestine'* is ultimately able to consider the conception of an Israeli identification alongside a Palestinian identification. This is reflected in the following activity:

> (The students are completing a poetry exercise where the teacher gives them 7 or 8 words and they have to glue them on a piece of paper along with any other words they deem appropriate. They have spent the last ten minutes preparing their poems and are now sharing them)

James: Liana is my name. I am moving from America to Palestine. I am confused ... Wait ... Some people say that this is Palestine and some people say that this is Israel. I don't ... I don't know what to think.

The teacher and the pupils use English to construct a more liberated phraseology, one that, within the context of this study, equalizes, rather than further dichotomizes, Arab-Jewish identifications. Moreover, albeit temporarily, they use English to dismantle an either/or national identification and to suggest the possibility of Palestine alongside Israel.

From its inception, the school has adopted, created and propagated a nationalist ideology not unlike that of its parent state. In the State of Israel, nation-state ideology frequently morphs into ethnic categories, where Israelis tend to be characterized as 'Jews' and Palestinians as 'Arabs.' Just as the State of Israel roots its nationalism in a fundamental Arab/Jewish divide, so too does the school, albeit with a different intention, which in this case is Arab/Jewish coexistence. This ideology appears in school materials, publications and protocols. Not surprisingly, in this study the observed students also often spoke in terminology that resounded of the school's very own nation-state identifications, despite the fact that they were speaking in English, a nonnational language. Whereas nationalist/ethnic terminology is normally used to divide peoples, at the school the terminology is used to create parallels and reinforce standards of equality between Jews and Palestinians. What we must ask ourselves then is whether an ideology like nationalism, which does not readily encourage multicultural/multiethnic identification, and in Israel privileges the Jewish, Hebrew-speaking majority, can ultimately provide the language for peace and coexistence.

That said, as evidenced by the discourse related to Palestine and Israel, the students, at times, use English to express more nuanced conceptions of themselves and the nation in which they live. The teacher and the students temporarily step outside of the monolithic nation-state ideology and offer a binational, Palestine/Israel phraseology. In the end, it is too much to expect that children would use English as a means to fully dismantle identifications perpetuated by adults, the surrounding school context and the wider societal context. The fact that they are at all capable of adopting language that is outside the mainstream nationalist agenda is no small feat.

Conclusion

This chapter investigated language use and, more specifically, potential instances of emancipation (and occupation) through language. One of the underlining considerations of this study was whether English, as a language that is outside the enduring Israeli-Palestinian conflict including its expression through the languages of Arabic and Hebrew, could serve as a force for emancipation when constructing conceptions of self and others. From the outset, we treaded cautiously around this hypothesis, fully aware of the multiple hegemonies sustained through English language dominance (see Phan Le Ha, 2005; Wong & Nasser, this volume). However, we wanted to explore further Crystal's contention that 'if English can facilitate the process of universal dispossession and loss, so can it be turned round and made to facilitate the contrary process of universal empowerment and gain' (Crystal, 2003: 25).

Through this study, we offer the possibility that students found some liberative/emancipatory expression in English. Through the English discourse utilized in the classroom, students were exposed to ideas, concepts and ideologies beyond what is culturally imbedded in Arabic and Hebrew and beyond what they hear in the school and home environs. Moreover, via English language use, at times, students were emancipated from the binary identifications perpetuated by the school and the wider social context.

Nevertheless, it is important to acknowledge that the scope of this study is limited and further research is required if we are to fully grapple with the emancipatory potential of English in areas of intractable conflict in general and in Israel and in Palestine in particular. At present, the authors are conducting a larger study that investigates the experiences of Palestinian Israeli and Jewish Israeli English language learners. One intention is to further explore the possibilities surmised in this study and to arrive at a clearer understanding of whether English offers the possibility of an alternative discourse, one that is emancipated from the innuendos associated with Hebrew or Arabic. The bridging or negotiating possibility of English remains a tentative implication, not devoid of critical analysis or speculation but rather a potential reconstitution of the constructs that currently occupy much of the discourse in the region.

According to Burr (1995), 'the person you are, your experience, your identity, your "personality" are all the effects of language. [...] we can only represent our experiences to ourselves and to others by using the concepts embedded in our language' (Burr, 1995: 39). The children involved in this study were exposed to new and different concepts embedded in the English language. Periodically, they used English as a means to rework the discourse the wider contexts provide. They constructed concepts unique to their experiences and, in most cases, unfamiliar to politicians, policy makers and theorists. Their interactions were based on real-time, previously uncharted encounters whose implications cannot be fully known.

Our conviction is that the conceptions embedded in their language and the categorizations they construct are worthy of translation. As much as any other initiative, such conceptions offer the possibility of a reconceptualization of the categorical systems we cling to so dearly despite their sometimes paralyzing nature.

At times, the perceptions constructed by the children involved in this study offer alternative and diversified identifications which contain the beginnings of freedom and possible change. Ultimately, there are no broad strokes, only small seeds in which we may hope to construct a more just society.

Notes

1. Throughout this chapter, we have chosen to use the delineation Palestinian-Israeli to refer to Arabs living in the State of Israel (see e.g. R. Suleiman, 2004). However, the discourse and materials that emerged from our research context utilizes the delineation Arab or Arab Israeli. We will therefore use Palestinian Israeli when offering our own analysis and Arab when referencing incidents or discourse from the research setting.
2. Code switching/code mixing can be defined as a fluctuation between two or more languages during the production of discourse (Myers-Scotton, 1997: 217).
3. Habibi (My Beloved) written by Naomi Shihab Nye and first published in 1997 by Simon & Schuster, Inc.

Chapter 5

The Presentation of Palestinians in Israeli Schoolbooks

N. PELED-ELHANAN

> *The national solution for Israel's Arabs lies elsewhere: in order to maintain a Jewish-Democratic state we must constitute two nation-states with clear red-lines. Once this happens, I will be able to come to the Palestinian citizens of Israel, whom we label Israel's Arabs, and tell them that their national solution is elsewhere.*
> Tzipi Livni, 10.12.08.

Introduction

The discourse of identity is also the discourse of difference, inclusion and exclusion. The construal of identity, and especially of national identity, includes strategies of denying other identities that seem threatening. The Jewish Israeli identity is achieved, among other ways, through the exclusion and rejection of different ethnic groups – both Jewish and Muslim – whose national, territorial and cultural rights are denied (Yona, 2005). The discriminated groups are those who lived on the land before the establishment of the state of Israel, namely the Palestinians, the Druze, the Bedouins and other 'non-Jewish' groups and those who came after the establishment of the state: Arab Jews, Ethiopian Jews and ex-Soviet Union Jews to name the largest groups whose heritage, traditions, customs and culture are not recognized either at school or in Israeli social and cultural life, and who are expected not only to be integrated in the Israeli society but to assimilate.[1]

This chapter is part of a critical study of one aspect of the Israeli-Zionist narrative as it is reproduced in school books of three disciplines: history, geography and civic studies. It consists of an analysis of the visual and verbal texts that represent the 'others' of Zionist Jews, namely the Palestinians – both the citizens of Israel and the noncitizens who are for the most part refugees of the 1948 war and have been living under a military regime in the occupied Palestinian territories since 1967.

Although the study relies on studies made in different countries, such as Holland (Essed, 1991; van Leeuwen, 2000), Sweden and Australia (van Leeuwen, 1992; Walls, 2010), it does not compare Israel with other places, nor does it deal in depth with the social and psychological reasons for the anti-Arab discourse that prevails in Israeli society, but rather analyzes one type of this discourse, prevalent in Israeli schoolbooks of history and geography, that which characterizes the representation of Palestinians.

Based on the premises of Critical Discourse Analysis and Social Semiotics, the analysis follows the assumption that no sign is neutral and that texts reflect the circumstances that engendered them (Kress, 2003). Therefore, any analysis of verbal or visual signs should explain its findings in the context of the culture and circumstances in which they were produced, in this case the Israeli-Zionist culture and the circumstances of the Israeli occupation of Palestine.

As the philosopher Michael Waltzer notes 'critics are not disembodied hermetic individuals, but interested members of specific societies and social groups with specific points of view' (Waltzer, 1987: 43). This view is shared by literary critics, philosophers, semioticians and discourse analysts, who agree that the act of reading consists of personal 'meaning-making', whereby the reader is 'filling elements with content and making sense of these elements' (Kress, 2003: 38). The 'sense' is never entirely dictated by the writer, as Renaissance French philosopher Michel de Montaigne had already observed, '*La parole est moitié à celui qui parle moitié à celui qui écoute*' (Montaigne, Essais III).[2]

My own reading and the intertextual connections that I found in the textbooks I analyzed are the basis of my interpretation. This reading is informed by my knowledge of Israeli political, cultural, social and educational discourse, and my ideological stance which is what M. Reisigl and R. Wodak describe as 'emphatic with the victims of discrimination' (Reisigl & Wodak, 2001: 35).

The discourse used by Israeli schoolbooks to represent Palestinians stems from an ideology of exclusion and is overtly compatible with the official discrimination against them, enhanced by the Israeli-Zionist project to 'Jewify' the Land and thereby 'de-Arabize' it (Yiftachel, 2006). It presents reality from the sole point of view of the Jewish dominant group and is founded on the fundamental principle that serves as the ideological 'common ground' of Israeli education, namely that Israel is the state of all the Jews wherever they dwell and not the state of its non-Jewish citizens. As Smooha (2002) points out:

> It is a diminished type of democracy for it takes the ethnic nation, not the citizenry, as the corner-stone of the state [...] At the same time this democracy extends various kinds of [individual] rights to 1 million Palestinian-Arab citizens (16% of the population) who are perceived as a threat. (Smooha, 2002: 475–478)

The de-Arabization of the Land finds its expression in all aspects of Israeli life. One example is Israel's language policy: Although both Hebrew and Arabic are Israel's official languages, there is only one college whose language of instruction is Arabic, there are no signs in Arabic in public places such as malls, hospitals or the airport. Other examples are the very recent law allowing the Jewish National Fund, which is responsible for allocating land, not to lease lands to Arab citizens;[3] the law of citizenship that prohibits family reunion of Palestinian citizens who marry Palestinians from the occupied territories and separates between spouses and between children and their parents,[4] the inaccessibility of most government posts to Palestinian citizens, the recent Nakba law, which followed the mentioning of the Nakba in the Arab-Israeli version of *Living Together in Israel* (a booklet of Geography and civics for third grade) in 2007 and the May 2008 supreme-court ruling in favor of the Islamic movement's commemoration of the Nakba in Israel.[5]

These laws, and the built-in discrimination against Palestinian citizens, in terms of budget both on the municipal and on the educational level, in terms of individual and municipal expansion,[6] lack of infrastructure and lack of services, are rationalized and reinforced in textbooks, in expressions such as: 'Their lands are diminishing' (SIS.: 60), their construction is 'illegal' (GLI 303), 'Arab villages are too far from the centre and therefore it is difficult to connect them to the water and power systems' (GLI 303) and so on. The Palestinians living in the occupied territories are deprived of all human rights and are treated as 'bare life' or Homini Sacer (Agamben, 1987: 37), namely as people who are subjected, by law, to a permanent 'state of exception', lack or are forcibly denied, all social or legal status and whose blood is 'dispensable with impunity'.[7] This perception is reflected in norms and regulations that permit collective 'punishments', excessive use of force, whether bullets or tear-gas, and extrajudicial assassinations of Palestinians; such a conduct is inconceivable in relation to Jewish citizens, or even to Jewish terrorists, nor does it match norms of appropriate behavior or justice in other democratic states.

The sample of schoolbooks, from which the following examples are drawn, was chosen according to the popularity of the books among teachers in mainstream secular Jewish elementary, middle and high schools, which constitute the majority of schools in Israel.[8] All books were published during the years 1996–2009, after the Oslo Peace agreements between Israel and the Palestinian Authority, in 1994. All books are currently used and claim to reflect the national curriculum. All, but one, were authorized by the Ministry of Education.

Methodology

The chapter presents a multimodal analysis of written and visual discourses. The analysis relies mainly on the theory of Social Semiotics, founded by Halliday (1978) and developed by Kress and van Leeuwen. The main assumption is taken from Kress:

> Since meanings are made as signs in distinct ways in specific modes [...] That which is represented in sign or sign complexes realizes the interests, perspectives, values and positions of those who make the sign [...] representation is always 'engaged'. It is never neutral. (Kress, 2003: 44)

This standpoint rejects the idea of arbitrariness (Kress, 2003: 42) for 'the relations between signifier and signified is always motivated, that is, the shape of the signifier, its "form", materially or abstractly considered, is chosen because of its aptness for expressing that which is to be signified' (Kress, 2003: 42). Therefore, 'we have to find ways of understanding and describing the interaction of such meanings across modes into coherent wholes, into texts' (Kress, 2003: 37).

The verbal analysis uses the categories of 'everyday racist discourse' established by Essed (1991), as well as van Leeuwen's critical – discursive categories regarding the representation of social actors (1996/2008), which were elaborated in Reisigl and Wodak's (2001) extensive study of racist discourse in politics and in the media.

The visual analysis will follow the work of Kress and van Leeuwen who laid the foundation of the grammar of visual design (van Leeuwen, 1992, 2000; Kress & van Leeuwen, 1996/2006), especially van Leeuwen's (1992, 2000) work concerning the racist visual representation of others in general and in textbooks.

The analyses of maps in geography textbooks will rely on observations made by geographers such as Bar-Gal, Yiftachel and Henrikson, especially regarding the manipulative use of cartography.[9]

Verbal and visual representation of Palestinians in Israeli schoolbooks

Schoolbooks are still powerful means by which the state shapes forms of perception, of categorization, of interpretation and of memory, which serve to determine national identity. Schoolbooks use an array of visual and verbal modes to transmit values and meanings. Therefore, a multi-modal analysis is required in the study of school books. Israeli textbooks, though they vary in the way they teach the disciplines serve as relays of the Zionist message regarding the exclusive 'historic rights' of the Jews on the Great Land of Israel that includes Palestine (Bar-Gal, 1993a; Firer, 1985, 2004). This ideology is the 'common ground' (Fairclough, 2003: 55) on which facts are selected and narratives are 'carved'.

The existence of Israel as a Jewish state and the crucial importance of a Jewish majority in Israel are the milestones of education, the basis on which all arguments and interpretations are founded. Although the ideal of an Arab-free country is never spelled out explicitly, schoolbooks use the importance of a Jewish majority as justification for the reluctance of Israel to grant Palestinian refugees the right of return or to annex the occupied Palestinian territories to the state of Israel and to accord civil rights to the inhabitants of these territories. As one secondary History textbook explains, such annexation would be a disaster whereby Israel would become 'a bi-national state with an Arab majority – an absurd situation where the Jewish people would become a minority in their own land and the Zionist dream [would turn into] a south-African nightmare' (*The 20th* Century: 249). The nightmare such an annexation would be for the Palestinians is never discussed.

Nevertheless, the West Bank, which has never been annexed to the state, is depicted in all Israeli maps as part of Israel. Bar-Gal explains this by the fact that curriculum planners have never resigned to man-made borders that seem to them an 'accidental consequence of cease fire commands which paralyzed military momentum' (Bar-Gal, 1993a: 125), nor have they given up teaching about the Greater Land of Israel that they consider to be 'a whole Geographic entity' (Bar-Gal, 1993a: 125). Bar-Gal explains that Israeli students do not learn about 'the "State of Israel" which has achieved international legitimation, but about the "Land of Israel" which has divine legitimation' (Bar-Gal, 1993b: 430). That is because 'in the field of Geography the curricula have always emphasized the nationalist goals as the principal goal' (Bar-Gal, 2000: 169). This goal has been 'to know and love our homeland', which is the biblical 'promised land' that includes Israel, Palestine, parts of Jordan (called Western Land of Israel) and portions of Syria and Egypt. As literary scholar Ariel Hirschfeld comments[10] the Zionist creed 'know your homeland' means forgetting 2000 years of civilization on this land, and seeing present Jewish life in Israel as a direct continuation of the biblical kingdom of Judea. This perception serves what Nora (1999) termed as the myth of continuity, typical of national narratives. According to the myth of continuity, the land, too, was condemned to a sort of exile as long as there was no Jewish sovereignty over it: 'it lacked any meaningful or authentic history, awaiting redemption with the return of the Jews' (Piterberg, 2001: 32). Piterberg explains that the known Zionist slogan, 'a land without a people to a people without a land', does not mean the land was literally empty, but that it was empty of its historic custodians and populated by insignificant intruders. This notion may be at the base of the statement made by R. Firer of the Truman Institute for Peace, in her analysis of Israeli school books of History: 'the sovereign state of Israel was *re-established* in 1948' (Firer, 2004: 22, my emphasis). Such a statement assumes that the current state of Israel is a direct successor of another, ancient 'state of Israel' or rather, kingdom.

The educational system continues, therefore, to present the 'distorted map as a miniature model of reality, and less often emphasizes that this map is a distorted model, which sometimes can "lie", and contain items that are completely different from reality' (Bar-Gal, 1996: 69). This is the reason why none of the schoolbooks is called 'The Geography of the State of Israel'. Geography schoolbooks are usually called 'Israel' or 'The Land of Israel', which entail the inclusion, in all maps, of territories beyond the state's official borders, and occupied areas that were seized during the wars but whose legal status does not make them a part of the state of Israel. As Bar-Gal emphasizes:

> The borders of Israel as presented on the map represent the right-wing ideological perception which refuses to see the area of the West Bank and Gaza as territory under a different sovereignty. (Bar-Gal, 1993a: 125)

In order to legitimate and eternalize Israeli dominance in those areas, schoolbooks use as a recurrent device the insertion of biblical phrases that reiterate the divine promise. For instance, *The Mediterranean Countries*, a geography textbook for the 5th grade, includes a chapter called One Sea with Many Names. But from the outset one realizes that 'many names' does not mean the names this sea has been given by the different nations living along its coastline but only the Hebrew biblical names of the Mediterranean, along with biblical quotes regarding the divine promise to Abraham, which in Israeli discourse legitimates the occupation of Palestine:

> The Mediterranean Sea is already mentioned in the bible. Is it also called the Mediterranean in the book of books? Exodus 23/31: 'And I will set thy bounds from the sea of Suf even to the sea of the Pelishtim, and from the desert to the river.' *Deuteronomy,* 11/24: 'Every Place whereon the sole of your foot shall tread shall be yours. ... From the river, the river Prath to the uttermost sea shall be your border.' Joshua, 1: 4: 'From the wilderness and this Lebanon as far as the great sea ... towards the going down of the sun, shall be your border.' *Genesis,* 28: 14: 'And thou shall spread out to the West and to the East and to the South and to the North (Yama-Kedma-Tzafona-Negba). The phrase means that your country will spread in the future to the North, to the South, to the east and to the West. (Vaadya *et al.,* 1996: 11)

This intertextuality with the Bible gives a holy stamp to the textbook and a scientific stamp of validity to the Bible (Lemke, 1998) (Figure 5.1).

Although Palestinian lands are depicted on this and other maps as part of the state of Israel, their inhabitants are never represented. This misrepresentation creates 'blind spots' where people are supposed to be seen but are not (Barthes, 1980: 855), or rather, as in Lacan's example of the book that is absent from the shelf and whose nonoccupied slot proves its existence as a missing book, they are represented as missing entities. In Geographical terms, there are 'toponomyc silences' on these maps, which are a cartographic way to deny the existence of people through Fragmentation (Thompson, 1987): separating people from the places where they live and work, or representing the land while ignoring or concealing the existence of its population. This is also done by changing the names of places (the West Bank is usually called by its Hebrew biblical name: Judea and Samaria and so are all former Arab cities and villages), or by depicting Palestinian areas as colorless spots defined as 'Areas without data' (Figure 5.2).

This representation creates 'toponomyc silences, [...] blank spaces, silences of uniformity, of standardization or deliberate exclusion, willful ignorance or even actual repression' (Henrikson, 1994: 59). Although this map depicts Arab population, Arab and mixed Jewish-Arab cities such as Nazareth and Acre are not marked. The 'toponomyc silences' regarding the presentation of Palestinian areas are the visual expression of the Zionist slogan 'A land without people for a people without land', which has always justified the policy of occupation and colonization.

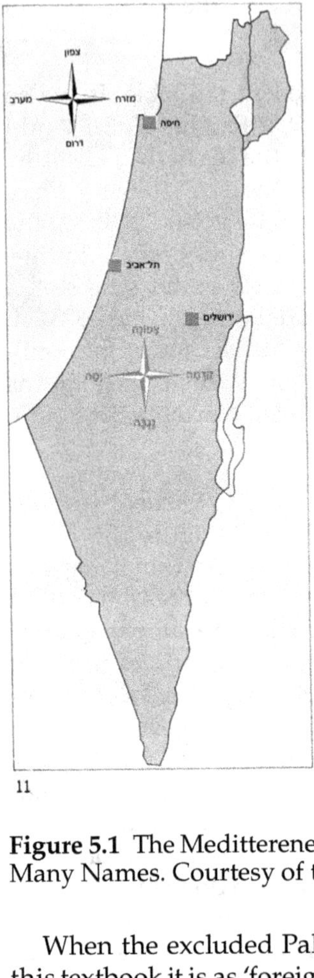

ים אחד ושמות רבים לו

הים התיכון כבר מוזכר בתנ"ך. האם גם בספר הספרים הוא
נקרא הים התיכון? וכך כתוב בתנ"ך:
בספר שמות כג 31:
וְשַׁתִּי אֶת גְּבֻלְךָ מִיָּם סוּף וְעַד יָם פְּלִשְׁתִּים.
בספר דברים יא 24:
...מִן הַמִּדְבָּר וְהַלְּבָנוֹן מִן הַנָּהָר נְהַר פְּרָת וְעַד הַיָּם הָאַחֲרוֹן יִהְיֶה
גְּבֻלְכֶם.
בספר יהושע א 4:
...וְעַד הַיָּם הַגָּדוֹל מְבוֹא הַשֶּׁמֶשׁ יִהְיֶה גְבוּלְכֶם.

2.   מהם שמות הַיָּם התיכון בתנ"ך?
3.   פָּרְשׁוּ שניים משמותיו של הים, כלומר: מה מקור השמות
     ועל פי מה נתנו השמות ליַם?

בתקופת המקרא (התנ"ך) השתמשו במלה יָם לציון צַד מערב.
בספר בראשית כח 14 נאמר:

וּפָרַצְתָּ יָמָּה וָקֵדְמָה וְצָפֹנָה וָנֶגְבָּה.

(פירוש הפסוק: בעתיד תתרחב ארצך מערבה, מזרחה, צפונה
ודרומה.)

4.   עיינו במפה א' 2 והסבירו: מדוע המלה יָם מציינת את
     הכיוון מערב?

5   האם גם במצרים נכון לכנות את צַד מערב בשם יָם?
    בדקו במפה שבאטלס והסבירו.
6.   באילו מדינות נוספות לחופי הים התיכון אפשר לקרוא לצד
     מערב בשם יָם?

מפה א' 2: יָמָּה וקדמה צפונה ונגבה

11

Figure 5.1 The Meditterenean Countries (Vaadya *et al.*, 1996: 11). One Sea with
Many Names. Courtesy of the Ministry of Education and Maalot Publishers

When the excluded Palestinian inhabitants of these areas reappear in
this textbook it is as 'foreigners' or 'host workers' – namely as illegal invaders or temporary human labor force:

> Some of the foreign workers are Palestinians who come from the areas
> controlled by the Palestinian authorities. They are employed in unpro-
> fessional jobs and their wages are lower than that those of the Israeli
> citizens who work in the same jobs. [...] This is characteristic of all
> developed countries. (Henrikson, 1994: 32)

This characterization of developed countries was regarded by Franz
Fanon as 'The other side of western modernity: colonialism, holocaust,

א9. תפרוסת האוכלוסייה הערבית במדינת ישראל
לפי נפות, בשנת 2000

Figure 5.2 Arab Population in the State of Israel 2000 (Israel-Man and Space, 2003: 16). *White spots: 'Area for which there are no data'. Courtesy of the Centre for Educational Technology

slavery, imperialist domination and exploitation' (quoted in Reisigl & Wodak, 2001: 17).

Treating the Palestinians as foreigners points to an odd geographical perception: The Palestinian territories are presented as part of Israel, yet the inhabitants of these same territories are presented as foreigners. As van Leeuwen notes, not representing people in contexts where, in reality they are present is a racist strategy of representing 'others' (van Leeuwen, 2000: 349). This is also apparent in the map of Jerusalem, 'The historic capital of the Jewish people', (Israel-Man and Space, 2003: 174–175) titled 'Jerusalem as capital – government, culture, administration and national sites', where no Palestinian cultural sites or administrative buildings are depicted in the eastern side of the city, which is inhabited almost exclusively by Palestinians. This map convinces the viewer that Eastern

Jerusalem is an empty place where the only important sites are Temple Mount and the Wailing Wall, marked as Jewish 'national sites'.

Racist verbal and visual discourse

Israeli educators and researchers are not always aware of the racist discourse of schoolbooks. In a recent study of Israeli textbooks Firer (2004: 75) claims that 'as political correctness has reached Israel it is no longer appropriate to use blunt, discriminatory language in textbooks,' and then adds that in the years 1967–1990 'the stereotypes of Arabs and Palestinians almost disappear' (Firer, 2004: 92). However, examining the schoolbooks that were published after 1994, one cannot avoid noticing that Palestinians are still represented, visually and verbally – if at all – in a racist stereotypical way, as an impersonalized negative element, or as a nonentity.

Van Leeuwen specifies the Strategies of verbal and visual racist representation (Van Leeuwen, 2001):

- Depicting people as agents of actions that are held in low esteem or are regarded as subservient, deviant, criminal or evil.
- Exclusion: not representing them at all in contexts where in reality they are present, live and work.
- Showing people as homogenous groups and denying them individual characteristics and differences.
- Emphasizing negative cultural connotations.
- Presenting negative racial stereotypes.

Palestinians are never depicted as modern, productive, individual human beings but as negative 'types'. The most common types are the classical 'primitive' Arab with a mustache, wearing a kaffiyah and followed by a camel (usually in the form of a caricature as in Figure 5.3), the 'Oxfam images' (Hicks, 1980: 13) of the primitive farmer, 'refugees' shown from a very long distance, situated in nonplaces and face-covered terrorists, namely the 'problems' or 'threats' these people constitute for the Israelis: ('Asiatic') backwardness, terrorism and the refugee 'problem' that 'stains Israel's image in the eyes of the world' (*The 20th Century*). None of these 'Arabs' really represent the Arabs living and working in Israel or Palestine, but all of them are depicted 'as the agents of actions which are held in low esteem or regarded as subservient, deviant, criminal or evil, [or] in a negative cultural connotation' (Van Leeuwen, 2000: 349). As Rabinowitz puts it, these representations 'nourish an amalgam of right-wing anti-Arab reasoning', and conceals an image of Palestinians which Israelis can identify as PLU (Person Like Us): 'rational and educated,

Figure 5.3 (*Geography of The Land of Israel*, 2003: 303): 'The Arabs refuse to live in high buildings and insist on living in one-storey land-ridden houses'. Courtesy of Lilach Publishers

possessing the positive characteristics Israeli students tend to associate with their own collectives, a rational, well spoken, responsible Arab – a civilized, stereotype-busting native, with a jacket, a degree and an understanding smile' (Rabinowitz, 2001: 76).

The icon below, from *Geography of The Land of Israel*, does not represent any living Arab but is rather modeled after old European drawings of imaginary 'Arabs'.

Van Leeuwen specifies that whereas photographs are factual cartoons are always expressing opinion. He summarizes the motivation for such a cartoon-like presentation:

> Cartoons are general without being abstract [...]. All Turks have moustaches and all Arabs have camels. This reality is replacing the reality of naturalism and individualism. (van Leeuwen, 1992: 56)

This cartoon appears throughout the book, whenever Arabs are discussed, implying that 'they all look alike' and restricting all Arabs to this ridiculous nonexistent racial stereotype.

The caption of the caricature is elaborated in the verbal text (Aharony & Sagi, 2003: 302–303):

> The Arab society is traditional and objects to changes by its nature, reluctant to adopt novelties that may change the character of the village. Modernization seems dangerous to them for it jeopardizes the status of the elderly and the honorables. Therefore, villages that have to allocate land for the building of public roads, as the Jewish sector

does, refuse to do so because [...] they are unwilling to give anything up for the general good.

Verbally, Palestinians are represented through the discursive devices of 'impersonalisation' and 'genericization' by which whole populations are labeled by 'a generic name in the plural without the article' (van Leeuwen, 2008: 35), such as 'non-Jews'.

Non-Jews

The population in Israel is usually divided into Jews and non-Jews. The 'non-Jews', who are considered less advanced, are excluded from developmental graphs as in *People in Space* (Rap & Fine, 1996/1998: 76) (Figure 5.4).

Israel is the last bar in a row of 'developed countries'. However, at the Bottom of a graph we find a note: 'The Israeli Data Refers only to the Jewish Population.'

The indigenous 'non-Jews', regardless of their origin and religion, are called by the generic hyperonym: Arabs. For instance, in Israel–Man and Space (2003: 12):

> The Arab Population [in Israel]: Within this group there are several religious groups and several ethnic groups: Muslims, Christians,

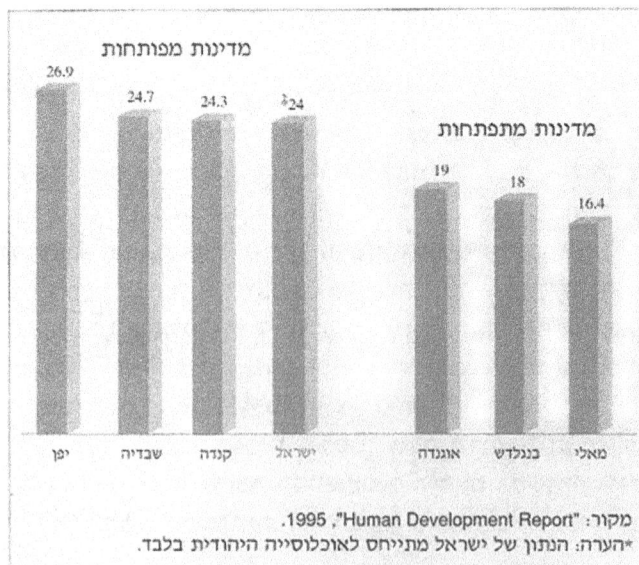

Figure 5.4 Average age of marriage for women in several countries, 1990. Courtesy of the Centre for Educational Technology. *People In Space 1996*, p. 76.

Druze, Bedouins and Circassians. But since most of them are Arab they shall be referred to henceforth as Arabs.

However, there is another group of citizens called 'others' who are the non-Jews who are not 'Arabs' – usually state-approved immigrants from the ex-Soviet Union – and these are included with the Jewish group in some statistics, as in Figure 5.5.

Students learn from this presentation that there are some non-Jews who deserve to be included in the Jewish group as long as they are not Arabs.

Mental Maps and the Marginalization of Palestinian-Arab Citizens

'Mental maps' are ideological constructs that may have little to do with geographical evidence. They reflect individual or societal perception or reflection of the world. For instance, in European maps Europe is the centre of the world. As Henrikson (1994) points out: 'Mental maps are a critical variable – occasionally the decisive factor – in the making of public policy' (Henrikson, 1994: 50). Henrikson adds that 'The map has always been the perfect representation of the state. [...] Maps are powerful and persuasive sometimes explicitly and nearly always implicitly. Every map is someone's way of getting you to look at the world in his own way. They do it by conveying that they have no such interest. They are convincing because the interests they serve are masked' (Henrikson, 1994: 58–59). 'It is through the lens of a map [...] that we see, know, and even create the larger world' (Henrikson, 1994: 52). For instance, In a history book for Grade 9 called *From Conservativism to Progress*, we learn that 'In the years 1881–1882 thousands of people arrived at Jaffa Port from Russia, from Rumania, from the Balkans and even from far-away Yemen' (Henrikson, 1994: 269).

Needless to say, Yemen is almost the closest to Jaffa Port, and the question is, why is it mentioned as the most 'far away'? The only answer is that the implied center of the 'mental map' of the writers is still Eastern Europe, the spiritual center of Zionism and the origin of the dominant social group in Israel. As Henrikson (1994) explains, 'One of the unfortunate consequences of colonialism and the condition it engendered, [...] is a feeling that the centre is elsewhere' (Henrikson, 1994: 55–56).

Maps, Henrikson maintains, have a synoptic quality (they show what is happening in an area), and a hypnotic quality – or a suggestive effect. 'Cartohypnosis' (Boggs, 1947) is the subtle persuasiveness of maps that 'causes people to accept unconsciously and uncritically the ideas that are suggested to them by maps' (Henrikson, 1994: 50). For instance, maps can

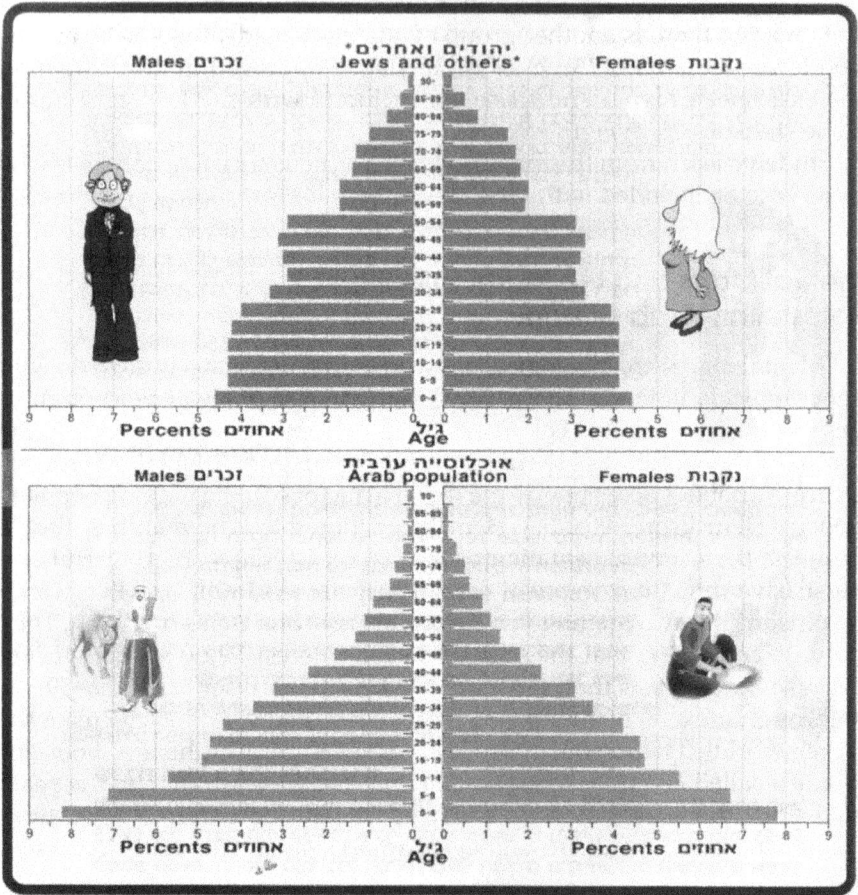

Figure 5.5 *Age Pyramid:* Title 'Jewish population versus Arab population.' Inscription inside the pyramid: 'Jews and others vs. Arabs.' *Geography of the Land of Israel* 2003: 149. (Aharony & Sagi, 2002) Courtesy of Lilach Publishers

shift the centre by means of perspective and color or differentiate between the centre and the focus of the map (van Leeuwen & Kress, 1995). The drawing of maps is highly influenced by mental maps or by the political ideologies the state is interested to diffuse. Thus, in spite of Israel's small size, the Palestinian, Druze and Bedouin citizens of Israel are pushed to the margins of consciousness and social reality, as it is well expressed in the following statement from *Geography of the Land of Israel*:

> Factors that inhibit the development of the Arab village: [...] Arab villages are far from the centre, the roads to them are difficult and they have remained out of the process of change and development, they are hardly exposed to modern life and there are difficulties to connect them to the electricity and water networks. (Aharony & Sagi, 2003: 197)

Most of these 'distant' villages are not specified on any map though they are all within the 'narrow waistline of Israel' that at its widest part is 50 km wide (30 minutes drive) and at its narrowest part is equal to the distance between Manhattan and JFK airport – 15 km, 9 minutes drive – as emphasized in Israeli maps issued by the Ministry of Foreign Affairs.[11] However, Jewish top-sites that are built on top of the hills overlooking these villages, and Jewish illegal colonies such as Ariel, Alon-Shvut and Bet-El, that are beyond the official borders of Israel, are presented in the same chapter as examples of high standard of living and not as marginal far-away deprived settlements. But as Henrikson (1994) writes: 'The sensation of peripheralness itself cannot be altered, of course, by simply shifting or reducing the graphic frame of the map' (Henrikson, 1994: 56).

Representation of Palestinians in the Occupied Territories

The Palestinian refugees, who were driven out of Palestine-Israel in 1948 and in 1967, are usually defined as 'the Palestinian problem'. van Leeuwen (2008: 41) counts as one of the features of racist discourse the reference to humans by an abstract noun that does not include the semantic feature '+ human', and represents 'social actors by means of a quality assigned to them' for instance 'the quality of being "a problem"'. This is well expressed in the following example from *The 20th Century* (p. 244):

> This chapter will explore the Palestinian problem, which stands since the beginning of the Zionist enterprise in the heart of the Middle Eastern conflict, and the attitudes within the Israeli public regarding the problem and the character of its solution. (Bar-Navi, 1998: 244)

Or in *Modern Times II* (1999: 239):

> The 'Palestinian Problem' incubated in the poverty, the idleness and the frustration that were the lot of the refugees in their pitiful camps. (Bar-Navi & Nave, 1999: 239)

This problem has no human face in any of the schoolbooks. It visually materializes in empty shanty towns or empty flooded streets (Figure 5.6), in hordes of faceless refugees or face-covered terrorists, all of which endow the 'problem' with the appearance of danger, security threats, environmental or ecological hazards.

The only information the reader receives about the Palestinian 'problem' is that of a sad 'lot' or of unfavorable circumstances that are presented in one of the following fashions (van Leeuwen, 2008: 67):

(1) In terms of 'existentialization' or 'naturalization', where action is represented as something that 'simply exists', natural and outside temporal boundaries. For instance:

'The population in the refugee camps is growing fast and the conditions of life are very hard, the rate of unemployment is high, the

Figure 5.6 *Modern Times,* 1999: 239: The 'Palestinian problem' matured in the poverty, the inaction and the frustration that were the lot of the refugees in their pitiful camps. Courtesy of the State of Israel Government Press Office

houses are crowded and poor and the standard of health services, education and hygiene is low.' (Rap & Fine, 1998: 110)

By using the auxiliary verb 'to be', the above quote presents Palestinians' dire situation as something natural. That simply exists, devoid of human agency or cause.

(2) As a self-directed phenomenon, which acts independently of human social actors:

'Although Israel came victorious out of the survival-war that was forced upon her, the Palestinian problem would poison for more than a generation the relationships of Israel with the Arab world and with the international community.' (*Modern Times II*: 239).

The 'Palestinian problem' is presented as an agent that acts on its own, to the disadvantage of Israel. It is not the problem the Palestinians have as a result of Israeli occupation, expulsion and domination but the problem of the Israelis themselves who are inflicted with this 'trouble'. Visually 'the Palestinian problem' is always shown as empty places struck by poverty and dirt. For instance, People In Space (PIS) (Rap & Fine, 1996/1998: 150) includes a subchapter called: 'Case study 4: Many refugees in the world are running for their lives'. This chapter is analytically structured: it shows many subkinds of what is classified as 'refugees'. A map shows concentrations of refugees in 1992, 1.2 million of whom, it states, are in the region of Israel. An interesting point to be made here is that the later version of this book, *Places and Settlements* (2006), turned the map into a graph that presents one bar for Central, Southern and Western Asia and north Africa, where the number of refugees is the highest in the world, without any specification.

In the 1996 version, there are altogether seven photographs: three 'close-shots' of Jewish refugees from 1945 and 1956, one close-up of Israeli soldier-doctors tending to a Rwandan baby, one 'long-shot' aerial photo of Rwandan refugees, one 'long-shot' aerial photo of Somali refugees, one 'long-shot' of Haitians, and one 'very-long-shot' of an empty shanty town defined as 'Jabalia refugee camp in the Gaza region'.[12] The 2006 version omitted the Jabalia case and replaced it with Darfur, emphasizing the help Israel has given to some of its refugees.

In the 1996 version, all the refugees except for the Palestinians are presented as human beings 'running for their lives', though all of them except for the Jewish ones are shown from a long distance, as 'phenomena' rather than as individuals. However, their troubles are detailed in the text and their escape routes are depicted on maps that contain all the necessary facts the reader might need to understand their circumstances: size of the country, composition of the population and so on. The only refugees that are not depicted 'running for their lives' are the 1.2 million refugees in the Israeli region, whose vicissitudes are neither described in the text nor depicted on any map.[13] These refugees are represented by an aerial photograph of the refugee camp of Jabalia. Van Leeuwen writes about such aerial photographs that appear in schoolbooks in the West, usually in relation to the third world:

> It is the angle of the omnipotent observer, placed high above the madding crowd [...] it is the kind of knowledge which education is still primarily concerned to reproduce. (Van Leeuwen, 1992: 49)

The caption of the aerial photograph of Jabalia reads:

> One of the big refugee camps, whose inhabitants live in over-crowdedness and poverty. (Rap & Fine, 1996/1998: 153)

This is the only caption that does not specify who the inhabitants are and how they became refugees. Poverty and over-crowdedness are presented in terms of *existentialization* – as given conditions or rather as timeless circumstances that 'simply exists' (Van Leeuwen, 2008: 67), a situation into which those inhabitants happened to fall or to be born, detached from any cause or human agency. The editorial text above the Jabalia photograph explains:

> The population in the refugee camps is growing fast and the conditions of life are very hard – the rate of unemployment is high, the houses are crowded and poor and the standard of health services, education and hygiene, is low.

This account is given without any specification. The phrase 'The population is growing fast', resembles reports about epidemics, such as the increase of mosquitoes or rats in places where *the standard of hygiene is low.*

On the back side of the page, as 'counterpart' or 'negative' of the Jabalia photograph (Rap & Fine, 1996/1998: 154), is a photograph of 'Jewish refugees on their way to Israel' during the 1950s, showing Kurdish Jews crowded in an airplane. Kress and Van Leeuwen (1995: 34) maintain that 'Connections are realized as vectors [...] on double spread, on two sides of a page or through pages'. The text above the photograph confirms the connection between the two sides of the page:

> Contrary to the Arab refugees, of whom many still live in refugee camps and their problem has not been solved [by the Arab countries] – the problem of Jewish refugees from Islamic countries has long been

solved [...] The state of Israel has invested a lot of effort in the absorption of these refugees.[14] (Rap & Fine, 1996/1998)

PAS (Segev & Fine, 2007: 111) specifies that the number of 'Arab refugees known by the label of 'Palestinian refugees' is controversial [...] The Arab countries refused to absorb them as citizens with equal rights and that is why to this day many of them live in refugee camps and slums'.

Legitimation of Massacres

'Justification' and 'legitimation' primarily refer to controversial acts or events of the past, which may influence the narrative of national history (Wodak, 2002). Coffin argues that in History textbooks events 'are appraised in their capacity to bring about good and bad changes' (Coffin, 1997: 220). Three major massacres of Palestinians, out of all the massacres that occurred during the various wars, are reported in the more 'progressive' textbooks. These reports seem to researchers as a courageous educational act (Firer, 2004; Podeh, 2002), although they are never told from the victims' point of view and although rhetorically, the reports are constructed in a way that legitimates them, for they have all brought about positive consequences for the Israelis. For instance, the massacre of the 'friendly village' Dir Yassin in 1948 (*The 20th Century*, 1998: 184–195), 'did not inaugurate the "Panic-stricken escape" of the Arabs [...] but accelerated it greatly'. Both 'inaugurate' and 'accelerated it greatly' are positive if not festive expressions. The 'panic-stricken flight' of the Palestinians, caused by this and other massacres, brought about a positive change for the Jews, for it solved 'a horrifying demographic problem' which could have been an obstacle on the way of 'the realization the dream the Zionist movement fought to realize for more than half a century: the declaration of the state of the Jews' and as the text emphasizes, 'even a moderate Zionist leader such as [the first president] Haim Weizman, considered it as a miracle' (*The 20th Century*, 1998: 195). The massacre in Kafer Kassim (on the first day of the 1956 war) had – according to the schoolbooks – positive results both for the Israelis and for the Palestinian victims themselves; for the Israelis – because it was the prompt for an unprecedented court ruling against obedience to 'manifestly unlawful orders' (Avieli-Tabibian, 2001). This court ruling was invoked by minister Yuli Tamir while speaking to high-school students during the last raid on Gaza: 'The Massacre of Kafer Kassem and the trial it entailed have become milestones in the national consciousness of the Israeli society, and has inculcated to generations of commanders and soldiers of the IDF the moral limitations of action' (Ha'aretz, December 2, 2009).

Tamir's speech implies, as other speeches of other politicians (i.e. Zipi Livni) at that time, that this ruling guarantees the alignment of what was done to the Palestinians in Gaza with universal and Jewish norms of behavior. However, from testimonies of Soldiers[15] who participated in the raids on Gaza, as in the occupation of the West Bank over the years, we learn that the implementation of this ruling has always been much more problematic. As soldiers confessed to Breaking the Silence, rules in Gaza and in the West Bank are completely different from the rules inside Israel. One textbook that addresses this problem honestly is *Being Citizens in Israel* (2001), which is being thoroughly revised now by the order of the head of the pedagogical council of the ministry of education because it promotes 'criticism against the state'.[16] This book discusses the nature of 'manifestly unlawful orders' and the impossibility of soldiers to identify them. Below are extracts from the report of Kaffer Kassim massacre as it is reproduced in this book and the discussion that follows it (headings added).

Chapter title: The Limits of Obedience to the Law in a Democratic Regime.

Sub-chapter: The duty of disobedience to the law.

Ground: It is important to note that not every disobedience to the law, to an order or to a decree is considered a felony. There are cases – especially in the military system – in which the soldier is obliged to disobey an order or a decree which are manifestly unlawful.

Explanation: A manifestly unlawful order is a rare case of a law or a decree that contradict in their content the fundamental values of a well-formed society, and is totally immoral. The individual is obliged then to disobey the unlawful order and those who obey it should be brought to trial.

Account:

Orientation: An example of a manifestly unlawful order is the one that was given in Kaferr Kassim, a large Israeli-Arab village east of Rosh ha Ayin, close to the Jordanian border.

Record of events: On October 29, 1956, with the onset of the Kadesh campaign, a curfew was imposed on Arab villages between 17:00 and 6:00 the following morning. All inhabitants of the Arab villages between Petah-tikvah and Natanya had to be at home throughout the duration of the curfew. The order was very stern: There would be no arrests, and curfew breakers were to be shot dead. The order was published the same afternoon, and the Arab villagers who had gone to the fields outside the village early in the morning knew nothing about it. When their working day was done, they returned home as usual, after 17:00. They were shot dead by a border guard unit stationed in the village. Forty-seven people including 15 women and 11 children aged 8–15 were shot dead by the soldiers, on the order of their commanding officer. It is important to note that Arab villagers from the villages neighboring Kafer Kassim who returned home after 17:00 were arrested for violating the curfew but were not shot. The border guards understood that they were not to execute the villagers who knew nothing about the curfew imposed in their area.

[...]

Discussion: The court definition of a manifestly unlawful order is problematic because it does not define clearly and accurately what it is. The definition determines the unlawfulness very ambiguously: 'unlawfulness that pierces the eye and revolts the heart'. The result of this ambiguity often puts many soldiers in a severe dilemma. The difficulty lies in that military law distinguishes between an illegal order which the soldiers must obey and an unlawful order they must disobey; for instance, when a commander orders his soldiers to search a house without a warrant [...] although the order is illegal the soldier must obey. Because of the importance of military discipline, military law obliges the soldiers to obey illegal orders. A soldier who refuses to obey an illegal order will stand trial. However, when the order is manifestly unlawful the soldier must disobey for if he obeys he will stand trial. The soldiers, who are required to make a moral deliberation, face a huge dilemma: should they obey an order that seems illegal to them because the military law obliges them to obey illegal orders or should they refuse to comply because the order is manifestly unlawful and they are bound by the military law not to obey such an order?

The soldier, who is often under stress and pressure, does not always know how to act. A soldier who has a sensitive conscience may risk disobedience to an order that revolts his conscience, and is actually legal or illegal but not manifestly unlawful. In contrast, a soldier may find himself obeying a manifestly unlawful order that did not revolt his conscience, at least not at the time of the action.

As for the Palestinian victims, most books do not mention them or their vicissitudes after the Kaffer Kassim massacre or any other massacre for that matter, except for one book, *The 20th Century* (1998: 211) that tries to convince the reader that the slaughter in Kaffer Kassim was a starting point of a long process at the end of which the military government in which Palestinian citizens lived since 1948 was abolished:

> The 1956 war was a good turning point for Israel's Arabs although it began with the tragedy of Kafer Kassim [...] but in the long run, the smashing victory, the relative peace on the borders and the self

confidence of the Jewish population turned the military government into an unbearable moral and political burden and ten years later it was abolished altogether. (1998: 121)

The text creates, through consequential explanation, a sort of logical argument by which the massacre becomes the starting point of a process whose end was beneficial for the 'Arabs'. However, the text seems careful not to give the impression that the massacre or empathy with the victims, or moral considerations alone had any direct connection with the abolition of the military government, emphasizing that it was the outcome of states of mind and circumstances of those who had imposed it in the first place, following their 'crushing victories' over other 'Arabs'. And indeed, as noted by Bauml, criticism of the military government within Israeli society at the time, 'rather than address the immense difficulty of the Arab citizens in living under the regulations of the military government or the need to stop the harsh institutional discrimination against these citizens, was focused on the need of the Jews to decontaminate their young state of the negative image of an undemocratic militaristic state that had adhered to it' (Bauml, 2002: 135).

Students learn from this text that Palestinian suffering does not deserve too much 'paper time' probably because for them 10 years of living under curfew pass very quickly.

Some books explicitly legitimate the massacres by their outcome. For instance, Kibya massacre, and other such 'reprisals' 'have restored somewhat the confidence of Israeli citizens' (Domka *et al.*, 2009: 160; Avieli-Tabibian, 2001) and rebuilt 'the morale and dignity of the IDF, helping the army to become a vigorous, bold army whose long arm could harm the enemy deep in its own territory. The IDF improved its operational capacity and its deterrent capacity' (Inbar, 2004: 244). Other books legitimate the massacres by biblical norms of 'eye for eye', describing these 'operations' as 'a punitive action' and 'an appropriate response to the murder of a woman and her two children in Yahud' (Avieli-Tabibian, 2001; Domka *et al.*, 2009), or by the norm of deterrence, relying on the biblical norm: 'kill whosoever sets out to kill you'. These norms are apparent in one of the questions in Nave *et al.*:

Do you think the reprisals were enough to deter the Arabs from acting against Israel? (Nave *et al.*, 2009: 205)

Some books give the outcomes of the massacres as causes: to empty the Dir Yassin of its inhabitants (Inbar, 2004), to restore confidence to the Jewish citizens of Israel (Domka *et al.*, 2009; Avieli-Tabibian, 2001), or to send a deterring message to the neighbours that they should control the Palestinian refugees or else. For instance:

> These actions [including the Kibya massacre] were meant to transmit a message to the host countries (especially to Jordan and Egypt) that they must prevent the infiltration from their lands. Otherwise they would be hurt. The actions were also intended to strengthen the feeling of security and the morale of the citizens of Israel. (Domka *et al.*, 2009: 160)

Or:

> The [101] unit acted for months and performed reprisals beyond Israel's borders, whose aim was to transmit the message that if the Israeli side did not enjoy peace and quiet, there would be no peace and quiet on the Arab side either. (Avieli-Tabibian, 2001: 331)

Sometimes the massacres are made to be seen like a series of mishaps, for instance:

> The loud-speaker encouraging the inhabitants of Dir-Yassin to leave the village did not work [...] the people did not leave the village and that is the reason why the number of casualties among them was so great. (Nave *et al.*, 2009: 113).

Or:

> The soldiers did not know the people were hiding in their homes that night. (Inbar, 2004: 244 Kibya massacre)

Visually, the soldiers who committed the massacres are often depicted as heroes by glorifying layout where photographs – placed above or aside mythicizing songs – show them as the role-models of Israeli youth. One such photograph (Figure 5.7) accompanies two of the reports about the Kibya massacre, depicting the 101 soldiers – headed by Ariel Sharon – with chief of staff Moshe Dayan who came to congratulate them. The soldiers wear the 'object-signs' of Israeli heroism – red military berets of paratroopers, dark khaki combat garb, parachutist wings and parachutist red boots. The photograph in this case is not only an elaboration of the verbal text – it does not just reveal who the 101 soldiers were – but a legitimatory device, for it shows the men who set the high standards of the Israeli army and later rose to the highest political positions. Such heroes could not have done unjustified wrong. Van Leeuwen notes that 'the mere fact that these role models adopt a certain kind of behaviour, or believe certain things, is enough to legitimize [their actions] and the actions of their followers' (Van Leeuwen, 2007: 103). Nave *et al.* explain that these soldiers who were endowed with 'extraordinary courage, improvisation, perseverance in the hardest conditions, tenacity and loyalty to wounded friends, became the myth of the combatant soldier in the IDF' (Nave *et al.*, 2009: 204) (Figure 5.7).

Whether they solve 'horrifying demographic' problems or any other problem such as lack of confidence in the Jewish population or low morale among the troops, the massacres of Palestinians – unfortunate as they may be – are presented, as any other action that decreases their number, as serving Israel and its project of the Judaization of the land and its de-Arabization.

The determination of the books to justify the wrong by creating legitimating narratives can also explain why in none of the reports do we find what La Capra (2001: 125) calls emphatic unsettlement, which is 'the response of even secondary witnesses (including historians) to traumatic events [...] that should register in one's very mode of address' (La Capra, 2001: 125).[17]

In the Israeli context empathy toward Palestinian victims means de-legitimating the national narrative and is therefore inadmissible. The massacres are presented as the 'founding crimes' on which the establishment of the state is based, which is why they are offered in the guise of heroic narratives. Israeli schoolbooks teach, with the aid of truthful but censored reports about massacres, that lead the reader to accept their point of view (see Peled-Elhanan, 2010), that positive outcome (for us) may condone or overlook evil (done to them), or as Žižek would put it: so much pain (inflicted on them) is tolerable if it prevents pain (for us) (Žižek, 1989).[18] They teach how to treat Palestinians 'as objects whose pain is neutralized', objects that have to be dealt with 'in a rational utilitarian calculus' (Žižek, 1989).

Israeli students embark on their military service with the conviction that empathy is race or religion related and is subject to interest.

Afterword

Coffin (1997: 205) argues that history (and one should add geography) textbooks often use the discourse of politicians, lawyers and other manipulators of language, who employ linguistic and discursive devices to persuade readers and listeners to accept interpretation as fact or truth, thereby putting the disciplinary politics of truth at stake.

The discourse used in Israeli textbooks regarding the Palestinians serves an explicit political agenda of exclusion. A recent example for the

מחוץ לגבולותיה של ישראל שמטרתן היחה להעביר את המסר כי אם לא יהיה שקט בצד הישראלי, לא יהיה שקט גם בצד הערבי. פעולה צבאית גדולה נערכה בכפר **קיביה** בירדן (אוקטובר 1953). פעולה זו באה בתגובה על רצח אישה ושני ילדיה בישוב **יהוד**. בפעולה פוצצו בתים בכפר ונהרגו 69 אזרחים ובהם נשים, זקנים וילדים. האו"ם גינה את ישראל על הפעולה. נוסף לפעולות העונשה נגד כפרים ערביים, שמהם יצאו מסתננים, ביצעה ישראל גם פעולות יזומות נגד מתקנים צבאיים במדינות ערב.

אולם בעיות הביטחון של המדינה החריפו בהתמדה. חוליות מסתננים חדרו ממדינות ערב לשטחי ישראל ובביצעו פעולות טרור קשות שזיעזעו את המדינה: **במעלה עקרבים** הותקף אוטובוס בדרכו מאילת לתל אביב, ו־11 מנוסעיו נרצחו (17.3.1954); חוליית מחבלים הגיעה למושב **שפריר** בקרבת רמלה, חדרה לבית הכנסת ופתחה באש על המתפללים (11.4.1956). בחזירת מסתננים לקיבוץ **נחל עוז**, בגבול

מצרים, נרצח אחראי הביטחון של הקיבוץ ומעשי התעללות קשים נעשו בגופתו (29.4.1956); חייל ירדני ירה על משתתפים בכינוס ארכיאולוגי **ברמת רחל** והרג 10 בני אדם (26.9.1956).

פעולות אלה גררו פעולות־נגד של צה"ל. ב־10 באוקטובר 1956, בעקבות רצח של שני פועלים יהודים בפרדס בקרבת הגבול, יצא צה"ל להתקפה על **משטרת קלקיליה**. פעולות התגמול אמנם חיזקו במידה מה את תחושת הביטחון בקרב האזרחים, אבל גררו בעקבותיהם ניגויים מצד האו"ם ומצד מדינות המערב.

Figure 5.7 *The Age of Horror and Hope* (Avieli-Tabibian, 2001:232). Courtesy of IDF Archives and the centre for educational technology

continuing efforts to be rid of the Palestinian-Arab citizens is found in the declaration by Zipi Livni that is quoted above.

Reality is presented in Israeli schoolbooks from the point of view of the dominant Jewish group, who considers Palestinians as a primitive, vile, threatening and undesirable element. The maps conceal Palestinian existence and show disregard for international laws and decisions. Human-caused evils are presented as natural processes and the killing and expulsion of the indigenous population are legitimized in the name of the highest Israeli cause – the existence of the Jewish state. Israeli students may be drafted to the army without ever having seen a Palestinian face to face let alone having talked to one. However, the information they receive from their school books prepares them to treat their neighbors as unwanted invaders and to feel no compassion for their suffering. This education is far from encouraging peace and coexistence.

Notes

1. The only group of immigrants who is strong enough not to obey these assimilative requirements is the Russian one, who has its own schools, papers, publishing houses, theatre and political parties.
2. The word is half the speaker's and half the listener's. For the act of reading as personal meaning-making see also Iser, *The Act of Reading*, Barthes' *The Pleasure of the Text*, S/Z, Umberto Ecco's *The Limits of Interpretation*, J. Bruner's *Acts of Meaning* to name but few.
3. This law is a response to the Supreme Court 2004 ruling in favor of the Arab citizen Adel Kaadan, who wanted in 1995 to buy land in the out-post of Katzir and was refused on the ground that the land is reserved for army veterans (Supreme Court File 8060/03). In 2004, after another petition to the court, the Israel Lands Authority was forced to allocate land to the Kaadan family in Katzir in spite of their rejection by the screening committee.
4. Both the UN Committee against Racism and Amnesty found the Law of Citizenship tainted with worrying racism.
5. http://news.bbc.co.uk/2/hi/8163959.stm. Israeli textbooks to drop 'Nakba'. 'The so-called "**Nakba** Law" aims to prevent public commemoration of the catastrophe – or "**Nakba**" in Arabic – that befell the Arab population of Palestine during the Arab – Israeli war of 1948 that gave birth to the State of Israel'.[16] The bill, approved at first reading, on March 15, 2010, authorizes the finance minister 'to decrease the budget for bodies receiving government funding if they allow marking Israeli-Jewish Independence Day and the founding of Israel with mourning ceremonies'. The Israeli Democracy Institute http://www.idi.org.il/sites/english/OpEds/Pages/NakbaaLaw.aspx. Accessed on 22.07.09.
6. Although the Arabs make up 20% of the population they have only 3.5% of the land [...] Over a half of land owners were expropriated by the state after 1948 and more than 500 Jewish settlements were built on these lands [...]

Since its establishment the state has built over 700 Jewish localities and 0 Arab localities. Yiftachel (2006: 133, 166).

7.　Yiftachel, O. (Un) Settling colonial presents, *Political Geography* (2008).

8.　Israeli schoolbooks are trade books and teachers may choose which book to use. However, they all need to be authorized by the Ministry of education or at least be compatible with the national curriculum. I chose the textbooks that were mostly bought according to bookstore reports. The Geography of the Land of Israel does not have the authorization of the Ministry of Education, though it claims to be written according to the national curriculum and is sold and used in schools. I thank the following publishing houses for letting me reproduce the photocopied pages from the textbooks: The Centre for Educational Technologies (*People in Space, Israel-Man and Space*), The Ministry of Education and Maalot Publishers (*The Mediterranean Countries*), Lilach Publishers (*the Geography of the Land of Israel*). IDF Archives.

9.　All the quotes and excerpts from schoolbooks were translated from Hebrew by me and validated by professional translators. All bolds are mine.

10.　*Haaretz*, December 27, 2008.

11.　http:/www.mfa.gov.il/MFA/facts about Israel/Israel in maps#threats& topography. Last accessed on 1.1.08.

12.　These terms are taken from van Leeuwen (1992, 45), who used the terminology of television and film.

13.　Million Palestinian refugees is not an accurate figure but the figure given by the book. Israel admits there are 3 million, UNRWA claims there are 3.5 million, and the Palestinians claim there are 5 million refugees, 1.5 million in Gaza Strip.

14.　This statement stands in contrast to statements in History textbooks (i.e. *The 20th Century*: 214) which assert that the Jewish refugees from Arab countries were actually deceived and treated badly by the state of Israel and their problems are still far from being resolved. However, it serves the Israeli claim that it should be absolved of all responsibility for the Palestinian refugees for it had Jewish refugees from Arab countries to absorb.

15.　Occupation of the Territories, Israeli soldier testimonies 2000–2010. Breaking the silence.org.

16.　Or Kashti, September 1, 2010 http://www.haaretz.co.il/hasite/spages/1187466.html. Accessed on 1.9.10.

17.　As is expressed in the suggested law approved by the committee of ministers on the May 24, 2009 – forbidding the commemoration of Palestinian catastrophe in 1948 – the *Naqba*.

18.　Term quoted from Yiftachel (2006: 105).

Part 2

Media

Chapter 6

Palestinians, Arab American Muslims and the Media

N. AYISH

Introduction

The conversation invariably goes something like this: 'Where are you from?' 'Palestine.' 'Pakistan?' 'No, Palestine.' 'Um, where's that?'

I have had this conversation with countless students and adults of all ages.

As an educator, I often wonder how it is possible for a place, Palestine, and a people, the Palestinians, to be so highly visible in popular culture, yet, at the same time, remain so seemingly invisible and misunderstood to the typical American. After all, it is difficult to grow up and/or live in the United States without being regularly inundated by images of Palestinians, the Israeli-Palestinian conflict or Arabs and Muslims in film, the media and other popular culture.

While many have pointed to Hollywood and the media as a cause for perpetuating stereotypes about Palestinians and maintaining myths and misinformation about the Israeli-Palestinian conflict, that so many in the United States remain ignorant about the world's most reported conflict and, in particular, about one of the key players in that conflict – the Palestinians – suggests that there are other factors impacting people's understanding (Ahmed, 1998; Alatom, 1997; Ayish, 2006, 2008; Haddad & Smith, 2002; Naber, 2000; Said, 1978, 2009; Shaheen, 2000, 2001, 2008; Zogby, 2010).

What I have discovered while teaching middle school for more than 21 years (as well as graduate school for the past six years) is that three key factors – in addition to popular culture – have negatively impacted the ability of many children and adults to know basic facts about Palestinians and the Israeli-Palestinian conflict, or, on an even more fundamental level, to simply see the humanity of the Palestinians. First, there has been a conflation of Palestinians, Arabs and Muslims into one 'other' in popular culture. Second, there is a psychological explanation as to why otherwise rational individuals seem unable to empathize with a people dispossessed of both land and liberty. And third, there is an absence of accurate and comprehensive information about Palestinians and the Israeli-Palestinian conflict in K–12 curriculum (Barlow, 1994; Brockway, 2007; Morgan, 2008).

This chapter analyzes how such mediums as film, the media and other popular culture – in the absence of accurate and comprehensive information in school curriculum – affect many people's understanding of the Palestinians and the Israeli-Palestinian conflict and why this makes seeing Palestinians as an indigenous population deserving freedom and human rights so complicated for so many.

Arab Americans and Islam

The conflation of Palestinians, Arabs and Muslims into one 'other' in popular culture stems, in part, from the way popular culture has historically reduced the tremendous diversity inherent among a quarter of the world's population. The intentional blending of many US and Israeli policies (based ostensibly on shared values and principles of democracy, the rule of law and strategic interests among other things relative to Arabs and Muslims) only reinforces this stereotyping (Haddad, 1991a; Haddad & Smith, 2002; Mearsheimer & Walt, 2007; Said, 1978; Shaheen, 2001, 2008). That the identity of Palestinians is subsumed by this conflation suggests that for many in the United States, distinguishing between Palestinians as a distinct nationality and Arabs and Muslims generally is neither easy nor even necessary – especially within the context of the Israeli-Palestinian conflict. In the absence of accurate information in popular culture and social and formal institutions such as schools, this has only complicated the ability of many Americans to see the Palestinians as an indigenous population dispossessed of their historic homeland by an illegal occupation (United Nations Report of the Human Rights Council (UNRHRC), 2009).

Complicating matters further, it is important to point out that there is a general misunderstanding in the United States of the terms 'Arab', 'Muslim', 'Arab American' and 'Arab American Muslim'. Such broad labels are often used interchangeably – and erroneously – and reflect an inaccurate but popular perception among many Americans (and perpetuated in popular culture) that Arab Americans – irrespective of their ethnicity, national origin or religious affiliation – are the same (Aswad, 1993; Salaita, 2005; Sarroub, 2001; Seikaly, 2001; Shaheen, 2008; Zogby, 2010).

Thus, it is difficult for one to talk about Palestinians without being reminded of the implicit or explicit connection they have with Arabs and Muslims. And because of the negative stereotypes associated with these two groups, Palestinians often experience a double indignity: They are overtly disparaged in popular culture, while also being disparaged by their association with Arabs/Muslims (i.e. when an Arab or Muslim, e.g. commits an act of violence Palestinians are likely to be implicitly [if not explicitly] associated with this act).

On a practical level, many Americans are confused as to whether Muslims constitute a religion or a race. Given that the average American is raised on a steady diet of Hollywood images in which the depiction of Palestinians, Arabs and Muslims is often blurred, such confusion might be expected. After all, as Shaheen pointed out, there is the 'real' version of Arabs and Islam and a 'reel' version created for the Hollywood set (2001, 2008: 7). Unfortunately, the contempt, fear and misunderstanding many Americans have of Palestinians, Arabs and Islam stems not from personal contact and experience with these individuals, but from Hollywood's depiction of them, and translates into practical consequences for Arab Americans (both Christian and Muslim) and non-Arab American Muslims (Abraham, 1995; American Muslim Council, 1993; Esposito, 1988; Haddad, 1991b; Shaheen, 2001, 2008; Zogby, 2010).

For example, after every major event that involved or purported to involve Muslims (e.g. the 1979 Iranian hostage crisis, the 1983 bombing of the United States marine barracks in Beirut, the 1990 Gulf War, the 1993 World Trade Center bombing, the 1995 bombing of the Alfred P. Murrah Federal Building in Oklahoma City and the 2001 attack on the World Trade Center), numerous instances of racial profiling, work place discrimination and hate crimes against Arab and Muslim Americans – or those that looked Arab or Muslim – were reported (ADC, 2009; Alavi, 2001). While such instances are not uncommon within the Arab and Muslim American community – even during times of relative calm – the fact that they increase dramatically during times of crisis reflects an underlying fear, misunderstanding and uncertainty that characterizes the relationship between Arab and Muslim Americans and others in the United States.

It is worth noting that, historically, one of the consequences of stereotyping has been a conditioning of the public to allow government a freer hand in policies that are discriminatory and that infringe on civil liberties (Haddad, 1991a, 2002). Numerous ethnic groups have experienced this, including African Americans, Asians, Latinos and Native Americans

(Dovidio & Gaertner, 1986). In the case of Palestinians and other Arab and Muslim Americans, legislation such as the USA Patriot Act of 2001, racial profiling and the use of secret evidence have been adopted with serious ramifications for civil liberties and civil rights (Salaita, 2005). The ongoing trial of Palestinian American professor, Sami Al-Arian, an outspoken critic of Israeli policies, is just the latest in a number of high-profile cases (Malloy, 2009). Thus, the cumulative effect of such misinformation and stereotypes often translates into real political and social consequences. As Haddad recognized early on, this makes Arab American Muslims feel that they are on 'a roller coaster on which they are forced to experience new heights of distortion and vilification' (Haddad, 1991a: 226) while living in a country that has grown more and more hostile to their ethnicity and faith.

Haddad also suggests that some people know that 'the truth about the Arab world, Islam and Muslims is being distorted for political expediency by those in office' (Haddad, 1991a: 26). Nonetheless, such mischaracterization and generalizations are regularly made by top government officials, opinion makers and others (Khan, 1998; Salaita, 2005; Zogby, 2010). The controversy surrounding the so-called 'Ground Zero mosque' in New York City is just the latest example. Silberstein confirms that 'In the recent past, rhetorics of Middle East occupation have centered on Palestine, an icon of grievance and Western domination for some, of terrorism for others' (Silberstein, this volume: 173). These comments contribute to an atmosphere of mistrust and suspicion between Arab American Muslims and the larger US society and lead to detrimental economic, political and social policies that affect all concerned. This is particularly true with regard to the Palestinians and charities and organizations created to assist them with everything from medical relief to food distribution.

The media further complicate matters by reinforcing the 'stereotyping of Islam and Arabs and their equation with radicalism and terrorism' (Esposito, 1996: 10). Indeed, the 'negative image of the Arab world and of Islam has been further distorted by those Western commentators who have in recent years portrayed Islam as a triple threat: a political, cultural, and demographic threat' (Esposito, 1996: 11). Berlin demonstrates how the media, based, in part on ideology, 'propagandize identical events' (Berlin, this volume) to the detriment of the other side. The days, months and years following the tragic events of September 11, for instance, highlighted the tenuous and uncertain status that many in the Arab American Muslim community felt. Israel, in particular, capitalized on the fear generated among many in the United States toward Arabs and Muslims and used

September 11 as a means to strengthen ties with the United States and as a justification for even harsher treatment of the Palestinians (Mearsheimer & Walt, 2007).

Palestinians, Arab American Muslims and Stereotype Research

To understand how stereotyping is used to impact people's understanding of Palestinians and the Israeli-Palestinian conflict, it is helpful to have a sense of the history of stereotype research in the United States and its relationship to Palestinians (and, by extension, Arabs and Muslims).

The term 'stereotype' was first used by Lippmann (1922) to refer to beliefs about groups (Miller, 1982: 3). He defined stereotypes as generalizations about social groups that are rigidly held, illogically derived and negative. He also described stereotypes as 'pictures in our heads', which constituted 'erroneous representations acquired other than through direct experience of the reality they claim to represent' (Lippmann, 1922: 12). Despite Lippmann's research, it has only recently been established that most devaluing group stereotypes are known throughout society. Indeed, while the field of social psychology, in particular, has surveyed the content of stereotypes, examined their effect on social perception and behavior, considered the motivational bases of prejudice, and, along with personality psychologists, analyzed the origins of prejudice, many researchers now agree with Devine (1989) that because communicative processes (such as public discourse, popular culture and school curricula) play such a central role in the acquisition of stereotypes, knowledge of cultural stereotypes is shared by people irrespective of one's level of prejudice – including those being stereotyped (Bandura, 2006; Fein & Spencer, 1997; Fishman, 1956; Katz & Braly, 1933; Tajfel, 1978, 1981).

Although stereotype research from the 1920s to the 1940s did not include Palestinians or even Arabs or Muslims, their images can nonetheless be gleaned from news accounts and film from that time. For example, the stereotype of the Arab/Muslim during the early part of the 20th century was that embodied by Rudolph Valentino as he appeared in the movie, *The Sheikh* (1921). These individuals were seen as 'exotic desert dwellers', 'brute savages' and 'lecherous sheikhs' out to harm the dashing Western hero and to seduce the fair Western heroine, while all but ignoring – or worse, enslaving – hoards of nameless, faceless and oppressed Arab women (Orfalea, 1988; Shaheen, 2001, 2008). This 'picture in our heads' remained intact throughout the 1920s and 1930s and shaped an entire generation's image of Arabs and Muslims. As Shaheen revealed, unlike stereotypes for some ethnic groups, this image has neither been eliminated nor replaced. Instead, it has been altered – with varying modifications – only to be recycled and resurrected in countless other films. As one movie producer explained, the image of the Arab is a 'ready-made stereotype' just waiting to be tapped (Shaheen, 2001; 28). Thus, Arab and Muslim stereotypes have and continue to serve a dual purpose; they are easily recognized by viewers with little or no prompting, and they are a convenient foil for scriptwriters and producers in need of a quick prop (Greenberg & Brand, 1994; Shaheen, 2001).

For the purposes of this discussion, therefore, a stereotype will be regarded as 'a representation of a culture which teaches that the people of that culture are by nature inferior' (Alatom, 1997: 24). This definition best reflects the type of stereotypes confronting Palestinians (as well as Arabs and Muslims) in the United States and also echoes Allport's (1954: 9) notion of 'refencing'. After all, such stereotypes contend that these individuals possess inherently flawed characteristics (e.g. terrorist, fundamentalist, oppressive, womanizer, greedy, unsophisticated and violent) and that nothing on their part can be done to alter this condition (Fishman, 1956). The consequences of such false conclusions can be detrimental for both individuals and groups. For instance, while it is true that a small number of Palestinians have used violence to resist Israeli occupation, the truth is that the vast majority of Palestinians regularly use nonviolence to assert their desire to be free. Likewise, while it is true that a small number of Arabs are fabulously wealthy and derive their wealth from oil, the truth is that many Arabs are, in fact, relatively poor and lack basic needs, such as access to clean water (UNDP, 2009). Over time, the effect of such erroneous stereotypes can adversely affect people's understanding of Palestinians and Arabs and negatively influence American domestic, economic and foreign policies (Shaheen, 2001, 2008; Zogby, 2010).

Given the nature of stereotype research in the early 1900s and considering the relatively small Arab and Muslim American population at the time, it is not surprising that this segment of society was overlooked. After all, immigration officials were just beginning to recognize Arabs as citizens of distinct nations. What is surprising, however, is that despite the increased number and visibility of the approximately 15 million Palestinians, Arabs and Muslims in the United States today, the growth of stereotype research into virtually every aspect of human interaction and the September 11 tragedy, this diverse population remains relatively excluded from such research (Abraham & Abraham, 1981; Pulcini, 1993; Salaita, 2005).

Disconfirming evidence

Along with the study by Katz and Braly (1933), most early research on stereotyping assumed that stereotypes were necessarily erroneous. After all, it had been demonstrated that stereotypes were neither based necessarily on facts nor fixed in time. An important confirmation of this assumption was the belief advocated by Allport (1954) that people's perceptions about others are emotionally defended, even in the face of disconfirming evidence (Kunda & Oleson, 1995). This is particularly true with regard to Palestinians and the Israeli-Palestinian conflict.

The concept of contact-hypothesis stems from Allport's (1954) research on prejudice – as well as from Tajfel's (1968) research on intergroup relations – and has been embraced by numerous social psychologists. The underlying theme of this concept is that interactions with members of stereotyped groups offer a means to reduce the level of discrimination and improve intergroup relations. Contact-hypothesis research assumed that the new evidence about members of a stereotyped group would contradict people's expectations and instigate a change in the content of their stereotype (Dovidio & Gaertner, 1986; Hewstone & Brown, 1986). Those that embraced this belief saw great promise in its implementation. To many, the concept of contact-hypothesis seemed intuitive, relatively easy to implement and a means to reduce and eliminate various stereotypes plaguing society at the time. The strategy of providing people with an opportunity to interact with stereotype-disconfirming members of another group, however, met with little success. In fact, it has been shown that stereotypes are often maintained over extended periods of time even after manipulation involving cooperation with atypical members of the group (Kunda & Oleson, 1995; Schneider, 2005). This is evident in the ongoing efforts of many to alter the general image of Palestinians.

Stereotypes and psychological research

This gap in understanding is nurtured in other ways too. For example, while the impact stereotypes have on individuals is well-documented (e.g. lower self-esteem, self-concept, self-perception and academic performance) and scholarship on this topic has expanded over the past few decades to include not only concern with African American student achievement but a greater recognition of other ethnic groups in the United States, some populations, such as Palestinians, remain insufficiently researched (Allport, 1954; Ayish, 2008; Erikson, 1968; Nieto *et al.*, 2001; Steele & Aronson, 1995). Unfortunately, Palestinian students have been excluded from such research, because unlike many other minorities, they have not been studied as a group with historic ties to the United States. This is not surprising considering that popular culture has consistently portrayed this segment of society as foreign. Indeed, in research studies, which tend to focus on issues of adjustment, Palestinian American children are almost always treated as foreign students (Ahmed, 1998; Haddad & Smith, 2002). This oversight is striking because the vast majority of these children are US born. Furthermore, they are part of one of the fastest growing ethnic and religious groups in major metropolitan areas in which distinct immigration patterns have produced an internally diverse community whose attitudes and behaviors vary by nativity, social class, religion and culture (Zogby, 1998, 2010).

What I find most disconcerting about the paucity of research on Palestinians, however, is that the voices of these individuals remain unheard at a time when historically disenfranchised groups are demanding more accurate representation and inclusion of their culture and narrative in society, in popular culture and in school curricula. Even multicultural education, which has elevated the voices of many marginalized groups, has not adequately addressed the needs of this growing population of students.

This is ironic, because while Palestinian Americans are considered part of an 'invisible' minority, they are nonetheless highly visible in a negative sense in popular culture (Naber, 2000; Salaita, 2005). And as Samhan notes, because Arab identity in the United States 'has historically been largely invisible and also racially ambiguous, falling between the cracks of the white/nonwhite binary and not officially recognized as an ethnic identity' (Samhan, 1999: 214), it is this negative visibility that has proven so detrimental to the ability of many Americans to relate to Palestinians. This, despite the fact that Palestinian Americans are considered one of the most assimilated ethnic minorities in the United States (e.g. typically losing their ability to read, write and speak their heritage language – Arabic – after only one generation) (Naber, 2000).

Persistence of stereotypes

Allport (1954) was aware of one process that could account for the persistence of stereotypes. He used the term 'refencing' to describe the strong tendency displayed by people to appraise disconfirming behavior as being performed by exceptions in the group. He also suggested that judging individuals to be atypical and not representative members of a group offers an effective strategy to maintain preexisting beliefs.

Other researchers have since confirmed his findings (Bodenhausen & Wyer, 1985; Schneider, 2005). This notion of refencing offers further insight into why certain stereotypes about Palestinians (and Arabs and Muslims) persist despite efforts to alter them. In fact, attempts to mitigate such perceptions by providing Americans with opportunities to interact with Palestinians and other Arabs/Muslims have been met with little success. Ayish (2006, 2008), Naber (2000), Shaheen (2000, 2008) and Zogby (2010) suggest that until a fundamental shift occurs in the environment in which such stereotypes are created, nurtured and sustained (i.e. in popular culture and school curricula), overcoming the effects of refencing by simply increasing contact among these various groups will remain insufficient.

Two particular studies offer insight into why stereotypes about certain groups (e.g. African Americans, Jews, Palestinians and Muslims) seem to persist and resist change over time. According to Schaller, Schaller and Conway (2001), some groups are more likely to be talked about than others. While there are many reasons why these groups figure more prominently in conversations (e.g. visual appearance and dress, religious differences and population size), it has been determined that the way people talk about others has a causal effect on stereotyping. That is, the more the traits are discussed, the more likely they are to be stereotypical (Schaller & Conway, 2001). In addition, those traits that are most discussed are also most likely to become and remain part of the popular stereotypes of ethnic groups.

Thus, traits that are identified as being stereotypical are likely to remain stereotypical for an extended period, especially if the traits are part of an ongoing conversation about a particular group. Because Palestinians and their images have been an integral part of Hollywood and popular culture for decades, it makes sense that such stereotypes remain alive more than the stereotypes for other groups that receive less attention.

For instance, one common stereotype about Palestinians that has existed for the past 60 years in film is that of the terrorist (Alatom, 1997; Haddad, 1991a; Shaheen, 2001, 2008; Zogby, 2010). This stereotype has been perpetuated in film, in the media and in popular culture to such an extent that many Americans are convinced that the stereotype is accurate. It slips into conversation as a fact known to all rather than as a means by some to caricature Palestinians.

The *kafeeya* (checkered black and white headdress) is the most visible manifestation of this stereotype. While many Americans may accept the stereotypical view that the *kafeeya* is the embodiment of Palestinian terrorism (just as the *swastika* symbolizes Nazis' genocide), the fact that most Palestinians perceive the *kafeeya* as a cultural and national artifact, in which few even wear the garment today, is lost (Antoun, 1994; Shaheen, 2008). That the *kafeeya* is talked about at all by individuals with otherwise little accurate knowledge of Palestinians or the Israeli-Palestinian conflict illustrates the notion that the more the stereotypes are communicated, the more likely they are to remain intact.

Given the lack of inclusion of Palestinians in stereotype research, it is necessary to look elsewhere for evidence of such stereotypes. In this regard, examining once again how Arabs and Muslims have been depicted in film over the years can be illuminating. Indeed, it was recognized early on that film was the most powerful tool to shape people's understanding of others. Following World War I and the lessons learned from producing war propaganda, for example, the head of Paramount Pictures claimed that 'as an avenue of propaganda, as a channel for conveying thought and opinion, the movies are unequaled by any form of communication' (as cited by Shaheen, 2001: 27).

Three phases of Palestinian/Arab/Muslim stereotypes in film have developed over the years. While each phase is distinct in many ways, all three share several fundamental characteristics. Stereotypes during the first phase did not explicitly include reference to Palestinians. Rather, the Arab and Muslim male stereotype emanating from Hollywood early in the 20th century was simply that of 'stooges-in-sheets, slovenly, hook-nosed potentates intent on capturing pale-faced blondes for their harems' (Shaheen, 2001: 19). Women were portrayed as 'bosomy belly dancers leering out from diaphanous veils' or as 'scantily clad harem maidens with bare midriffs, closeted in the palace's women's quarters' (Shaheen, 2001: 22). Movies such as *The Sheikh* (1921), *The Arab* (1924), *Son of the Sheikh* (1926) and *The Desert Bride* (1928) are representative of the type of genre that emanated from Hollywood at the time. Although it is worth acknowledging that Hollywood did not necessarily create these stereo-types, but rather inherited them from British and French colonial litera-ture and propaganda, film is nonetheless responsible for making these stereotypes more widely known to American (and international) audi-ences (Shaheen, 2001).

The second phase of stereotypes took shape after the Arab-Israeli War of 1948. And while it incorporated many of the stereotypes from the first phase, it also developed its own characteristics. Arabs and Muslims – and, in particular, Palestinians – came to be seen as terrorists out to kill Americans, Europeans, Israelis and even other Arabs (Haddad & Smith, 2002; Shaheen, 2001). *Sward in the Desert* (1949), *Exodus* (1960) and *Cast a Giant Shadow* (1966) are a few of the movies associated with this period.

The 1967 Arab-Israeli War contributed to the widespread image of this genre in films produced to this day.

The third phase of Arab and Muslim stereotypes came about after the 1973 Arab-Israeli War and subsequent Arab oil embargo. This phase incorporated a familiar image, but with new, more sinister overtones in which oily-sheikh billionaires, invariably sporting sunglasses and goatees, were out to buy up America. Stereotypes during this phase evolved further by incorporating earlier elements in which Palestinians, Arabs and Muslims came to be seen, with few exceptions, as fundamentalist terrorists, identifiable by particular garb (i.e. the *kafeeya*), and still coveting the blonde-Western heroine, but now seeking to dominate all that is valued in Western civilization or destroy all that cannot be dominated (e.g. *Prisoner in the Middle* (1974), *Black Sunday* (1977), *The Delta Force* (1986), *Wanted Dead or Alive* (1987), *Navy Seals* (1990), *True Lies* (1994), *Executive Decision* (1996) and *Rules of Engagement* (2000)).

Although this third phase effectively captures the essence of Shaheen's 'reel' or celluloid Arab (2001: 7), many had hoped that the events of September 11, 2001, would usher in a more nuanced phase of Arab and Muslim stereotypes in which image makers moved away from such overt and rigid stereotypes. Yet, little has fundamentally changed, with the possible exception of a few films such as *Syriana* (2005) and *Kingdom of Heaven* (2005) that offer slightly more complex portrayals of Arabs and Muslims (Salaita, 2005; Shaheen, 2000, 2001, 2008). Consequently, all the original stereotypes of Palestinians, Arabs and Muslims remain ready to be resurrected whenever they are needed, especially that of the 'Islamic' fundamentalist terrorists. And, as US foreign policy has tilted even more in favor of Israel, such images have only increased (Salaita, 2005; Shaheen, 2000, 2001, 2008).

Of course, some Palestinians, Arabs and Muslims have committed horrible acts of violence. The problem, however, is that the 'picture in our heads' of these individuals or groups have come to represent 10 million Palestinians, 300 million Arabs and 1.5 billion Muslims (Haddad & Smith, 2002, *inter alia*). Discourse among many Americans and others is dominated by the images and the acts of these few individuals, complicating the ability of Palestinians, especially after 9/11, to be accurately portrayed or understood.

Overcoming part of the challenge of understanding how the stereotyping of Palestinians and/or Arabs/Muslims impacts many Americans is connected to research that has been done on the influence of media exposure on social beliefs. However, while this is an increasingly popular area of psychological study, much of this research is dedicated to the examination of media portrayals of gender stereotypes. In contrast, little research has examined the effect of the media on racial stereotyping and even less on its influence on cultural, religious and political stereotyping (Beasley & Standley, 2002; Nathanson *et al.*, 2002; Nieto, 2000).

Nonetheless, considering the three main ways in which the media may influence stereotypes (through underrepresentation, selective presentation and stereotypic presentation) offers some insight into the effect such influences have on Palestinians. For example, minorities depicted on US television and other US media are often underrepresented in proportion with census data (except in the case of Palestinians where the reverse is true), presented in only selective situations, and frequently portrayed in stereotypical ways considered condescending and negative (Busselle & Crandall, 2002; Greenberg & Collette, 1997; Schneider, 2005). And although it is difficult to determine the true consequences of minority stereotyping in the media – as it is impossible to examine these effects in isolation from nonmedia influences on stereotypes – it has been shown that negative stereotyping (including gender, religious, ethnic and racial) in the media results in negative responses by young viewers toward the group portrayed, just as positive depictions result in more complimentary views (Durkin & Judge, 2001; Mullen *et al.*, 2000). This suggests that in the absence of reliable and accurate information about Palestinians, Arabs/Muslims in school curricula, 'It is time to recognize that the true tutors of our children are not schoolteachers or university professors but filmmakers' (Barber, as cited by Shaheen, 2001: 31). The same can be said of politicians and those in the field of political commentary, including television news and talk radio who help shape public opinion (Silberstein, this volume). Indeed, the underrepresentation and selective and stereotypic presentation of Palestinians in popular culture illustrates the inevitable effect such discourse can have on our ability to rationally understand a particular people and a particular conflict.

Conclusion

As Jo Kent, Sibii and Napoleone assert, 'When we teach students how to deconstruct media in all its forms, we must also show them how to build alternative interpretations tha generate desired meaningfulness' (Jo Kent, this volume). Doing so will begin the process of analyzing the complex reasons why Palestinian stereotypes persist and why so many in the United States remain misinformed and ignorant about the Israeli-Palestinian conflict. As an educator, I am cautiously optimistic that recognizing the relationship that exists between popular culture and K–12 curriculum development and psychology can be a critical step in bringing about the kind of comprehensive shift in thinking that is necessary for meaningful and sustained change in people's understanding. Through such concerted efforts, altering the discourse that dominates much of the rhetoric surrounding the Palestinians and the Israeli-Palestinian conflict is possible.

Chapter 7

The Political Discourse of the Israeli Occupation: The Spirit of Orientalism[1]

A. ATAWNEH

> *The Arab-Israeli conflict makes smart people dumb, sensitive people*
> *brutal, and open minded people pigheaded fanatics.*
> Ron David, 1993: 2

> *Arabs, undisciplined people, dogs, go back dogs*
> Fadwa Touqan, 1970[2]

Introduction

Ron David, a contemporary Israeli writer, and the late Fadwa Touqan, a Palestinian woman poet, challenge us to consider the language of occupation in the case of Palestine. According to Menz (1989), a concern of critical linguistics is to relate language to its users and to seek some principled way of bringing out the ideologies inherent in their communications. In the case of Ron David and Fadwa Touqan: how can we relate their political perspectives and ideologies to an international readership that may not be familiar with the history of the conflict? The quotes which open this chapter by David and Touqan index ways in which language can justify, mediate, reproduce or resist oppression in the case of occupied Palestine.

Critical Discourse Analysis (CDA) is a tool to look into language used in a specific context such as promoting war or peace (van Dijk, 2001). Among the objectives of CDA is to uncover inequality and injustice is language behavior in natural speech situations of social relevance, that is, media and racism (Wodak, 1989). All situations which are threatening or involve a power play between individuals are of interest. CDA is a tool to investigate how language serves war or peace. This chapter explores the language of occupation in Palestine and analyzes how language in the media reflects power or weakness in the two sides of the conflict (van Dijk, 1994). Occupation is defined as the invasion and control of a country or area by enemy forces.

In the two opening quotes in this chapter, the seemingly irresolvable horror of the conflict is highlighted by Ron David's trio of negative transformations:

(1) *Stupidity*: ('smart people dumb').
(2) *Brutality* ('sensitive people brutal').
(3) *Fanaticism* ('open-minded people ... pigheaded fanatics').

In the early 1970s, the Palestinian poet Fadwa Touqan wrote the poem *Waiting at the Allenby Bridge Begging for Crossing* quoting an Israeli soldier addressing Palestinians: 'Arabs, undisciplined people, dogs, go back dogs.' Echoed in Fadwa Tuqan's ('dogs, go back dogs') is the allusion to the historic justification of British colonial subjugation of Palestine which predated the Israeli occupation. The reference to Orientalism (Said, 1978) in which colonial subjects are represented as exotic, uncivilized or animal like in need of Western enlightenment and governance is an example of the way in which poetry can serve as a counterdiscourse or writing-back of the colonial subject and engage the reader in an awareness or (re-) examination of the injustice of occupation. Edward Said understood and responded to the precarious nature of how the Palestinians struggle is represented in the West. He knew how the historic position of Jews in European history silenced all attempts by Palestinians to narrate their story, and how the predicament of the Palestinian people as the 'victims of the victims' of Europe conditioned the West's refusal of support or sympathy. The spirit of Orientalism is seen through the contrastive picture of the Israelis and the Palestinians. The Palestinians have no known Einsteins, no Chagall, no Freud or Rubinstein to protect them with a legacy of glorious achievements. The Palestinians have had no Holocaust to protect them with the world's compassion. They are 'the other,' and opposite, a flaw in the geometry of resettlement and exodus. The negative counterpart of Orientalism has been demonstrated by the Oslo deal which was made on the basis of naked power, while the outside image was one of normativity. It was rape portrayed as a love story. Despite the one-sidedness, the Palestinian leadership went along with the image of 'historic compromise' to avoid putting its weakness on public display (Zreik, 2003: 39–49).

One question for CDA is how opposing sides of a conflict are identified textually. By 'naming' the problem *occupation* the participants have already taken a political stance toward the framing of the dialogue (Wong *et al.*, this volume). Of interest to those readers who are not familiar with the case of Palestine is how to reference the two sides of the conflict: Is it the *Arab-Israeli conflict* as Ron David has identified the problem in the quote above? Or is it the British and subsequent *Israeli occupation of Palestine* with Palestinians and other people who were driven from their homes? In the first narrative of 'Israeli-Arab' conflict, Israel is surrounded by Arab countries and is the continuing underdog of history – victims of the Nazi holocaust. By use of 'Arab' instead of 'Palestinian' the colonized subjects are ignored or submerged into the background. This is reminiscent of the 'discovery' and subsequent European conquest of the Americas and Africa as if the people who already lived there did not count as part of the civilized world, thereby nullifying their claims to their land and justifying their expulsion and confinement into reservations or Bantustans.

Where does one begin the story of occupation? How does it relate to the speakers or authors: Ron David and Fadwa Touqan? And how do those readers who do not know the history of Palestine/Israel come to understand the ideological perspectives of the participants as members of divergent speech communities?

In this chapter we analyze the language of occupation by comparing the language of Israeli and Palestinian leadership in the media, using a corpus of 22 pages having 8904 words of '135' quotes[3] from Israeli leaders and '2624' words in '43' quotes from Palestinians mostly said after the year 2000.

Key Factors in Shaping the Language of Occupation

Under occupation, speech between the two parties (occupiers and occupied) over a period of time may develop into expressions of hatred and self-hatred. Hate speech has been defined by Neisser as: 'all communications (whether verbal, written, symbolic) that insult a racial, ethnic and political group, whether by suggesting that they are inferior in some respect or by indicating that they are despised or not welcome for any other reasons' (Neisser, 1994: 337). This definition matches the spirit of Orientalism which makes the superior only see the inferiority of the inferior. We will discuss how this relates to power, spinning of media and ideology.

Power

Power seems to be a dynamic factor in shaping behavior in general and language performance in particular in media reports of the statements and the views of politicians on political issues across the world. According to Kramarae *et al.* (1984: 10), the concept of power and politics are closely linked. We choose power over politics because not all expressions of influence and control are governmental. According to Wrong (1979), power is the capacity of some persons to produce intended and foreseen effects on others. Intentional influence may be achieved through authority, manipulation, persuasion and force.

Media spinning

Governments often make demands on the media to serve what they define as the national interest. They classify information and withhold access. They stage media events, frame the issues and articulate positions that are, in essence, pure propaganda (Amer, 2009). The Israeli occupation has been justified for all these years as necessary for Israel's security. On the other hand, Palestinians believe that the future of Israel will only be secured after a settlement that also secures the rights of the Palestinians. Reporting the news of the Israeli occupation has never been fair according to Schechter (2003).

Israel is one of the top countries regularly reported in media. According to Schechter (2003: 163), Israel features high on the international news list of the major television channels in the United States and the United Kingdom. In Germany, it is sixth and in South Africa, fifth. More than 60% of the news coverage in these four countries deals with the conflict situation in Israel and Palestine. Violence is a major topic covered. Of the coverage that is of a violent nature, Germany rates almost 50%; in the United Kingdom and South Africa more than 66%, and in the United States about 90%. South African television gives 65% coverage to the Israel side of the conflict and 35% to Palestine, U.K. channels give 8% coverage to Palestine. Although in many Arab countries, the Palestinian narrative of a disposed people dominates the scene, in the United States, however, the narrative that dominates is that of Israel, which is portrayed as 'a democracy under siege'. Such spinning and staging of media supports and justifies Israeli occupation of Palestine and enforces hate and injustice.

Ideology

According to Schjerve (1989: 59), ideology is a system of ideas based on value judgments and attitudes, which aids certain forces within a society to further their interests or to stabilize their power. One of the prominent issues in political language is how ideology shapes the themes of political statements. A critical study of political texts may reveal the ideological and pragmatic functions of propagandistic discourse. For example, analysis of political texts of Futurism ideology in Italy revealed glorification of war through presenting war positively as a revolutionary force renewing the world (Schjerve, 1989).

The language of ideology is emotionally charged as it hinders reflection by the recipient or reader of the contents of the message. The concept of war is transformed into something desirable or noble through the production of mythology. The stereotypical use of concepts such as 'blood', 'race' and 'heroism' creates an emotional hotbed on which prejudices are activated (Schjerve, 1989). Such notions will be the framework which encompasses hate speech between enemies.

One way of understanding the harm caused by hate speech is by comparing it to that caused by other insults such as nasty comments, deprecating a person's or a group's intellect, beauty, athletic ability, technical skill, height, weight or any other characteristic that is valued in a society (Neisser, 1994: 338).

The Study

Data collection

The corpus

The corpus for this study was drawn from print media during the period of 2000 and after. Some of the quotes were given before this time. A corpus of 22 pages having 8904 words of '135' quotes from Israeli leaders were found under the title of 'hate speech'. Given the fact that the Zionists started talking about the occupation of Palestine as early as 1895, the number of quotes is not surprising; Actually, most of the quotes were said in the year 2000 and after, during the years of the second Intifada. The site of the Israeli Ministry of Foreign Affairs published 2624 words of '43' quotes from Palestinian Authority leaders besides quotes of '3690' words by Hamas leaders. Considering the fact that the Palestinian leadership only appeared 14 years ago, the small number of quotes is reasonable compared to the bigger number of the Israeli quotes. Data sources were taken from the following newspapers and websites:

> *The Jerusalem Post* (Israel).
> *New Statesman* (UK).
> *New York Times* (USA).
> *Washington Post* (USA).

Yediot Ahronot (Israel).

Haaretz (Israel).

Judische Rundschau (small Jewish periodical in Germany).

A-Sharq Al-Awsat (Saudi newspaper based in the United Kingdom).

al-Ayyam (Palestine).

Al Hayyat Al-Jadedah (official Palestinian Authority daily newspaper).

Novsimaya gazeta (the Israeli Ministry of Foreign Affairs).

Al-jazeera (TV Channel- Qatar).

A-Sabeel (Jordan).

http://www.wakeupfromyourslumber.com/node/5820 November 15, 2008.

http://www.mfa.gov.il/MFA (Israel Ministry of Foreign Affairs).

http://www.ifamericansknew.org/ and http://whatreallyhappened.com/.

Analytical procedure

To establish a theoretical background for the analysis of data in this study, Vaughan's (1995) model was utilized as she looked at a similar situation of animosity during Lebanon war in 1982. She tried to answer research questions by analyzing newspaper editorials of countries involved in the war mainly, the main arguments in the editorials, the key words supporting arguments, use of imagery and metaphors supporting arguments and the concepts of war and peace forming ideology. The key concepts viewed in the editorials were responsibility of the United States, the need for Israeli security and the need for Palestinian self-determination. Newspapers representing weaker nations view them as helpless against powerful ones; waging their just war is morally superior. Along the same lines, Bhatia (2009: 281) analyzed the discourse of terrorism pointing to the dichotomies of good versus evil; law versus lawlessness; civilization versus barbarism; and freedom versus tyranny as discourse features. The linguistic features of 'prejudiced speech' are investigated by Quasthoff (1989: 187), noticing that social prejudice as a source of power is directed against the weak.

Given this background, three aspects are focused on here as an attempt to put the corpus of quotes from the Israeli and Palestinian sides into a theoretical context: (1) the Israeli discursive position as power in view of Vaughan's model; (2) the discursive position of the Palestinian side as the weak side; and (3) the asymmetrical discursive relation between the Israelis and Palestinians. In the next section, the statements of Israeli leaders will be analyzed to discuss underlying Israeli ideology and then there will be an analysis of the quotes from various Palestinian leaders which reflect Palestinian ideology.

The Israeli side

Looking at the themes of the Israeli quotes, we were interested in analyzing the ideology of the Israeli leaders. Along the lines of Vaughan's (1995) analysis, the discursive position of the Israelis was manifested in the following five aspects:

(1) Depictions of Palestinians.
(2) Reports of killing or threats to kill.
(3) Statements concerning deception and lying.
(4) Statements of superiority.
(5) Excluding the other.

These themes serve to rally the public behind this ideology to justify war, make the life of the Palestinians difficult and force them to leave their land.

Insulting Palestinians

Quotes from the Israeli leaders include curses, and insults in which the victim is in principle not able to do anything about it (Brekle, 1989). Vaughan (1995: 61) believes that distrust and hatred beget violence and war between peoples. They are nurtured and rationalized in everyday discussion. In modern society, the interpretations expressed in the elite newspapers and websites carry great weight in influencing opinion especially during times of war.

The following are examples of insulting animalistic metaphors for Palestinians: 'crocodiles', 'beasts walking on two legs', 'grasshoppers', 'cockroaches' and 'creatures not belonging to the world of humans'. The speech act forms in the quotes are assertions as opposed to propositions in the sense that an assertion is an illocutionary act, but a proposition is not an act at all (Searle, 1969). Such speech acts in the form of statements are meant to produce an effect intended by speaker; the hearer would then react in hopelessness due to a lack of power.

(1) '[The Palestinians are] beasts walking on two legs.' (Menachim Begin, *New Statesman*, June 25, 1982.)
(2) 'When we have settled the land, the Arabs will scurry around like drugged cockroaches in a bottle.' (Raphael Eitan, Chief of Staff, *The New York Times*, April 14, 1983.)
(3) 'The Palestinians would be crushed like grasshoppers [...] heads smashed against the boulders and walls.' (Israeli Prime Minister, *The New York Times*, April 1, 1988.)
(4) 'The Palestinians are like crocodiles [...]' (Ehud Barak, Prime Minister, *The Jerusalem Post*, August 30, 2000.)

(5) 'There is a huge gap between us (Jews) and our enemies. [...] They are people who do not belong to our continent, to our world, but actually belong to a different galaxy.' (Israeli President, Moshe Katsav. *The Jerusalem Post*, May 10, 2001.)

The above quotes from the Israeli leaders range from denial of Palestinian existence to images of all kinds of animals. The Israeli leaders were either prime ministers or chiefs of staffs who have been important governmental officials and decision makers for the future of Israel. Such pronouncements of hate speech on the part of those at the ultimate level of political and military authority have grave repercussions with respect to the power to incite massive hatred against those targeted. As previously mentioned, according to Schjerve (1989: 59), ideology is a system of ideas based on value judgments and attitudes, which aids certain forces within a society to further their interests or to stabilize their power. Degrading stereotypes of Palestinians as less than human enables them to be as seen as a monolithic enemy and justify brutal measures against them. Ideology serves to instruct the public of the proper attitude to adopt toward the enemy and what they should think of their enemies. Enemies have been pictured as different types of animals that bring disgust and require caution in dealing with them. On the other side, Palestinians hearing such language may react in defiance and reject such names reflecting the hatred and ideology of occupation.

As the case of the Futurism movement in Italy (Schjerve, 1989), insults arouse prejudices on the psychological level that could be exploited politically. Patriotism and love of war are nurtured by these quotes to feed a fertile environment for willingness to spill blood. That is why killing Palestinians was seen as necessary for the Israelis to achieve their objectives. Hence, inciting the public and the army to kill has become open policy declared by the Israeli leaders and stated clearly in their quotes as seen in the following examples.

Reports of killing or threats to kill

Thirteen quotes were found out of 135 taken from the aforementioned websites and newspapers related to killing besides the seven quotes about insults that is 15% of the whole sample. Actually, insults incite people to kill. Killing as promoted by political leaders is the ultimate level of hatred and taking revenge on people who were displaced from their land. During the period from 2000 to 2009, 1487 Palestinian children and 123 Israeli children were killed according to the *If America Knew* web site (http://www.ifamericansknew.org/) as shown in Figure 7.1.

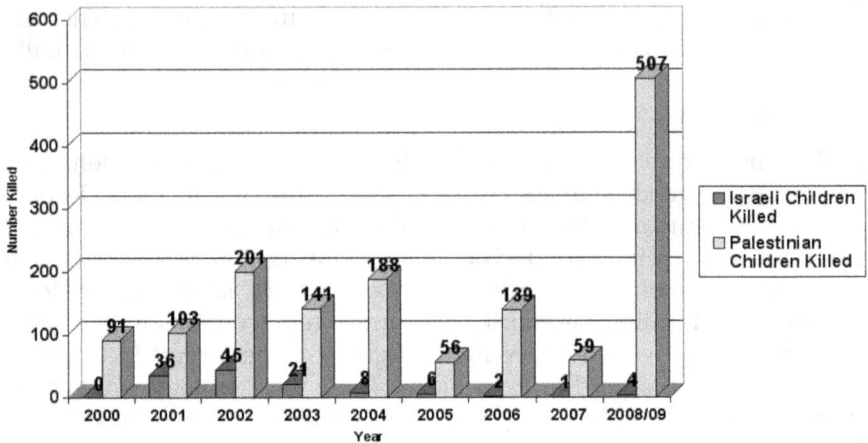

Figure 7.1 Israeli and palestinian children killed

The following are examples of brutality in killing and suffering inflected on the Palestinians:

(6) 'We have to kill all the Palestinians unless they are resigned to live here as slaves.' (Chairman Heilbrun, Mayor of Tel Aviv, October 1983)

(7) 'We must use terror, assassination, intimidation, land confiscation, [...].' (Israel Koenig, 'The Koenig Memorandum' April, 1976)

(8) 'We'll make a pastrami sandwich of them, [...]' (Ariel Sharon, 1973)

(9) '[T]here is no single fixed method for murder and not even for genocide. [...] The government of Israel, using the military and its instruments of destruction, is not only spilling blood, but it is also suffocating?' (Shulamit Aloni, March 2003)

(10) 'On October 29, 1956, soldiers of the Israeli Border Police murdered 43 civilians, after curfew was imposed on the Israeli Arab village of Kafr Qassem [...] killing villagers who were returning from work in the fields without knowing anything about the existence of a curfew.' (Aviv Lavie, October 31, 2003)

(11) 'During the three years of the Second Intifada the Israelis have killed three times as many Palestinians, most of them innocent civilians, including babies and pregnant women.' (Gerald Kaufman, November 22, 2003)

According to Lakoff (2000), the Israeli policy promotes a sharp polarization between the 'we' and 'them', 'them' being less human, more bestial and more satanic. Because we cannot win over them, they threaten our very existence, and we have to fight back with whatever we have. To Bhatia (2009) the dichotomies are civilization versus barbarism. It is noticed that the kind of verbs used in the quotes either like 'Israel/we must', 'we have to', 'we will' or commands like 'make their life' to mean the intended actions are obligations that must be carried out. Other quotes are reports of killing in the past given as models for the future obligations. In analyzing threats and appeals in media discourse of the Israelis and the Palestinians during the second Intifada, Atawneh (2009) found that Israelis used threats; while Palestinians used appeals.

Israeli statements concerning deception and lying

Politicians are not reputed to be the personification of credibility. According to Holly, the epigram by Friedrich von Logau (1604–1655) referred to the politician as *politish* in that he knows how 'to be different, to seem different, to speak differently and to mean differently' (Holly, 1989: 115). Some might even say that the very profession of being a politician involves a certain amount of *implicit* deception or lying. However, in the Israeli quotes given below there is *explicit* admission to lying as a strategy to achieve objectives. What does it mean to believe what someone says? A simple answer would be that we do not consider that person a liar. A liar is a person who asserts something and does not believe it himself. Therefore, we need to know a person's thoughts in order to judge him a liar. This is in many cases impossible to do because it is difficult to know someone else's thoughts. What makes an utterance credible or a person trustworthy (not taking into account characteristics of nonverbal behavior)? The answer may be based on Grice's (1969, 1975) explanation of 'meaning' in his cooperative principle for speaking whereby telling the truth is a key element in being cooperative. Lack of trustworthiness is because the way of conveying meaning is obscured, and above all, the speaker's intentions are not overt. The Israeli quotes below are in violation of Grice maxims in relation to the element of truth. Therefore, there is no need for Grice's explanation of 'meaning' or implicature; rather, it is obvious confession to lying to achieve different political purposes. The percentage of these 15 quotes given below to the whole sample (135) is 11%.

(12) 'The hiding behind anti-Semitism may make an impression on the Europeans.' (Meron Benvenisti, November 6, 2003)

(13) 'We have not been seeking peace for twenty-five years – all declarations to that effect have been no more than colored statements or deliberate lies.' (Yeshayahu Leibowitz, November 30, 1973)

(14) 'I have learned that the state of Israel cannot be ruled in our generation without deceit and adventurism.' (Moshe Shertok, Second Prime Minister of Israel, 1950s)

Lexical items used to reflect the meaning of lying are *'deceit', 'deliberate lies', 'hiding behind', 'makes an impression'* and *'bluffing'*, showing a key element in the Israeli ideology. Avi Shlaim, who is considered a key member of a group of Israeli scholars known as the 'New Historians', said the following about the lies of Ben Gurion:

(15) Ben-Gurion [...] denied any IDF involvement [in the Qibya massacre]. [...] This was not Ben-Gurion's first lie for what he saw as the good of his country. (Avi Shlaim, 2000)

In line with Ben-Gurion policy, Shamir, the ex-Israeli Prime Minister, says:

(16) 'It is permissible to lie for the sake of the Land of Israel.' Yitzhak Yizernitzky, date unknown (Yitzhak Yizerntzky was known later as Yitzhak Shamir, Prime Minister of Israel).

The following quotes were made by Akiva Eldar, a distinguished journalist for the Israeli *Ha'aretz* newspaper. He uncovers Israeli lies from his field work as a journalist.

(17) 'Without lies, it would be impossible to talk about peace with the Palestinians. [...] Without lies, it would be impossible to claim that there is no partner for the road map. [...] Without lies, it would be impossible to promise 'painful concessions' in exchange for peace.' (Akiva Eldar, November 24, 2003)

Like Akiva Eldar, Gideon Levy is another Israeli journalist for the *Ha'aretz* newspaper. He is a prominent left-wing commentator. He formerly served as spokesman for Shimon Peres from 1978 and 1982. He is quoted about the Israeli Defense Forces (IDF) lies:

(18) 'On numerous occasions, the IDF has put out lying accounts of incidents, and in the end, the Palestinian version turned out to be true.' (Gideon Levy, November 23, 2003)

(19) 'The thesis that the danger of genocide was hanging over us in June 1967 and that Israel was fighting for its physical existence is only bluff.' (Israeli General Peled, *Ha'aretz*, March 19, 1972)

The above statement is a clear confession from an Israeli General stating that the claim of genocide in June 1967 was bluffing. This is a typical example of deception as a war strategy. In March 1972, Israeli Air Force General Weizmann reported, 'there was never any danger of extermination' (*Ma'ariv*, April 19, 1972).

Statements of superiority

The Israeli leaders' discourses of superiority and of being better than others in leadership, intelligence, vision and political perspectives have been linked to the arrogance of Orientalism (Said, 1978). One million Palestinians are seen by the Israelis not worth a fingernail of an Israeli. Palestinians should come crawling like animals and become woodcutters or waiters. This ideology of superiority on the part of the leadership disallows any spirit of reconciliation or peace. They dehumanize others on grounds of their superiority which led them to destroy Palestinian homes (shown in Figure 7.2). However, there are voices in the Israeli society that call for peace; but such voices are weak and have little influence in making policies. Therefore, the rift between the two enemies widens everyday and hope is lost for a solution as seen in the following examples of superior boasting:

(20)   'We, the Jewish people, control America, and the Americans know it.' (Ariel Sharon, Israeli Prime Minister, October 3, 2001)

(21)   'One million Arabs are not worth a Jewish fingernail.' (Rabbi Yaacov Perrin, February 27, 1994. (*The New York Times*, February 28, 1994: 1))

(22)   'We declare openly that the Arabs have no right to settle on even one centimeter of Eretz, Israel. [...] We shall use the ultimate force until the Palestinians come crawling to us on all fours.' (Rafael Eitan, Chief of Staff, *The New York Times*, April 14, 1983)

(23)   'We shall reduce the Arab population to a community of woodcutters and waiters.' (Uri Lubrani, Prime Minister Ben-Gurion's Special Adviser on Arab Affairs, 1960). (From *The Arabs in Israel'* by Sabri Jiryas)

(24)   'We Jews, we are the destroyers and will remain the destroyers. We will forever destroy because we want a world of our own.' (Maurice Samuels, *You Gentiles*, 1924: 155 (N.B. 18,147 Palestinian homes were demolished from 1967 to 2009 [*If Americans Knew* website]))

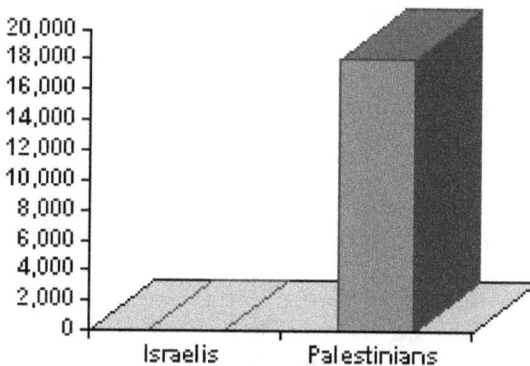

Figure 7.2 Israeli and palestinian homes demolished

(25) 'We possess several hundred atomic warheads and rockets and can launch them at targets in all directions. [...] Our armed forces, however, are not the thirtieth strongest in the world, but rather the second or third. We have the capability to take the world down with us.' (Martin van Creveld, 2003)

All of the above quotes begin with 'We' (except (21)) followed by the complement 'the Israelis' or 'Jewish people' to demonstrate the strongest level of declarative or 'assertive' speech act. The first person pronoun here is intended to present the speaker as the focal point of the statement or assertion. Haider and Rodriguez (1995: 128) view personal pronouns as discursive indicators of power and ideology. The dominant group has the frequent use of 'I' which manifests subjective illusions of originality and discourse freedom. Asymmetrical respect treatment in the language of power is manifested in the use of 'you' and frequent use of inclusive 'we'.

Excluding the other

Between total denial of existence and exclusion of the other, the Israelis widen the gap between themselves and the Palestinians. The quotes given below show the intent of the Israeli leaders in confirming their ideology of discrimination and exclusion like saying 'Palestinians never existed' and 'there is nobody to return land to' despite the fact that undercover negotiations and even open talks were underway telling the world that they take serious steps toward peace. Despite the claims of the Israeli willingness to have peace with the Palestinians, they promote the ideology of segregation and exclusion in social studies and geography books. Ronald Bleier (2006) from http://desip.igc.org/bleierpubs.html, a Jewish writer in New York, critiques Zionist ideology, which sees no place for Palestinians in Palestine. That is why, to create a Jewish State in 1948; Zionists expelled 750,000 Palestinians from their homeland and never allowed them or their descendants to return.

Nurit Peled-Elhanan (this volume), an Israeli professor, reports that Israeli schoolbooks are a manifestation of 'Israeli education which promotes racism, both towards the Palestinian citizens and towards the Palestinian non-citizens' (Peled-Elhanan, 2006: 114). She found that they inculcate Jewish exclusive rights of the Land, and encourage the oppression of Palestinian identity and culture.

Peled-Elhanan also noticed that the Israeli students were misinformed about the geopolitical situation of their country, and were denied the information necessary in order to regard their immediate neighbors as partners for shared life and coexistence. They learn that democracy may segregate citizens according to ethnicity and that human suffering and empathy are race dependent or religion dependent.

(26) 'Palestine will be as Jewish as England is English.' (Chaim Weizmann, 1921)

(27) 'How can we return the occupied territories? There is nobody to return them to.' (Golda Maier, Israeli Prime Minister, March 8, 1969)

(28) 'There was no such thing as Palestinians, they never existed.' (Golda Maier, Israeli Prime Minister, June 15, 1969)

Looking at the United States arrogance which is similar to that of Israel, Lakoff (2000) criticizes the separation between 'them' and 'us'. 'We' stands for normality, decency and civilized behaviors while the enemy; 'they' represents perversion and strangeness (Berlin, this volume). 'The other side' commits wrongs such as 'terrorism', but 'we' never do. The 'we', a powerful side, ignores all or most of the information on the 'enemy' that could result in words of positive value when describing the enemy. The 'we' is good and the enemy is evil (Haider & Rodriguez, 1995). Since the enemy is such 'a genuinely evil character', 'our' violence against him is morally justified even if exactly the same violence against 'us' is most immoral. This is how value-loaded words are used to unite the population in a nation at war. That is the language of occupation which reflects the power and cruelty of the dominant ideology to the extent of excluding the other.

The Palestinian side

The Palestinian leaders have no army, no wealth but verbal support from the Muslim world. Being in this position makes their image of inferiority ideal for the spirit of Orientalism. The imbalance of power has a strong impact on shaping their language. They lead a struggle to achieve freedom. They are under siege and they have to beg for Israeli permission for leaving the country or making contact with the outside world. Yet the Israelis take them as the prime enemy whose aim is to destroy Israel. Therefore, animosity is nurtured between the two sides through language.

Kathleen Christison (November 8//9, 2003), former CIA political analyst, is quoted in her article 'Zionism as a racist ideology' on how the Israeli ideology necessitates the creation of an enemy by victimizing the Palestinians portraying them as murderers and predatory as said in the following quote:

Indeed [...] a political philosophy like Zionism [...] requires an enemy in order to survive and, where an enemy does not already exist, it requires that one be created. In order to justify racist repression and dispossession [...] those being repressed and displaced must be portrayed as murderous and predatory. (CounterPunch, *Newsletter*)

The source of the Palestinian quotes is an Israeli web site which selected what the Israelis believed to be the enemy language. Though some Palestinians such as the Palestinian President Abbas belong to the peace camp and others such as Hamas belong to the resistance camp, both are seen by the Israelis as enemies. The Hamas movement leads the ideology of resistance and wants to liberate all Palestine from the Sea to the River. They have been issuing threats against the Israelis in response to their losses in raids. They also used to shoot home-made missiles against the neighboring town of Sederot near the border. However, most of their threats never materialized even when their top leaders were assassinated by missiles from Israeli helicopters in 2004.

The following quotes from Abbas, the Palestinian president show the peace camp ideology:

(29) 'There is absolutely no substitution for dialogue.' (*A-Sharq Al-Awsat*, March 3, 2003)

(30) 'The armed struggle necessitates certain conditions and opportunities that do not exist for us in Palestine. Therefore, military activities under these circumstances and means are ineffective. For this reason, we stated that we have no choice but to stop it [i.e., military activities].' (*A-Sharq Al-Awsat*, March 3, 2003)

The leader of the Palestinians decided that dialogue is the only way to achieve freedom given the inequality in military power. However, submission to defeat is always rejected and face and dignity must be maintained. After the long years of Intifada against the occupation, no freedom was achieved. Peace initiatives never worked. Therefore, the top Palestinian leader wanted to achieve security and economic growth:

(31) 'The little jihad is over, and now we have the bigger jihad – the bigger battle is achieving security and economic growth.' (Abu Mazen, 2005)

(32) 'I renew my commitment to continuing the road he [Arafat] began and for which he made a lot of sacrifices, until the Palestinian flag flies from the walls, minarets and churches of Jerusalem.' (Abu Mazen, 2005)

Marwan Barghuthi, the second Fatah leader, toned down his language to keep dignity and advance peace as in the following quotes:

(33) 'And while I, and the Fatah movement to which I belong, strongly oppose attacks and the targeting of civilians inside Israel, our

future neighbor, I reserve the right to protect myself, to resist the Israeli occupation of my country and to fight for my freedom.' (2002 *Washington Post* op-ed) (Abu Mazen, 2005)

(34) 'I am not a terrorist, but neither am I a pacifist. I am simply a regular guy from the Palestinian street advocating only what every other oppressed person has advocated – the right to help myself in the absence of help from anywhere else.' (2002 *Washington Post* op-ed) (Abu Mazen, 2005)

The powerless language is that which expresses the injustice inflicted on the occupied people and appeals to world leaders and communities to garner support for the struggle against occupation. That is why the Pope was given the Bethlehem passport. The past struggle led by Arafat was a guerilla struggle against the great power of Israel; all Palestinians have been invited to participate in the holy resistance. All that they could do was to sacrifice their life as freedom fighters. Such a struggle has been portrayed by Israel and the United States as terrorism. The following are quotes from Yasir Arafat:

(35) 'The oath is firm to continue this difficult Jihad (holy war), this long Jihad, in the path of martyrs, the path of sacrifices.' (June 15, 1995)

(36) 'The Palestinian Rifle is ready and we will aim it if they try to prevent us from praying in Jerusalem. [...] the "Generals of the Stones" are ready.' (*al-Ayyam*, November 16, 1998)

(37) 'Palestinians are "irrigating the land with their blood" in the struggle for "Palestine".' (Organization of the Islamic Conference, Qatar, May 26, 2001)

The leader is affirming the objectives of his movement seeing the Israeli killing will not stop the movement for freedom. He compliments the young fighters calling them generals of the stones. However, nothing in the quotes is insulting to the Israelis; it is only complaints against the killing of his own people. Seeing the peace process going nowhere, the Palestinian leaders talked about options in case negotiations failed to raise future hopes in freedom for the public. Nabil Sha'ath, a Palestinian Cabinet Minister and leader, sums up the strategy in the following quote in January 1996:

(38) 'We decided to liberate our homeland step-by-step. [...] Should Israel continue – no problem? Therefore, we honor the peace treaties and non-violence [...] if and when Israel says "enough". [...] in that case it is saying that we will return to violence. But this time it will be with 30,000 armed Palestinian soldiers and in a land with elements of freedom.'

(39) 'We still believe, however, that we are entitled to use all means available to us to face the enemy.' (*The Jerusalem Times*, June 8, 2001)

(40) 'The Intifada came to end occupation, not to allow for a return to negotiations.'

(41) 'I believe that a return to negotiations would be nothing but a waste of time and that seeking the mediation of the US is useless.'

(42) 'He who seeks peace with Sharon is pursuing a mirage. There is no chance for peace with Sharon. The only way to deal with Sharon is resistance.'

According to Lakoff (2000), such statements fall in the category of 'war propaganda'. She talks extensively about language war and propaganda. The aim of war propaganda is to unite the nation and rally support of the domestic population as well as of third parties for the war effort and to encourage them to accept decisions made, as well to discourage the enemy. Actually, seeing peace never materializes with never-ending negotiations, the public voted for Hamas, the resistance movement, whose leaders led an ideology of freeing all Palestine and no more believing in futile peace negotiations. Therefore, the public has given support for such movement though the consequences have been more suffering and killing under the Israeli attacks against what they claim as terrorists hiding among civilians. The quotes given below from Hamas leaders were based on religion ideology to rally support for their fight against occupation.

These following are the Hamas principles on which we raise our children and in which we believe:

- Armed resistance.
- Nonrecognition of the occupation in any form.
- All Palestine from the river to the sea.
- The holy places and Jerusalem.
- The right of return. (Abu-Zuhri, TV, April 6, 2007)

(43) 'We have been advocating the establishment of a Palestinian state within the 1967 borders with Jerusalem as capital and the return of the refugees. For this we will declare a truce, not recognition of Israel. This is our view in Hamas.' (Haniyya, *Al-Jazeera*, April 2007.)

(44) 'Our government affirms that all resistance to occupation by all methods is the legitimate right of the Palestinian people.' (Haniyya, *Novsimaya Gazeta*, March 19, 2007)

(45) 'We saw the Oslo Agreement as a political mistake. [...] Resistance has aims which can be temporary or permanent. One of the temporary aims is to remove the occupation from part of the occupied

territories. [...] What is needed now is for the resistance to act in all occupied areas such as Jerusalem and use all means possible.' (Al-Zahhar, A-Sabeel, Jordan, April 10, 2007)

(46)   The Hamas spokesman, Isma'il Radwan, March 30, 2007, urged fighting and killing the Jews. He quoted from the Hadith (sayings attributed to the prophet Muhammad) declaring: 'Judgment Day will come when the Moslems kill the Jews.'

Looking at the quotes from Hamas leaders, it is interesting to note that they talk about the same ideology in different ways, all of which is rooted in Islamic ideology. They are willing to sacrifice themselves for the sake of freedom, accept truce, and will not recognize Israel. In the last quote there is a prediction about killing the Jews at the end of time based on religious sources but it is not part of Hamas ideology. However, none of the quotes include dehumanizing or insulting the Israelis as those found in the Israeli quotes.

There are two extremes here: the Israelis on one side wanting all the land by force, and the resistance on the other wanting all the land based on religious ideology. The problem for Hamas is that they have no equal power to finish the fight quickly. Consequently, like the ideology of Arafat, they adopt steadfastness until they achieve their objectives. The Israelis have the power to control and kill and evict people from the land refusing to share the land. That is why the struggle has been continuing since the creation of Israel.

Conclusion

This study has shown how language is shaped by power. This power of the West (Occidant) against that of the Orient furnishes the grounds for the concept of Orientalism as illustrated by Edward Said (1978). The Israeli language reflects the ideology of aggressiveness and belligerency including making threats, killing, insulting, arrogance, deception and excluding the other. However, the Palestinian language reflects the appeal for help, defensiveness and attempts to save face and maintain dignity while seeking peace with the Israelis at the same time. The Israelis view the Palestinians as terrorists not belonging to humankind, and consequently present them in the media as victimizing others and not the victim of others. Palestinians, on the other hand, view the Israelis as occupiers settling their land by force and maintaining their occupation by means of military power and US support. The peace camp among Palestinians accepts partitioning the land and has been trying to reach a peace agreement with the Israelis to no avail. That is why the peace camp has lost support from the public and consequently has been weakened giving rise to radical movements.

Notes

1. Parts of this chapter was published in *Hebron University Journal –B (Humanities)*, Volume (5) No. (1), July 2010. under the title 'The language of occupation in Palestine'.
2. This poem was Fadwa's reaction to insults after seven hours waiting at the Allenby Bridge in the heat of summer. Other lines are: *Ah, humiliation, my hatred is immeasurable, only eating up their livers can satisfy my hunger for revenge. They killed love in my blood changing it into fire and tar.* http://www.aklaam.net/forum/showthread.php?t=15913. Accessed on 19.11.09.
3. See website: WHATREALLYHAPPEND.COM, Examples of hate speech. Accessed on 19.11.09.

Chapter 8

The War on Gaza: American and Egyptian Media Framing

N.H. EL-BILAWI

Introduction

The beginning of the 21st century can be described as a revolutionary and unpredictable in at least one important respect: the profound trans-formation of media. At present, new global media bring images from around the world into our living rooms to make the world smaller. However, the advancement of technological communication combined with the privatization of television and the deregulation of media own-ership make it possible for media giants to establish powerful distri-bution networks which can, in turn, influence world public opinion (Schwartz, 2008).

Perhaps now more than any other time in human history when human rights violation and political polarization seem unbridled, and respect for international law that protects national sovereignty is tarnished, objective news media are desperately needed to inform the masses, provide voice to the voiceless and function as a counterbalance that scrutinizes the power-ful. Instead, the mainstream media are gaining more power by gaining the spread of an international perspective, claiming to narrow the gap between global citizens in the advancement of a common understanding. Even more insidiously, the media are abusing their power by broadcasting misleading truths serving the interests of the political institutions they represent and serve (Bronner, 2009).

Wolfsfeld argues that '[t]he authorities' level of control over the political environment is one of the key variables that determine the role of the news media in political conflicts' (Wolfsfeld, 1997: 36). Wolfsfeld further explains that political conflicts arise from the moves and countermoves enacted in an attempt to control the course of events; such moves include dominating political discourse and mobilizing as many supporters of their cause as possible. In order to accomplish these moves, governments have histori- cally enlisted the media. Hence, it can be suggested that governments and mainstream media act together to influence the world community, in some cases creating a certain public opinion to serve their own political agendas (Caldas-Coulthard, 2003).

The Rationale/Stating the Problem

Focusing on the media and their role in transacting the dissemination of political agendas into the social arena, I examine the reporting in news print media coverage of the Middle East, particularly Palestine and the war waged on Gaza starting December 26, 2008. The Israeli incur- sion represents the heaviest aggression against the Gaza Strip since the 1967 Six-Day War and has taken an enormous toll on the territory's civil- ians, especially children. The Israeli offensive has resulted in nearly 1000 Palestinian deaths with more than 4000 wounded, and inflicted incalcu- lable damage to homes, hospitals, schools and businesses in the Gaza Strip. In contrast, since the bombing began, it was reported that 10 Israeli soldiers and four civilians were killed (A.N.S.W.E.R. Coalition, 2009). Despite the inequities, however, most of the mainstream media have given equal or greater coverage to the casualties and views of the Israeli side than the Palestinian side. The same media sources have also con- tinually represented a one-sided view of the crisis, invariably blaming the Palestinian side while ignoring Palestinian reports of the Gaza block- ade, air strikes and 'targeted assassinations' carried out by Israel against the people in Gaza. Tracing media coverage on the Israeli-Palestinian conflict leaves the hope for objective, transparent and just media to be a long way off.

According to Arman (2009), while media around the world (including the Middle East) are gradually reaching new heights in promoting unprec- edented political openness, the quality of news coverage of the American mainstream media is losing its credibility; hence, it is declining in the direction of misleading propaganda. For instance, a study conducted by the *If Americans Knew* organization (2004) indicates that *The New York Times'* significantly distorted coverage on topics related to the Middle East. For example, *The Times'* coverage of children's deaths was even more skewed. *If Americans Knew* showed that in the first year of the current uprising (i.e. 2000), Israeli children's deaths were reported at 6.8 times the rate of Palestinian children's deaths. In 2004, this differential in news cov- erage increased even further with deaths of Israeli children covered at a rate 7.3 times greater than the deaths of Palestinian children. However, given that in 2004, 22 times more Palestinian children were killed than Israeli children (If Americans Knew, 2004), this area of investigation is especially striking in demonstrating this inequality in coverage.

The aim of this chapter is to unveil the 'portrayed reality' that each of several investigative print news media present to their public on the Gaza situation and the broader Israeli-Palestinian conflict. This chapter attempts to shed light on media framing, narrative theory, news decontextualization and dramatization in order to explain how and in what ways public opinion, in general, and the American perception, in specific, is shaped and altered. Two familiar American news sources *The Washington Post* and *The New York Times*, were allowed for the individual analysis and side-by-side comparison of the newspapers' portrayal of realities; the 'we-they dichotomy', which Caldas-Coulthard (2003: 275; see also Berlin, this volume) refers to, led to the inclusion of the *Daily News*, a prominent Egyptian newspaper printed in English, for further comparison with a Middle Eastern media perspective. The rationale behind my choice of these specific newspapers is that as an Arab American, who lives in Washington, DC, I was mainly interested in exploring American media biases, especially in newspapers in Washington. *The Washington Post* is one of the largest newspapers and media venues here in the area, so I picked it as my first choice. Then, I decided to use *The New York Times* to give *The Washington Post* the benefit of the doubt by comparing it to another largest newspaper venue in the East Coast. To maintain the dialogue theme, I had to choose a well-known Egyptian newspaper *Daily News Egypt* (established in 2005 and owned by Egyptian Media Services). It is affiliated with the *International Herald Tribune*. This paper is the only independent English language daily in Egypt and the Middle East and as such does not belong to or is controlled by the State (claimed by the newspaper home web site). These three newspapers will provide me with the view points of the outsiders away from the entanglement of the Palestinian-Israeli conflict.

Using a critical discourse analysis (CDA), the newspaper categories of analysis examined are (1) headlines; (2) first paragraphs on the Israeli-Palestinian conflict; and (3) coverage of casualties (in particular, the recounting of children's deaths). As such, the power of media vocabulary choice in constructing readers' knowledge about the world, particularly incidents beyond their experiential perception, is well documented (cf. Atawneh, this volume; Berlin, this volume; Cohen *et al.* 1990; Lederman, 1992). Following in this line, I present a graph of the lexical items used in each news article and take into consideration the various media outlets.

Questions and design

Questions

The analysis of all the coverage by the various media sources allows for the exploration of certain questions about these different sources. The main questions of interest in this study are:

(1) What type of 'reality' on the Israeli-Palestinian conflict is constructed in each of the selected news sources?
(2) How can we describe the representation of discourse of each side of the conflict? That is, are there inherent biases in the US news coverage?

Design

In order to tackle these questions, the theoretical framework chosen to uncover the ideology behind media positioning is CDA. CDA claims that 'the mode in which an action is presented, either as transitive or as non-transitive, is not a matter of truth or of reality but rather a matter of the way in which that particular action is integrated into the ideological system of the speaker, and the manner in which such an action is therefore articulated in a specific discourse' (Wodak, 1989: 33–41). In other words, decontextualizing events from their actual situations distort realities; the choice of lexical items can change form and place from one context to another to cause an absolute change of meaning. Thus, CDA aims to reveal potential biases in the media discourse. The current study utilizes the following categories for analysis in its attempt to identify distorted realities implying a media bias which is then imposed on the public: word choice, absence of information, inaccuracies, decontextualization, falsification and exaggeration, and journalists' prejudice. At the end of the chapter, main ideas and concepts are compared from the separate perspectives of the US and Egyptian media sources.

A Framework

The role of media in Middle East conflicts

Media coverage can have a large role not only in shaping worldwide public opinion regarding international conflicts, but also in serving the governments' political agendas. International media sources such as the *BBC, CNN, Al-Arabiya and Al-Jazeera*, to name a few, have global reach and, as such, can have an 'agenda-setting effect'. This effect, as Livingston (1996: 18) explains, revolves around the ideological components of political disagreements and, more specifically, the way key actors in conflicts seek to manipulate public perceptions of the disagreement. That is, actors in any conflict will seek to either minimize or exaggerate the conflict, depending upon their relative position of power: those who are weak will seek to draw media coverage to the conflict while those in power will seek to minimize the extent of the problems.

Said refers to the propagandizing of Israeli-Palestinian conflict by claiming that 'never have the media been so influential in determining the course of war as it was during the Al-Aqsa Intifada[1] which, as far as the Western media are concerned, has essentially become a battle over images and ideas' (Said, 2001: 2). Israel has already poured hundreds of millions of dollars into funding for producing information marketed to the outside world; in particular, they have used the media in the United States effectively over a long period of time. Said called this kind of misinformation a 'double standard propaganda' with the intention of covering up criminal actions, especially killing people unjustly, with a mask of justification and reasoning labeled the 'war on terror'. What makes this propaganda campaign so effective is the sustained, well-illustrated Western sense of guilt for anti-Semitism by the Zionists (Said, 2001). Nothing could be more efficient than to displace that guilt onto another people – in this case, the Arabs – and thereby feel not only justified, but also unburdened from the guilt complex of the Holocaust; in so doing, Westerners are not only at peace with Israelis, but are allied with them against the Arab world.

Critical discourse analysis (CDA)

CDA is an approach that studies language as a social practice; it also studies the relation between language and power (Fairclough & Wodak, 1997). In this chapter, the focus is on three dimensions of CDA: language and discourse, power and discourse, and coded discourse.

The first dimension is language and discourse. CDA requires the analyst to be continuously conscious of the underlying meanings of words. Given the power of the written and spoken word, CDA is useful in describing, interpreting, analyzing and critiquing social life reflected in text (Luke, 1997). According to Wodak (2007), CDA deconstructs the inferred and indirect linguistic devices, as well as explicitly prejudiced utterances, to turn texts into a 'pragmatic toolbox' to systematically enable the detection and analysis of the media's word choice, absence of information, inaccuracies, decontextualization, falsification and exaggeration and journalist prejudice.

The second dimension is power and discourse. CDA explores how texts construct representations of the world, social relationships and social identities, and emphasizes practices and texts that are ideologically shaped by relations of power (cf. Chouliaraki & Fairclough, 1999; Fairclough, 1992, 1993, 2005). The relationship is illustrated when analyzing the discourse of narratives by two rival parties in a dispute; the discourse always implies the status quo of each party in terms of either being powerful or powerless (Atawneh, this volume).

The third dimension is coded discourse. In political discourse in particular, it is potentially damaging for politicians to utter discriminatory or biased statements explicitly in public domains; therefore, coded expressions are created which embed prejudices and can be labeled the 'discourse of silence' (Wodak, 2007: 41). When uttered as part of an interview, the contents of media statements and news announcements can only be inferred by readers and viewers. If any 'hidden' accusations take place, the writer or speaker can always deny them or justify them by saying he/she did not *mean* what was implied. According to Wodak, this coded discourse is challenging for analysts and linguists because the broad and narrow contexts and cotext of the respective utterances have to be systematically integrated into the analysis.

Methods

The newspapers chosen for the investigation, as mentioned earlier, are *The Washington Post* (the United States), *The New York Times* (the United States) and the *Daily News* (Egypt). The articles analyzed were chosen because they met certain criteria: first, they were found in the 'Middle East' or 'World' news sections, not from the opinion or the commentary pages. Second, they were published between December 27, 2008 and January 3, 2009, corresponding with the commencement of the Israeli airstrikes on Gaza. Third, the articles focused primarily on Gaza, not on any marginal news related to the extant Israeli-Palestinian conflict.

In analyzing the articles, the particular focus was given to the headlines and the first two paragraphs in an attempt to uncover any media biases. In doing so, the above theoretical framework was used. Applying CDA, six important features were coded and then analyzed: lexicon (L), lack of information (LI) versus descriptive details (DD), lack of accuracy (LA) versus informative (I), de-contextualization (DC), falsification and exaggeration (FE) and journalists' prejudice (JP).

As is always the case, there were some limitations to this study. First, finding articles that met all the criteria within the established dates was sometimes challenging. In some cases, there were no 'news-only' articles published on a given date; as a result, no entries were included and the consecutive day was examined. Commentary accompanying photographs was not included even if it represented only news coverage for a particular day. Finally, considerations of space did not allow for the inclusion of the articles analyzed; however, referential information is provided in the Appendix so that readers are able to review the pieces in their entirety.

Data analysis

The Washington Post

The first article written by Michael Abramowitz on December 28, 2008, is titled 'Israeli Airstrikes on Gaza Strip Imperil Obama's Peace Chances.' The word choice in the title indexes Obama's unexplained silence from the beginning of the Israeli aggression on Gaza. In the first paragraph,

> Israel's airstrikes on Gaza yesterday, in retaliation for a nonstop barrage of rocket attacks from Hamas fighters, raised the prospect of an escalation of violence that could scuttle any hopes the incoming Obama administration harbored of forging an Israeli-Palestinian peace deal. (Abramowitz, 2008: A20)

implies that the only reason for the Israeli airstrikes is Hamas' continuous bombardment. The analysis of the cotext shows that references to the Israeli assaults are repeatedly followed by 'retaliation', suggesting that the lexicon used throughout the article by the author is justifying the strikes without intimating any initiation of aggression on the Israeli part. This example of media framing coincides with a study by an American organization called *Fairness and Accuracy in Reporting* (FAIR),[2] which monitored the use of the term 'retaliation' in the nightly news broadcasts of the three main American networks – CBS, ABC and NBC – between September 2000 and March 2002. The study found that:

> From the start of the Intifada in September 2000 through March 17, 2002, the three major networks' nightly news shows used some variation of the word 'retaliation' (retaliated, will retaliate, etc.) 150 times to describe attacks in the Israeli/Palestinian conflict. About 79 percent of those references were to Israeli 'retaliation' against Palestinians. Only 9 percent referred to Palestinian 'retaliation' against Israelis. (Approximately 12 percent were ambiguous or referred to both sides simultaneously.) (FAIR: 317)

On December 29, Griff Witte's article's title 'Israel Poised for Long Fight' presents the word 'poised' that implies self-control and dignity in relation to 'fight' when referring to Israeli stand in the conflict when, in fact, Israel declares war on 'the other'.

Also, in the first paragraph the juxtaposition when providing the number of Palestinian deaths with the Hamas calling for 'suicide' strikes portrays Hamas as the villain who is leading the Palestinian people toward a more collective massacre:

> The Palestinian death toll approached 300 after two days of violence, making this the deadliest operation in Gaza since Israel seized control of the coastal territory from Egypt in 1967 .... Hamas officials said Sunday that they would continue to fight back, and they called for suicide operations to counter Israeli military strikes. (Abramowitz, 2008: A01)

This was another example whereby the author is able to impose certain impressions on the readers.

The use of 'suicide strikes', or more pointedly 'suicide bombers', is a lexical choice fundamentally disputed between Middle Eastern media and Western media; in the Middle East, the individuals who die as part under the occupation are referred to as 'martyrs' while in the West they are depicted as terrorists (cf. Ayish, this volume; Nasser & Wong, this volume).

The repetition of the words 'retaliation' referring to Israeli and 'smugglers' referring to Palestinians highlights the propaganda model used by the US media in order to reify an ideology toward the conflict which supports Israel and demonizes Palestine.

The second paragraph quotes Israeli and Palestinian official spokesmen. The author attempts to give an impression of Israeli 'retaliation' and Palestinian 'aggression'. For example, Israeli officials said 'We will continue to attack as long as they fire,' while Hamas officials said they;

> would continue to fight back [...] Palestinian fighters launched more than 20 additional rockets Sunday, including two that reached deep into Israeli territory, falling just short of the port city of Ashdod. The rockets, which the Israeli military said were Katyushas, traveled about 20 miles, significantly further than previous rockets from Gaza. (Abramowitz, 2008: A01)

Witte talks about the Palestinian rockets and never mentions any information about the Israeli assaults, the weapons they are using, their targets or the resultant damage in property and casualties. The lack of parallelism is a feature identified in CDA as indicative of hegemonic ideology.

An article written by Philip Rucker on December 30 titled 'Pro-Palestinian Activists Picket Obama Compound in Hawaii' describes an example of public support for the Palestinian cause against the traditional American support of Israel. In the first paragraph, the author explains that protesters gathered in the early morning in front of Obama's vacation home, as they know he exercises outside at that time. However, the article states 'but as of 9:20 a.m. [...] Obama had not left his residence', which indexes the official US position toward the dispute.

In a January 1, 2009 article, also written by Griff Witte, the title 'Israel's Attacks on Gaza Deepen Palestinian Rift' foregrounds the conflict between Palestinians and draws attention away from Israel's attack on Gaza. Witte frames the discourse as if the Palestinians live in a muddle; concomitantly, no Israeli assault will be so harmful and cause more rift than what they already live in. He indicates that the Palestinians – 'the other' – need Israeli democracy in order to fit in with this civilized neighbor. The decontextualization and lack of accuracy disavows a pro-Palestinian reading by stating

> Israel's assault on the Gaza Strip has exacerbated the deep divisions between Palestinians who want to make peace with Israel and those who support Hamas's militant struggle against the Jewish state. (Witte, 2009: 44)

Witte never explains the foundation of what he calls 'a rift' between Palestinians; all that he does is elaborate that there are many 'good' Palestinians who want peace with the Jewish state against those 'violent' Hamas followers who are nothing but 'smugglers'.

The last article of the weeklong coverage in *The Washington Post* is Witte's piece titled 'Israeli Forces Enter Gaza Strip.' Analyzing the lexicon used in describing this Israeli action, the word 'enter', from the title, is an understatement; usually, if the military force of one country 'enters', or crosses, the territory of another, it is typically called an 'invasion' or 'occupation'; yet, the word 'invasion' was mentioned at the middle of the article:

> The invasion came under cover of darkness around 8 p.m., after electricity was cut to much of the strip. Teams of soldiers with night-vision goggles advanced on foot, while others traveled in tanks and armored personnel carriers. The only light came from Israeli flares that periodically illuminated the sky, and from the towers of bright orange flame that followed missile strikes, revealing scenes of devastation on the ground. (Witte, 2009: 10)

Decontextualization occurs in the article by stating the Hamas officials' words:

> called on Palestinians to rise up against Israel with suicide attacks and vowed to make Gaza 'a graveyard' for Israeli soldiers. (Witte, 2009: 10)

The author does not give a cultural or an ideological background for this statement. Indeed, putting the statement in a different framing could have led to a different reading, like calling on for martyrs to defend the land from the invaders.

The New York Times

On December 27, 2008, Taghreed El-Khodary and Isabel Kershner coauthored an article titled 'Israeli Attack Kills Scores Across Gaza.' The headline gives the impression that the reader is going to learn more about the statistical information regarding the exact number of deaths and murders caused by the Israelis – which, at the end, appears to be a play with generic wording that lacks accuracy. The first paragraph continues with an obvious journalist prejudice by stating: 'the Israeli Air Force [...] launched a massive attack on Hamas targets throughout Gaza in retaliation for the recent heavy rocket fire from the area, hitting mostly security headquarters, training compounds and weapons storage facilities, the Israeli military and witnesses said'. The use of the word 'retaliation' is part of the propaganda model, which is repeated to reinforce an underlying political ideology. The sentence 'attack on Hamas targets throughout Gaza' falsifies and omits information when claiming that the strikes of the air force did not hit or cause any damages to anything or any civilian targets other than Hamas. The exaggeration in the sentence 'heavy rocket fire from the area' maintains the impression that Hamas is the aggressor. Finally, when the reader reads through the article, there is no Palestinian 'witness' talking about the damages caused by Israeli; instead, the reader is left with a number rather than a human account of the facts and the victims.

Another article on December 27 by Taghreed El-Khodary and Ethan Bronner is titled 'Israelis Say Strikes Against Hamas Will Continue.' The word choice in the title specifically suggests that the Israeli strikes are merely on Hamas and have nothing to do with the Palestinian people. Even when identifying the damage and deaths caused by the Israeli attack in the first paragraph, the authors' statement make a vague reference to casualties without indicating who they are 'in a crushing response to the group's rocket fire, killing more than 225 – the highest one-day toll in the Israeli-Palestinian conflict in decades'; in other words, there is no reference if the deaths included children, women, or Hamas leaders.

Another article written by Taghreed El-Khodary and Isabel Kershner titled 'Israeli Troops Mass Along Border; Arab Anger Rises' was published on December 28, 2008. The lexical choices in the headline objectively indicate the Middle Eastern feeling toward the Israeli invasion and ground strikes. Also, in the first paragraph, the authors write 'Israeli aircraft pounded Gaza,' presenting the first time in the articles examined where a US newspaper depicts Israel as the aggressor.

On December 29, 2008, Isabel Kershner wrote an article titled 'A Captured Israeli Soldier Figures in Military Assessments and Political Calculus.' The whole article focuses on Gilad Shalit, the Israeli corporal who was held captive in Gaza for more than two years. The teasing point in this article is when Kreshner indicates that Ehud Barak – an Israeli politician, former Prime Minister; current Minister of Defense, Deputy Prime Minister, and leader of Israel's Labor Party – states that the only reason they would consider a truce with Gaza is to secure Shalit's safety, even after learning that the corporal was hurt in one of the Israeli attacks on Gaza).

Ethan Bronner's article, published on December 31, is titled 'Israel Rejects Ceasefire, But Offers Gaza Aid.' The article is a clear example of lack of information which further serves the Israeli propaganda model.

> Israel fend[s] off growing international pressure over civilian casualties from its military assault on Gaza, saying it would expedite and increase humanitarian aid and work with its allies to build a durable, long-term truce. But, Israel would not agree to a proposed 48-hour cease-fire. (Bronner, 2008: A1)

The text insinuates that Israel will facilitate aid – medical and food – and anything required by the Palestinians; in reality, however, the Red Cross and other organizations coming to provide the help needed by the Palestinian civilians complain about the hardships they have faced with the Israelis when trying to provide subsidies. Moreover, the use of provocative words like 'civilian casualties' describes Palestinian deaths and suffrage in an attempt to minimize the losses and implies that they are trivial matters. Referring back to Said's 'Orientalism' and the definition of 'the other', words are chosen deliberately and depersonalize the Palestinian deaths by referring to them simply as 'casualties'.

On December 31, 2008, Mark Mazzetti published his article, 'Striking Deep Into Israel, Hamas Employs an Upgraded Arsenal.' The headline displays prejudicial journalism and exaggeration. First, it describes the Hamas strikes as 'deep', rendering them incomparable to what Israel does to Gazans. Second, for the first time in the Israeli-Palestinian coverage analyzed herein, a journalist gives exact names and information about the weapons used by Palestinians in the strikes; whereas, there was no mentioning of the sophisticated technological weapons used by the Israelis throughout the whole article.

> By firing rockets deep into Israeli territory, the militant Palestinian group Hamas has in recent days displayed an arsenal that has been

upgraded with weapons parts smuggled into Gaza since it seized control of the territory 18 months ago, according to American and Israeli officials. (Mazzetti, 2008: A12)

Moreover, the author's source of information is clearly identified as 'American and Israeli officials' when covering an incident of a rocket hitting a vacant Israeli school. The attempt at being informative is even more poignant when considering the general lack of information about Palestinian targets, such as the UN school that Israel hit causing a score of Palestinian deaths and injuries).

Looking at the title of an article written by Steven Erlanger on December 31, 'An Egyptian Border Town's Commerce, Conducted via Tunnels, Comes to a Halt,'

The Israelis are there alone; Hamas has nothing up there,' he said. 'But on the ground it's different. They're deep underground in cement tunnels just over there, 20 meters deep. (Erlanger, 2008: A12)

The first paragraph represents another falsification in describing the tunnels used to transport aid to Gaza as 'BorderTown's Commerce.' The decontextualization and lack of providing complete statements of the person being quoted in the first paragraph creates the impression that there are groups of traitors using the tunnels who are trying to make a living regardless of the deaths and aggression in Gaza.

'In Dense Gaza, Civilians Suffer,' is another article written by Taghreed El-Khodary and published on December 31, 2008. The whole article reflects a pro-Palestinian stance which is unusual to see during the period under examination. It is also one of the few articles written solely by an Arab reporter. It is clear from the title that the focus is on civilians. Out of the sum total of articles analyzed in this study, this is the only article that discloses facts about Palestinian victims.

On January 1, 2009, Isable Kershner wrote 'In a Broadening Offensive, Israel Steps Up Diplomacy.' In the lexicon used in the headline, 'Israel steps up diplomacy'; the use of propaganda model is clear in the word choice of 'Israel' in relation to 'diplomacy' indicating that Israel finally brings diplomacy and steps it up in the region where it is needed the most. Israel is using its strategic tools to influence the public opinion; the implication is that 'the others' are just a group of smugglers and terrorists who deserve to be destroyed. The author's tone embeds a bias when describing Israel's offense as victory in the quote: 'destroying important symbols of the government and, for the first time in its six-day-old campaign, killing a senior leader of the militant Islamic group'.

In the last sample article from *The New York Times,* Isabel Kreshner and Taghreed El-Khodary's article 'Escalation Feared as Israel, Continuing Bombing, Lets Foreigners Leave Gaza' appeared on January 2, 2009. The article emphasizes the suffering of Palestinians who do not have the leverage of being saved from the bombardment. The lexical choice of 'enclave' in the following part:

> Israeli warplanes pounded Hamas targets in Gaza for an eighth day on Saturday while Israel allowed hundreds of foreigners, many of them married to Palestinians, to leave the enclave, raising fears there that Israel was planning to escalate its week-old campaign. (Kreshner & Khodary, 2009: A01)

This part connotes that Gaza is an isolated territory, politically and culturally, from the rest of Palestine. In the same article, however, it is stated that 'Palestinian militants continued to launch salvos of rockets at southern Israel on Friday, with several hitting the coastal city of Ashkelon, lightly injuring two Israeli women there.' The choice of the word 'salvos' denotes a heavy burst of firing or bombing. Juxtaposing that use with the lack of mention of Palestinian deaths and injuries, portrays Palestinians as the aggressors and shows falsification, exaggeration and lack of accuracy.

Daily News

The *Daily News* is Egypt's only independent (i.e. from any governmental influences) newspaper in English. In the sample coverage of the Israeli-Palestinian conflict, the first article, 'Egypt Accused of Being Part of Israeli Conspiracy', is by Yasmine Saleh and was published on December 29, 2008. The word choice is stronger in the use of 'accused' and 'conspiracy', describing how the Arab misinterpret Egypt's stand from opening the Rafah gate permanently. From the Egyptian politicians' point of view, they are trying not to fall into the trap of being a third part in the conflict, which might allow Israel to justify an attack on Egypt's lands (Rafah) as means of 'retaliation'. Likewise, the lexical choice in describing the Israeli 'assault' (also used in US media sources, such as *The Washington Post* and *The New York Times*) is used differently than the framing of 'Israeli raids on Gaza' and 'massacre and blockade' (used in the Saleh article).

On December 30, 2008, Abdel Rahman Hussein's article, 'Increased Security on Gaza Border to Prevent Further Breaches,' appeared. The use of the term 'breaches' appears in direct contrast to the word 'smugglers' from the US media indicated earlier. In the first paragraph, the author gives informative details on what he means, explaining that the people who are trying to transfer medical and food supplies or who are trying to escape are a direct consequence of the strong and rapid Israeli airstrikes.

'Israeli Assault Targets Symbols of Hamas Power' is an article by Ibrahim Barzak and Matti Friedman published on December 29. In the second paragraph, in direct opposition to US news coverage, there are descriptive details and statistical numbers of Palestinian losses. In another article by Ibrahim Barzak and Amy Tiebel published the following day, the lexicon is different. The tone in the headline, 'Israeli Warplanes Continue Striking, Kill Two Sisters,' seems to sympathize with the Palestinian suffering by identifying actual human loss.

On January 1, 2009, Ibrahim Barzak wrote 'Israel Wants International Truce Monitors.' His article carries more contextualized and descriptive details; the statement 'Israel also appeared to be sounding out a possible diplomatic exit from its campaign by demanding international monitors as a key term of any future truce with Hamas in the Gaza Strip' is a clear indication of counter-hegemonic discourse because Israel is the one in control on Gaza with the enforced siege banded on the Strip; Palestinians are paralyzed and they are the ones who needed the international interference to save them. Another January 1 article is '400 Killed and 1,700 Wounded as Medical Aid Crosses Through Rafah'. The article is an objective and descriptive account, full of concise and explicit statistical information about the situation within Gaza:

> Trucks from Egypt crossed over carrying much-needed medical supplies to the embattled Gaza, under fire for a sixth day. So far more than 400 Gazans have been killed, including 34 children, and some 1,700 have been wounded since Israel embarked on its aerial campaign on Saturday, Gaza health officials said. In no man's land between the Egyptian and the Palestinian sides of the Rafah border, 15 wounded Palestinians arrived from Gaza hospital and were transferred from Palestinian to Egyptian ambulances. (Barzak, 2009)

The choice of the word 'embattled' to describe Gaza reveals a pro-Palestinian stance.

On January 2, 2009, Abdel-Rahman Hussein wrote the article 'Transfer of Aid and Wounded at Rafah Crossing only Outlet for Gaza.' After media attacks on Egypt were initiated by other Arabic mainstream media to express their distrust and rejection of the passive role the Egyptian government was playing, the Egyptian media started to fight back. In his article, Hussein provides an explanation for Egypt's role in the situation. The choice of lexicon is very intentional, especially when trying to indicate Egypt's power and significance in the area by using phrases like 'only outlet'.

'Three Boys Killed in Fresh Israeli Raid on Gaza, Thousands Protest in Hebron' is an article published on January 2, 2009. This article is interesting as it incorporates new details about Hebron protests in direct response to the attacks on Gaza. Since growing anti-Israeli sentiment might seem too sensitive to publish in the US media, the mainstream American media fail to publish any reports on the incident. The direct reference to 'boys killed' in the headline seems to be an appeal for public sympathy.

On January 4, 2009, two articles appear in the *Daily News*: the first one is titled 'Egypt Calls for Humanitarian Corridors in Gaza'; the second written by Ibrahim Barzak and Matti Friedman is titled 'Israel Forces Sever Gaza, Surround Major City.' The first article emphasizes Egypt's tactical political agenda. The lexicon in the headline expresses this role of Egypt as the protector of Gaza's 'corridors'. Also, the claim that 'The Egyptian proposal is aimed at avoiding, as much as possible, the horrors of military operations' explains the Egyptian position in this conflict which has been disputed and criticized by other Arab countries. The second article provides additional informative details:

> Israeli ground troops and tanks cut swaths [...] cutting the coastal territory into two and surrounding its biggest city as the new phase of a devastating offensive against Hamas gained momentum. At least 24 Palestinians, mostly civilians, were killed. (Barzak & Friedman, 2009)

On January 5, 2009, Theodore May contributes 'Shelling Near The Border But Rafah Remains Open.' In this article, May gives informative and descriptive details on the blockade situation in Gaza. His choice of words draws public sympathy to Gaza's misery. On the same day, Ibrahim Barzak's article, 'Israel Pounds Gaza, Vows to Continue,' appears. The choice of lexicon is very strong; the words 'pounds' and 'continue' illustrate a cruel situation in Gaza. Barzak gives descriptive and informative details throughout the article to support his report:

> Israeli forces pounded Gaza Strip houses, mosques and tunnels on Monday from the air, land and sea, killing at least seven children and six other civilians, as they consolidated a bruising land offensive. (May, 2009)

Theodore May and Yasmine Saleh wrote 'Egyptian Doctors Denied Entry into Gaza,' published on January 7, 2009. The strong lexicon and the descriptive details appear in direct contradiction with the Israeli officials' claims of providing aid to the Palestinians 'even if they are not seizing fire'. The article is a counterattack on Israeli political propaganda which claims that the Israeli officials' cooperation with all sources of medical aid by coming in to help Palestinians on the borders. May and Saleh state:

> For the second day running frustrated Egyptian doctors were denied entry into Gaza through the Rafah border crossing, as Israel continued its shelling campaign near the border. (May & Saleh, 2009)

Discussion

The clear US media biases revealed in the support of Israel's assault on Gaza shadows what happened in the Iraq war news coverage: they followed blindly what the US Administration dictated and failed to objectively report the effect of the invasion on the locals (i.e. Iraqis) to produce impartial 'realities'. According to *If Americans Knew* (2004) there are many untold realities happening in Palestine and other Middle Eastern countries that cause great damage to American news' credibility.

Yet, as the Israeli bombs are dropping on occupied Gaza – and where there are clear reasons to challenge the legality, wisdom and morality of such brutal attacks with widely available public information – America's major newspapers fall in line behind official US foreign policy talking points, with an erroneous and one-sided picture, avoiding serious debate at all costs. Also, the use of Israeli officials' statements, as sources of information, were used in a wider range than using quotes from Palestinian officials in most of the chosen articles.

Findings

Looking at the two American newspapers and the Egyptian newspaper, I found that through a close reading of *The Washington Post* and *The New York Times'* seven days of articles on the Gaza siege, there were more articles written by Israeli or pro-Israel authors in the respective media sources than those by Arabs or pro-Palestinians. On the other hand, by virtue, *The Daily News'* seven days articles were all written by Arabs (pro-Palestinian conflict). Consequently, a question arises: What are the differences between each reality of both sides and the actual reality of the situation? To be able to answer this question, it is necessary to experience the reality in its totality, to be able to experience the conflict from both sides, impartially. However, it is almost impossible for this to be the case. First, there is the issue of personal opinions: people's preconceptions of certain situations and their subsequent interpretations of certain events. Then, there are the information sources, the tools for the construction of these personal opinions and preconceptions. Any expression of an event or situation that we receive through the mainstream media will inevitably consist of at least an element of the narrative of the elite powerful, since they maintain a hegemonic position within the dissemination of information (Wolfsfeld, 1997). It is also likely that other sources of information, not considered to be part of the mainstream media, will also include biases and will also use information which is likely to further their own interests. There is the inescapable impression that any information received is never likely to allow a true picture of reality.

The advantage in the 21st century is the ease with which so much information is available all over the world, if only the time and inclination to look for it exist. There are more reliable alternative sources of information since there are more independent news sources, such as the *UN News Centre*, that can provide information that is missing from the mainstream media. And, although many of the alternatives also have their own biases, at least there are variations in opinions and analyses that allow us to make up our own minds about what is happening to our world instead of simply having the events interpreted for us. For it is no longer a question of whether or not we are receiving objective reporting, but rather it is a question of our ethical concern about the events that are unfolding in our 'globalized' world and what we are willing and able to do about them.

Notes

1. The British Broadcasting Corporation (BBC) is the world's largest broadcaster. In common with the public broadcasting organizations of many other European countries, it is funded yearly by a television license fee charged to all UK households. Cable News Network (CNN) is a major US cable news network founded in 1980 by Ted Turner. Al Arabiya is an Arabic-language television news channel. It was established on March 3, 2003. The international news station is based in Dubai Media City, United Arab Emirates, and is partly owned by the Saudi-controlled broadcaster Middle East Broadcasting Center (MBC).
2. FAIR; FAIR, the national media watch group, has been offering well-documented criticism of media bias and censorship since 1986. They work to invigorate the First Amendment by advocating for greater diversity in the press and by scrutinizing media practices that marginalize public interest, minority and dissenting viewpoints. As a progressive group, FAIR believes that structural reform is ultimately needed to break up the dominant media conglomerates, establish independent public broadcasting and promote strong nonprofit sources of information.

Appendix

Table A.1 The selected articles from the three chosen newspapers. Data sources

Washington Post	The New York Times	Daily News Egypt
Nothing is on the 27th http://www. washingtonpost.com/ wp-dyn/content/ article/2008/12/27/ AR2008122700962.html By Michael Aramowtiz Features: L, FE, LA, JP December 28, 2008	http://www.nytimes. com/2008/12/28/ world/middleeast/ web28mideast.html http://www.nytimes. com/2008/12/28/ world/middleeast/ 28mideast.html By Taghreed El-Khodary and Isabel Kershner By Taghreed El-Khodary and Ethan Bronner Features I: LI Features II: L, JP, LI, LA December 27, 2008	Nothing in on the 27th or 28th http://www. thedailynewsegypt. com/article.aspx? ArticleID=18752 http://www. thedailynewsegypt. com/article.aspx? ArticleID=18755 http://www. thedailynewsegypt. com/article.aspx? ArticleID=18757 By Yasmine Saleh By Abdel-Rahman Hussein By Ibrahim Barzak and Matti Friedman Features I: L. Feature II: DD.Feature III: I. December 29, 2008
http://www. washingtonpost.com/ wp-dyn/content/ article/2008/12/28/ AR2008122800115.html By Griff Witte Features: L, JP, FE December 29, 2008	http://www.nytimes. com/2008/12/29/ world/middleeast/ 29mideast.html By Tghreed El-Khodary and Isabel Kershner Features: L December 28, 2008	http://www. thedailynewsegypt. com/article.aspx? ArticleID=18785 By Ibrahim Barzak and Amy Tiebel Features: L December 30, 2008
http://voices. washingtonpost. com/44/2008/12/30/ pro-palestinian_ protesters_pic.html By Philip Rucker Features: L December 30, 2008	http://www.nytimes. com/2008/12/30/ world/middleeast/ 30shalit.html By Isabel Kershner Features: JP December 29, 2008	Nothing is on the 31st http://www. thedailynewsegypt. com/article.aspx? ArticleID=18810 http://www. thedailynewsegypt. com/article.aspx?Article ID=18812 By Ibrahim Barzak By Abel-Rahman Hussein

Table A.1 *Continued*

Washington Post	*The New York Times*	*Daily News Egypt*
		Features II: DD Features III: L, DD January 1, 2009
Just photos on December 31 http://www. washingtonpost.com/ wp-dyn/content/ article/2008/12/31/ AR2008123103112.html By Griff Witte Features: D January 1, 2009	http://www.nytimes. com/2008/12/31/ world/middleeast/ 31mideast.htmlBy David Grossman Features: LI, JP December 30, 2008	http://www. thedailynewsegypt. com/article.aspx? ArticleID=18835 http://www. thedailynewsegypt. com/article. aspx?ArticleID = 18839 By Abdel-Rahman Hussein By Agencies Features I: L, DD Features II: DD, L January 2, 2009
http://www. washingtonpost.com/ wp-dyn/content/ article/2008/12/31/ AR2008123100467.html By Sudarsan Raghavan Features: LI, JP January 1, 2009	http://www.nytimes. com/2009/01/01/ world/middleeast/ 01mideast.html http://www.nytimes. com/2009/01/01/ world/middleeast/ 01rockets.html http://www.nytimes. com/2009/01/01/ world/middleeast/ 01rafah.html?_r = 1 http://www.nytimes. com/2009/01/01/world/ middleeast/01gaza.html By Ethan Bronner By Mark MazzettiBy Steven Erlanger By Taghreed El-Khodary Features I: L, LI Features II: JP, LI, FE Features III: D Features IV: L December 31, 2008	Nothing is on the 3rd http://www. thedailynewsegypt. com/article. aspx?ArticleID=18854 http://www. thedailynewsegypt. com/article. aspx?ArticleID=18868 By AFP By Ibrahim Barzak and Matti Friedman Features I: I Features II: I, DD January 4, 2009
http://www. washingtonpost.com/ wp-dyn/content/ article/2009/01/01/ AR2009010102061.html By Sudarsan Raghavan and Abdel Kareem	http://www.nytimes. com/2009/01/02/ world/middleeast/ 02mideast.html By Isabel Kershner Features: L January 1, 2009	http://www. thedailynewsegypt. com/article. aspx?ArticleID=18887 http://www. thedailynewsegypt. com/article.

Table A.1 *Continued*

Washington Post	The New York Times	Daily News Egypt
Features: L January 2, 2009		aspx?ArticleID=18893 By Theodore May By Ibrahim Barzak Features I: DD Features II: L, I, DD January 5, 2009
http://www. washingtonpost.com/ wp-dyn/content/ article/2009/01/03/ AR2009010300320.html By Griff Witte Features: L, D January 4, 2009	http://www.nytimes. com/2009/01/03/ world/middleeast/ 03mideast.html By Isabel Kershner and Taghreed El-Khodary Features: L, E, LA January 2, 2009	Nothing is on the 6 http://www. thedailynewsegypt. com/article. aspx?ArticleID=18919 By Theodore May and Yasmine Saleh Features: L, I January 7, 2009

Chapter 9

Language and the Art of Spin: Commendation and Condemnation in Media Discourse

L.N. BERLIN

Introduction

Within democratic societies, the notion of *freedom of the press* has long held an important place. The fourth estate, responsible for monitoring governmental conduct for the people, is only successful when allowed to operate independently and free from outside influence. Yet while the so-called 'free press' has long been aware of and often railed against media sources in parts of the world which function as little more than propagandists for oppressive, totalitarian states, critical discourse analysis brings into question the extent to which modern press media can be said to operate truly independently.

In *Talking Power: The Politics of Language*, R. Lakoff (1990) described the Chinese government's blackout of internal media coverage on any piece referring to the student uprising at Tiananmen Square. So complete was the government's suppression of reports on the incident within China that it appeared not only as if the call for democracy in the country was being exaggerated, but also that the entire event was a fabrication of the foreign press, thereby stifling any further action by the student or general population. Thus, even with the advent of the internet and access to instantaneous information from around the world, R. Lakoff's suggestion that the public cannot be fooled for long appears to apply only in nontotalitarian states. Yet in her reference to the long-term inability of regimes to use the press to maintain control over public opinion, the concept of 'spin' becomes particularly relevant, especially in an era when former bastions of the freedom of the press are functioning through corporate sponsorship. Spin, or the way a story is framed to favor one particular interpretation, plays a pivotal role in the way the populace construes a stated perspective. Thus, when a relatively acquiescent public wants to believe or has simply lost its ability to question its leaders for whatever reason – even in a democracy – the coercion (or even collaboration) of the press and a clever hegemonic entity, whether political or economic, can keep the public duped for an extended period of time.

Caldas-Coulthard (2003) describes the conditions necessary for the press media to influence the public and create a 'we-they' situation Weigand (1999: 35) has referred to as 'dialogue in the grip of the media' through the representation of 'otherness'. By creating a we-they dichotomy that essentially positions the press as operating on behalf of public interest (i.e. *We are with you* or *We are one of you* mindset) – an expectation further exacerbated by the notion that the press is indeed operating on its own accord – the 'scapegoat', whomever it may be, is presented as the 'other', operating against the interests of the people.

In one example, Berlin (2005) performs an analysis of newspaper headlines centered on the coverage of the 'No Child Left Behind Act of 2001' (NCLB),[1] a sweeping piece of educational legislature, passed in the United States in the wake of the attacks on the World Trade Center and Pentagon in September 2001, which is still considered contentious in many educational settings today. In Chicago, a barrage of newspaper articles being published on a daily basis immediately preceding the 2002–2003 school year positioned the schools and the teachers themselves as the 'other', describing them as inadequate and ultimately failing to provide the education they were charged with. The results within the local context left the Chicago populace, similar to the public in many parts of the United States where similar media attacks were occurring, with the impression that the immediate compliance with NCLB was necessary. Regardless of the inherent flaws and inequalities represented in the law which educators have attempted to bring to light and are still battling, NCLB emerged as a veritable government-imposed panacea destined to fix the many problems in public education.

In another example which has had a devastating impact, the media coverage within the United States leading up to the US invasion of Iraq presents a series of US government fallacies regarding connections between Saddam Hussein's regime and the attacks by Al-Qaeda on New York and Washington. Despite intelligence from numerous polities around the world and international organizations (e.g. United Nations, International Atomic Energy Agency), repudiating the connection or even the capacity of Iraq under sanctions to mount such an organized attack, popular opinion fomented by erroneous information broadcast in the United States regarding the guilt of Iraq was so strong that more than 60% of the US citizenry polled at the time believed Iraq to be directly responsible. Subsequently, the US Congress in both houses overwhelmingly voted to support former president George W. Bush in his pursuit to extend US influence in the Middle East (G. Lakoff, 2004; Rudd, 2004).

In the two preceding examples, news media sources operating in an alleged stronghold of democracy – the United States – can be seen taking positions, advancing a particular agenda (cf. Atawneh, this volume; Ayish, this volume; Bell, 1991; El-Bilawi, this volume; Kress & van Leeuwen, 1996; G. Lakoff, 2004; R. Lakoff, 1990, 2000; van Dijk, 2003). In fact, the commendation or condemnation used to create the we-they dichotomy spins, or frames (cf. Goffman, 1981; G. Lakoff, 2004), information in a way that takes advantage of sociocultural norms in the extrasituational context, functioning to construct, ratify and/or reinforce specific ideologies, especially during times of conflict between regimes (cf. Ehlich, 1989; Silberstein, this volume).

In an effort to answer the general question, then, about whether modern press media operate independently of outside influence – public (i.e. governmental) or private – this chapter explores the following issues. First, by taking a single topic and comparing the coverage of identical stories over the same time period, the study examines the texts of media sources operating in ideologically different regimes to determine whether they cover the same story similarly or differently. Along the same lines, the textual analysis combined with an investigation of how the news sources interact with their respective audiences (i.e. interactional context) can determine whether the media are exercising unbiased journalism. Finally, a look at the situational (sociolinguistic) and extrasituational (sociocultural and sociopolitical) contexts will expose the extent to which the various political ideologies within which the news sources are functioning can be said to influence the coverage on some level.

Methodology

Corpus

The corpus was comprised of transcripts from live news broadcasts collected during the period between December 2003 and February 2004. The focus identified was the reporting on the Israeli-Palestinian conflict (second Intifada). Two distinct news sources were selected for the research for the following reasons: (1) they both broadcast in English and could easily be compared on a number of levels; (2) their transcripts were readily available online; and (3) they operated from two countries in different parts of the world with disparate ideological stances. The first source, *Al-Manar*, is the news source of Hezbollah and operates out of Lebanon; the news program had previously been available in the West via satellite television, but access to the signal was blocked in December 2004 when the former US Secretary of State, Colin Powell, identified the news station as a 'terrorist organization' within the meaning of the US Immigration and Nationality Act due to its open affiliation with Hezbollah. The designation, in turn, caused the channel to be placed on the Terrorist Exclusion List. The second source, *CNNWorld* (Middle East edition), operates throughout the world, essentially proffering the US version of world news and events. *Al-Manar* and *CNNWorld* were compared on their representation of the totality of their reporting on the Intifada during the three-month period and identical events as they occurred.[2]

Analysis

Using a framework for conducting a critical discourse analysis suggested by Fairclough (1989, 1995) (see Figure 9.1), the investigation begins with the text itself and the concomitant attempts to describe what it contains and, to the extent possible, what is suggests. In the case of the current study, this was done with the assistance of a concordance program. Next, the process of text production leads to the process of interpretation. The transcripts being analyzed here are recognized as media discourse, produced through an institutional process of writing, revising and editing – a coconstructed message – that involves the participation of multiple entities, not the least of which is the editor-in-chief and producer of the broadcast who assumes responsibility for what is uttered by the

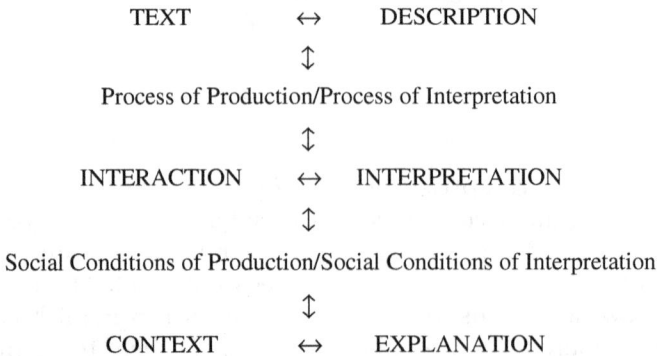

TEXT   ↔   DESCRIPTION

↕

Process of Production/Process of Interpretation

↕

INTERACTION   ↔   INTERPRETATION

↕

Social Conditions of Production/Social Conditions of Interpretation

↕

CONTEXT   ↔   EXPLANATION

Figure 9.1 CDA as an analytic framework

newscaster. At this level, the nature of the interaction is revealed; the presentation of the news is an attempt to connect with and perhaps influence the listening audience (Berlin, 2005; Caldas-Coulthard, 2003; R. Lakoff, 1990), removed in space and perhaps time, especially if the transmission is not live. However, Scannell argues that:

> the liveness of broadcasting, its sense of existing in real time – the time of the programme corresponding to the time of its reception – is a pervasive effect of the medium. The talk that goes out on radio and television is recognizably produced in actual institutional settings and intended for and addressed to actual listeners and viewers, listening and viewing in real-world circumstances. As such this talk is intentionally communicative. [...] All talk on radio and TV is public discourse, is meant to be accessible to the audience for whom it is intended. [...] A central concern in the study of broadcast talk is to specify the ways in which communicative intentionality is organized in the form and content of programmes. (Scannell, 1991: 1)

The focus of the critical analyst, then, is to interpret the outward and sometimes underlying intentions of the news agency cum speaker. This analytic process is further aided by an examination of the context within which the news agencies operate; in some cases, the analysis of the social conditions of production and interpretation lead to a deeper understanding of the context, which not only allows for a richer, 'thick description' (Geertz, 1973: 27), but also goes beyond a merely descriptive rendering and touches on the explanatory.

As a result of this analysis, the three items raised at the end of section one were investigated accordingly; that is, the differences in the texts suggests that the ideology of the regime can lead to substantially different coverage even when the stories are supposed to be comparable. The manner in which the broadcasters interact with their respective audiences can suggest that their reporting is more subjective and hegemonic, as opposed to objective, dispassionate and unbiased. Moreover, the context surrounding the news broadcasts and their interactions with listening and viewing audiences can potentially indicate the influence of outside sources operating within the various regimes as political ideologies or private agenda are uncovered in the analysis.

Findings and Discussion

Description

A concordance program was used to examine the corpus of the assembled news broadcasts (see Table 9.1). A simple count was done for the total

Table 9.1 Corpus data overview

	Al-Manar	CNNWorld
Period	*12/03/2003–02/26/2004*	*12/03/2003–02/26/2004*
Number of stories:	103	23
Number of words	34,976	10,983
Average number words/story	339	477

number of stories run by each news agency, as well as a count for the total number of words and average number of words per story. This initial analysis showed that *Al-Manar*, the smaller of the two media sources, presented more than four times the number of stories than that of *CNNWorld*.[3] A total word count also showed that *Al-Manar* produced more than three times the number of words, although the same analysis revealed that the average number of words per story was higher in *CNNWorld*.

Additionally, a lemmatizer included in the concordance program was employed to search for high-frequency lexical items. The 30 most frequent words were first identified in the combined corpus; then, the same lexical items were calculated for number of occurrences and overall percentage in each of the subcorpora (i.e. the separate compilations of the *Al-Manar* stories for the same period versus the *CNNWorld* stories). Tables 9.2 and 9.3, respectively, present a side-by-side comparison between the two sources of the five most frequently used lexical items and the least frequently used lexical items in an effort to connect those key content words (or 'signifiers' in the text) with the referents (or 'signified' in the interaction) (cf. Chouliaraki & Fairclough, 1999; Fairclough, 1989, 1995).

Table 9.2 Concordance for highest lexical frequency

Al-Manar			CNNWorld		
Lexical item	*#occ*	*%corpus*	*Lexical item*	*#occ*	*%corpus*
1. occup*	306	0.008749	1. attack	75	0.006829
2. settle*	139	0.003974	2. barrier	68	0.006191
3. separation	76	0.002173	3. terror*	58	0.005281
4. martyr*	72	0.002059	4. military	32	0.002914
5. security	72	0.002059	5. security	32	0.002914

Note: Items marked with an asterisk (*) represent common roots (i.e. occup* could appear in the transcripts as occupation, occupier, occupy, etc.).

Table 9.3 Concordance for lowest lexical frequency

Al-Manar						CNNWorld		
Lexical item	#occ	Comp rank	Lexical item	#occ	Comp rank	Lexical item	#occ	Comp rank
25. defense	7	10	20. assassinat*	2	17	25. casualties	1	26
26. casualties	5	25	21. incursion	2	18	bulldoze*	0	20
27. democracy	3	27	22. separation	2	3	democracy	0	27
28. militant	2	9	23. stone*	2	16	intifada	0	24
29. suicide	1	16	24. aggress*	1	6	martyr*	0	4

Note: Items marked with an asterisk (*) represent common roots (i.e. occup* could appear in the transcripts as *occupation, occupier, occupy*, etc.).

In Table 9.2, a major difference was found in the way each news source selected its language to represent the same events. Indeed, the only keyword that cooccurred in the top five most frequent words from *Al-Manar* and *CNNWorld* is 'security', albeit not always signified in the same manner. To highlight the disparate coverage of the same events further during the same timeframe, Table 9.3 demonstrates that items such as 'democracy' and 'bulldoze' which appear in *Al-Manar*'s list do not occur at all in the various pieces broadcast by *CNNWorld*. 'Separation', which occurs more frequently in *Al-Manar*'s list, only appears twice in *CNNWorld*, whereas 'defense' and 'militant', which occur very infrequently in *Al-Manar*'s 103 pieces appear more frequently in *CNNWorld*. Words such as 'Intifada' and 'martyr' with their specific use and meanings within *Al-Manar* are not to be found anywhere in *CNNWorld*.[4]

Headlines

In the exploration of the interaction between news agency and viewer (or in the case of reanalyzing the transcripts, author and reader), the headlines for stories on the same events were compared. As van Dijk suggests:

> the proposition expressed by the headline is also a strong strategic suggestion to the readers to construct this as the top macro proposition of their mental model of the event to be represented – or to add or modify an opinion already formed in an earlier model when readers heard about this case [...] the actual formation of the headline is also a function of the context model, in particular of the socal and political aims of the editorial and the newspaper. (van Dijk, 2003: 99)

or in this case, the broadcaster, its broadcasts and their subsequent transcripts.[5]

Textual description

In the first comparison, headlines (1a) and (1b), there are textual similarities between the two news sources in terms of the signified. The use of 'Cairo' in (1a) and 'Egypt' in (1b) refers to the Egyptian government and its role in attempting to broker an agreement between Israel and Palestine. Likewise, 'truce' and 'ceasefire' in the respective headlines are synonymous. Thus, even though the presentation is rather different with regard to the actual lexical items and their order, the content of the two headlines are clearly alike, setting a baseline that demonstrates that both sources are reporting on the same events and can, when desirable, represent the same facts in a relatively objective manner.

(1a) Al-Manar 12/05/2003
Cairo Proposes a One-Year Truce with 'Israel'[6] to Factions

(1b) CNN 12/04/2003
Egypt Calls for Palestinian Ceasefire: Conference of Palestinian Factions Opens in Cairo

Another example of textual and descriptive similarities can be seen in (2a), (2b) and (2c).[7] Nonetheless, there is a slight difference in the representation of the propositional content where the *CNN World* headline suggests the culpability for the inability to reach an agreement lies with the Palestinians; though the same situation can also be implied from (2a), (2b) sounds hopeful where the content of (2c) clearly indicates that the leadership of the Palestinian Authority has 'little to negotiate' with.

(2a) Al-Manar 12/06/2003
Palestinian Factions Insist No Ceasefire without Israeli Guarantees

(2b) Al-Manar 12/08/2003
Palestinian Authority Says It Will Continue Efforts to Reach a Comprehensive Ceasefire with 'Israel'

(2c) CNN 12/07/2003
Palestinians Can't Agree on Ceasefire: Militant Groups Leave Qorei with Little to Negotiate

In each of the previous comparisons, textual similarities are apparent whether the same or different words are used to signify the same propositional content. In the next example, though, the signifiers themselves

lend clues to the different perspectives of the two distinct media sources
– seemingly aligned with different sides in the Israeli-Palestinian conflict
as well as the separate extrasituational contexts (i.e. ideological) within
which each of these sources operate. *Al-Manar* refers to the Israeli army as
the 'occupation army' in (3a) compared with the *CNNWorld* signifier for
the same in (3b). Consequently, textual representations which would be
otherwise identical (i.e. 'X Kills 3 Palestinians') use different labels for the
same entity to indicate an ideological position toward the agent, *Al-Manar's*
depiction being politically loaded versus *CNNWorld's* more neutral stance
in this headline.

(3a) Al-Manar 01/07/2004
Occupation Army Kills 3 Palestinians

(3b) CNN 01/07/2004
Israeli Forces Kill 3 Palestinians

Interaction-interpretation

As previously stated, the 'interaction' of the news broadcast is essentially one way in nature. The agency reporting the news transmits information to the listening and viewing audience, following an idealized
model of speaker–hearer communication. The audience, displaced in
space and potentially time, does not have direct opportunities to interact
in the traditional sense of dialogue models or communicate its intentions
(Scannell, 1991); instead, the audience plays a relatively passive yet important role in the fulfillment of ideological indoctrination (Berlin, 2005;
Caldas-Coulthard, 2003). As such, the power of the news sources to frame
or 'spin' the propositional content has a real outcome in terms of the way
information is portrayed to and concomitantly perceived by the listeners
(cf. Atawneh, this volume; Ayish, this volume; El-Bilawi, this volume). For
instance, the propositional content embedded within the two headlines
(4a) and (4b) contains the same information, yet the way it is presented is
vastly different. In a side-by-side comparison, *Al-Manar* clearly provides
more detail while at the same time positioning Israel as the enemy with
references again to the 'occupation army' and the use of the term 'assassinates'. In contrast, however, *CNNWorld* omits most of the details, such as
the perpetrator of the strike. In so doing – although familiarity with the
context leaves no doubt who is responsible – the full interpretation is com-
promised as far as the 'social and political aims of the editorial' are concerned (van Dijk, 2003: 99), the attack having been left agentless and the
proposition simply indicating where the attack occurred (i.e. Gaza) and
whence it came (i.e. *airstrike*).

(4a) Al-Manar 12/25/2003
Israeli Occupation Army Assassinates a Palestinian Resistance Leader,
Kills 4 Others

(4b) CNN 12/26/2003
Gaza Air Strike

In another example of differential positioning, (5a) provides an interpretation for how the audience should understand the event by including
the quotation from the Palestinian perspective regarding the dismantling
of the settlements. Like (4b), however, the responsible party is omitted
although once again apparent in the situational context. Moreover,
Al-Manar appears to absolve itself of taking sides in the headline by using
evidentiality (i.e. quoting the Palestinian Authority). *CNNWorld*, on the
other hand, by neglecting to include the Palestinian response – neither in
the headline nor in the story – spins the piece in such a way that leaves
Israel in a favorable light, portraying the gestures of the Israeli government in (5b) as magnanimous.

(5a) Al-Manar 12/30/2003
Palestinian Authority Says Dismantling of 4 Settlement Outposts Is a
'Stunt'

(5b) CNN 12/29/2003
Israel to Dismantle Outposts, Ease Travel Limits: Four Outposts
Scheduled for Demolition

Besides positioning, news agencies may choose to represent the same
event differently in terms of degree, such as in (6a) and (6b). The two
verbs selected by each of the broadcasters are uniquely presented to
inculcate a vastly different reaction in the recipient audience. While 'crit-
icize' can be understood to have a negative connotation, the interpretation in the interaction is essentially left to the audience whereas the
measured reaction associated with the word 'violate' and imposed on
the listening and viewing audience is decidedly stronger. Nevertheless,
Al-Manar can claim objectivity in its headline by once again citing its
source while *CNNWorld* merely provides its own rendition of the statement by the Red Cross, mitigating the force of the assertion through
evidential reference.

(6a) Al-Manar 02/18/2004
ICRC Says 'Israel's' West Bank Separation Wall Violates Humanitarian
Law

(6b) CNN 02/18/2004
Red Cross Criticizes Israeli Security Barrier

Employing the same device used by *Al-Manar* in the previous two comparisons – (5a) and (6a) – *CNNWorld* uses evidentiality in (7b) where it releases itself from any responsibility for the claim made in the proposition by indexing the 'Palestinian sources' as the party responsible for the assertion.

(7a) Al-Manar 01/03/2004
Israeli Occupation Kills 3 Palestinians including a 15-year-old Boy

(7b) CNN 01/03/2004
Palestinian Sources: Israeli Forces Kill 4 Palestinians

However, the discursive practice of distancing itself from absolute claims of first-hand knowledge by *Al-Manar* is enacted quite differently because the statements signified are opinions to begin with; that is what the Palestinian Authority thinks in (5a) and what the ICRC thinks in (6a). The effect of *CNNWorld's* assignment of responsibility to Palestinian sources in (7b) is the mitigation of the force of the claim about an action – the killing of four Palestinians – thus bringing the truth value of the entire proposition into question (cf. Aikhenvald, 2004; Berlin, 2008).

The news stories and their contexts

Finally, for the investigation of the discourse context (i.e. the text with its extended linguistic context and the interaction with the audience), the pieces were juxtaposed together to identify the positioning of information and its possible spin within the stories, as well as how spin manifests commendation or condemnation of the signified. For the sake of expediency and the ease of comparison, excerpts from the extended transcripts are included herein.[8] The specific items to be discussed are underlined in the texts provided and numbered with comparable subscripts for easier identification. Where applicable, references to the wider situational and extrasituational contexts are made to provide some explanation and identify the underlying ideological stances of the distinct media sources (cf. Berlin, 2007, for a definition of the multiple layers of context).

In excerpts (8a) and (8b), it is again possible to establish a baseline for simply covering the facts of the story. The underlined, numbered text (hereafter referred to as 'sub1', 'sub2', etc.) demonstrates that the two media sources are completely capable of reporting similar, if not identical, facts on the same stories (cf. sub1 and sub3 in the respective pieces). While some small expressions may vary and one source may add some small details that the other does not include, the proposition of the reported information is the same. For instance, sub2 in *CNNWorld* provides additional extrasituational context – explaining the meaning of throwing shoes in the Arab world – which could be due in part to the expectation of a wider viewing audience that would be unfamiliar with the significance. Other bits of the story simply appear in a slightly different order: *Al-Manar*'s broadcast opens (sub1) by indicating how Maher returned to Egypt: 'safe and sound' whereas *CNNWorld* embeds the fact that he was 'not hurt' in sub3.

(8a) Al-Manar 12/23/2003
Egyptian FM Attacked by a Mob inside Al-Aqsa Mosque ₁Egyptian Foreign Minister Ahmed Maher has returned home safe and sound₁ later Monday after his one-day visit to lands occupied in 1948 turned into a show of non-welcome by Palestinians who labeled him as traitor and collaborator. Maher was there holding talks with Israeli premier Ariel Sharon and his foreign minister Silvan Shalom, over to get the so-called roadmap back on track. [...] But the foreign minister, who was the first high- ranking official to visit Israeli leaders since the intifada erupted in 2000, ₄*did not meet Palestinian chairman Yasser Arafat.*₄ [...] ₂On Monday afternoon and as Maher arrived at the Al-Aqsa Mosque, for prayers a group of Palestinians started shouting at him and threw shoes on him.₂ ₃Bodyguards surrounded Maher and immediately took him to hospital after suffering from breathing difficulties₃ He was released three hours later. [...]

(8b) CNN 12/23/2003
Seven Arrests after Egyptian Official Attacked: Egyptian Foreign Minister Harassed after Sharon Meeting

₃Foreign Minister Ahmed Maher was not hurt in the melee at the Al-Aqsa Mosque in Jerusalem, but he was taken to a hospital after complaining of shortness of breath and tightness in his chest.₃ ₁He has since returned to Egypt.₁

₂Dozens of people inside the mosque, *upset by the visit with Sharon,* shouted insults at Maher and threw shoes at him – a sign of disrespect in the Arab world.₂ He was hurriedly escorted from the area by his security detail and Israeli police.

Despite the matching coverage through most of the two stories, minor differences can still be detected in the explication of the cause of the event, differences which reveal two divergent perspectives. In (8b) sub2, the phrase 'upset by the visit with Sharon', the Israeli prime minister, has been italicized; it suggests that the meeting was the root cause of the unrest. In (8a), the visit is also mentioned in the second sentence of the piece, immediately following the labeling of the visiting Egyptian foreign minister as a 'traitor and collaborator'. But *Al-Manar* does not finish that portion of the story there; it goes on to provide more of the relevant situation context that offers more of an explanation for its characterization of Maher. In sub4, it reveals that Maher 'did not meet' with Arafat, suggesting that the feeling of betrayal from the Palestinian perspective is not unsubstantiated, a sentiment further strengthened when coupled with the coverage from the previous day seen in (8c). Thus, the decision taken by the foreign dignitary and fellow Arab, to delay his meeting with Palestinian leaders and possibly *not* meet with them at all was taken as a slight. The question that remains open, however, regards what was actually said by Maher and what the media may have incited by suggesting that there was no intention to hold the meeting with Arafat.

(8c) Al-Manar 12/22/2003
Egyptian FM Visits 'Israel,' Calls for Revival of Negotiations [...] In an apparent concession to 'Israel,' Maher is not expected to meet Palestinian President Yasser Arafat on this visit but may meet Arafat and Qorei sometime next week.

In the following excerpt from *Al-Manar* (9a), the positioning of the various actors within the story demonstrates a difference in the interpretation of the situational context which may be due to either the actors' expressed opinions as suggested by the evidential attributing of 'said' to specific individuals or groups, or to the covert attempt on the part of the media source to propagandize.

(9a) Al-Manar 12/04/2003
Palestinian Factions Start Discussions in Cairo on a New Ceasefire with 'Israel' amid Ongoing Aggressions Twelve Palestinian factions began talks in Egypt aimed at reaching a new ceasefire with 'Israel.' ₁Hamas and the Islamic Jihad groups said they would not target *so-called Israeli civilians* but made it clear they would not offer free concessions to Israel. Said Siyam, a Hamas leader, noted that *Israeli settlers are not civilians because they are all armed.*₁
[...]

₂Islamic Jihad leader Mohammed al-Hindi voiced similar stance saying Israel could not be offered a free ceasefire if it keeps up its aggressive policy, the settlement activity and the construction of the

separation wall.$_2$ $_3$Jamil Majdalawi, the head of the Popular Front of the Liberation for Palestine said the Israeli occupation is the basic problem and the resistance is the only means to defy it.$_3$
[...]

And on the ground, $_4$nine Palestinians were injured in Balata refugee camp in Nablus when occupation forces in Israeli tanks and vehicles opened fire randomly at unarmed Palestinians. 15-year-old Rami Abu Wardah was injured in the head by Israeli fire. The raid came after occupation forces detained 17 Palestinian in Jenin, 11 others in Ramallah and six others in Qalqilya. Israeli occupation troops also blew up a house in the West Bank town of al-Khalil early on Thursday as residents watched from nearby buildings. The house belonged to the family of, Alaa El Sohouri, a Palestinian who was killed five months ago by the occupation army.$_4$

In sub1, despite the claim of seeking a ceasefire, the reported speech uses the adjective 'so-called' in referring to the Israeli civilians, the addition of which qualifies the corresponding treatment in (9b) sub1. The *Al-Manar* piece goes on to clarify the statement by the Hamas leader, adding that 'Israeli settlers are not civilians' (i.e. those who are settling within Palestinian territory), a detail that *CNNWorld* completely omits by merely making a passing reference to those 'inside Israel'.

(9b) CNN 12/03/2003
Palestinian groups may call for halt to terror attacks: Factions meeting in Cairo include members of militant groups

CAIRO, Egypt (*CNN*) – Palestinian factions meeting in Cairo are expected to call for a halt to all attacks on civilians and to ask the international community to pressure Israel to do the same, *CNN* learned Wednesday.

$_1$Delegates to the meeting – including members of Palestinian militant groups – said there is a preliminary agreement among different Palestinian political parties to stop the killing of Israeli civilians, thereby implying an end to all attacks *inside Israel.*$_1$
In return, these delegates said, they will ask the Quartet, composed of the United Nations, the United States, the European Union and Russia, to pressure Israel to end its military strikes on Palestinians.
[...]

$_4$Such Israeli operations have been directed against members of Palestinian terrorist groups – who have claimed responsibility for attacks on Israeli civilians – but have sometimes killed bystanders as well.$_4$

$_3$The factions at the Cairo talks also are expected to affirm Palestinian rights to resist Israelis through a variety of means, including continuing armed attacks on Israeli soldiers and settlers inside the 1967 borders, a Palestinian delegate said.$_3$

$_2$Some factions have proposed a complete ceasefire – inside and outside Israel – with conditions and timelines. These conditions include halting Israeli raids on Palestinian towns, stopping all Israeli settlement activities, removing illegal Israeli outposts, halting current construction of a separation barrier, lifting Israel's siege on Palestinian Authority President Yasser Arafat and withdrawing Israeli troops to the September 28, 2000 borders.$_2$

A major difference in the spin of the two segments emerges with the way the story is covered and the corresponding characterization of the 'other' in the story, as well as *whom* is positioned as the 'other'. Though the difference may seem virtually imperceptible to the general listening and viewing audience, it highlights not only the differential framing of those signified (i.e. evidence of a 'we-they' dichotomy), but also reveals indicators of separate ideological stances on the part of the two media sources (cf. El-Bilawi, this volume). The notion of personalizing becomes relevant as *Al-Manar* tends to identify the individual responsible for making statements in (9a) whereas *CNNWorld* in (9b) simply refers to 'factions' (compare sub2 and sub3 in the respective pieces). In sub4, *Al-Manar* once again provides names of the persons affected (the 'we') by the Israeli occupation army (the 'they'). Contrastively, *CNNWorld*'s sub^4 generally refers to the Palestinians (*CNNWorld*'s 'they') as 'terrorists', assuaging its own culpability for inducing a public opinion by including a disclaimer that the groups themselves have claimed responsibility for attacks on Israelis and adding a depersonalized postscript about the 'bystanders' who 'have sometimes [been] killed.'

As the comparisons to this point have attempted to demonstrate, a superficial viewing (or reading) of the broadcasts could suggest that there is more alike than different in the coverage by the two news agencies. While there are some differences with regard to the point of view taken, *Al-Manar* telling the story from the Palestinian perspective and *CNNWorld* from the Israeli, the substance remains generally unchanged and intact. However, in the following comparison between (10a) and (10b), the 'other' positioning is epitomized. While similarities can be drawn between the reporting in the two excerpts (sub1 and sub2 in both), it is now *CNNWorld* which is leaning toward a more personal stance, naming the Israeli criminal in sub2 while *Al-Manar* takes a more objective posture toward the information. What underscores a tendency toward biasing the listening and viewing audience is the inclusion of the added statement in sub2 by *CNNWorld* that 'officials weren't ruling out terrorism' even though the corresponding quote that *Al-Manar* obtained from Israeli police[9] points away from 'a Palestinian operation'.

(10a) Al-Manar 12/11/2003
Explosion in Tel Aviv Kills 3 ₁Israeli television said three people were killed and 15 wounded Thursday in an explosion which rocked central Tel Aviv.₁ According to witnesses quoted by the television, the explosion took place near the Aroma cafe close to the busy Allenby street in the commercial district of the city. ₂Israeli police said a mafia leader was among the dead, hinting that the explosion was criminally motivated and not a Palestinian operation.₂

(10b) CNN 12/11/2003
Tel Aviv blast kills 3: Police: Suspected crime figure may have been targeted
JERUSALEM (*CNN*) – ₁A large explosion went off Thursday in a major thoroughfare in Tel Aviv, killing three people and wounding at least 19, Israeli police said.₁

₂Police said the explosion was apparently an attempt to kill Ze'ev Rosenstein, a suspected leading figure in Israel's crime underworld. But officials added they weren't ruling out terrorism in the blast.₂

They said the explosion took place near a foreign currency exchange shop in a three-story building. Police and witnesses said they saw Rosenstein entering the currency exchange around the time of the blast. Witnesses said he was among the injured.

Rosenstein, who returned to Israel on Sunday, was detained by police earlier this week in the investigation of an alleged hit involving leaders of a rival Israeli gang. Israeli newspaper Ha'aretz reported Rosenstein, the owner of casinos in Israel and abroad, has survived at least four attempts to kill him since 1996.

₃If the attack was a criminal hit,₃ it would be one of the most deadly in Israel's history.

The blast ended a period of relative calm in Israel. ₄The last terror attack in the country killed more than 20 people in the northern city of Haifa in October.₄

In an even more subtle attempt to influence the audience, the use of the conditional 'if' in (10b) sub3 sheds doubt on the absolute certainty of an Israeli criminal connection and hints that terrorism is a viable culprit. Using a tactic that expands and supports the tangential story – essentially editorializing – *CNNWorld* provides details about the last terror attack within Israel in sub4, leaving the audience with the perception that the explosion most likely *was* the result of terrorism which appears to be consistently equated with Palestinians in the *CNNWorld* linguistic context (cf. Atawneh, this volume; Ayish, this volume; Halabi, this volume; Silberstein, this volume).

If the function of the news is to inform the public, then what could possibly justify the presentation of a story with a slant (i.e. spinning the story)? Is it simply the case that cultural references resonate differently in different parts of the world? The previous comparison where *CNNWorld* extends the story to include additional and unrelated information seems to indicate something more. It is indeed clear that much of the coverage could be nearly identical and not risk confusing anyone in the respective situational contexts. For instance, sub2 in (11a) and (11b) provides virtually identical information with the exception that *Al-Manar* goes on to mention the act as retaliation, referring back to the opening line in (11a) where details are given about what the retaliation was for (i.e. 'Israeli aggression'), using lexical items that resonate in its interactional and situational context. It also identifies the 'martyr'/'suicide bomber' and tells the story primarily from the Palestinian perspective with specifics about the individuals affecting and affected by the events, including one reference to the decision made by the Israeli defense minister.

(11a) 12/25/2003 – Al-Manar
Martyrdom Operation in Tel Aviv Leaves 4 Israelis Dead, including 3 Soldiers
Palestinian resistance fighters resumed martyrdom operations after the wide-scale Israeli aggression on Rafah that killed 9 Palestinians and injured many others. $_1$A Palestinian self-bomber killed four Israelis, three of them soldiers, at a bus stop in Tel Aviv during the rush-hour on Thursday,$_{r1}$ a month after a female bomber blew herself up in Haifa. $_2$The Popular Front for the Liberation of Palestine claimed responsibility, vowing that it 'is the first operation in a series of retaliations.'$_2$ It named the martyr as 18-year-old Said Hanani from the village of Beit Fouriek east of Nablus in the West Bank.

$_3$The occupation forces demolished the home of martyr Hanini, and imposed a curfew on his home city. On Thursday evening Israel imposed a 'total closure' on the West Bank and the Gaza Strip following the martyrdom operation,$_3$ due to the orders of defense minister Shaul Mofaz. Israeli police were placed on high alert and multiplied their security checks, especially on roads connecting the West Bank to eastern Tel Aviv.

In contrast, *CNNWorld* tells the story from a completely different point of view, revealing the identities of the Israeli representatives and sharing their perspectives without including any data from the Palestinian side. Moreover, it adds the US perspective with the condemnation of the 'wanton act of terror'. In so doing, *CNNWorld* itself could be said to advocate an anti-Palestinian stance that goes beyond simply neglecting to obtain a Palestinian comment, official or otherwise. The reference to the act being 'wanton' (sub4) asserts that it is unjustified from the *CNNWorld* perspective, a view that does not coincide with the Palestinian account reported in *Al-Manar* – though the use of the evidential reference (i.e. quoting Boucher) alleviates any direct responsibility on its own part.

(11b) CNN 12/26/2003
Suicide bomber kills 4 in Tel Aviv: Six reported killed in Israeli helicopter strike in Gaza

JERUSALEM (*CNN*) – ₁A suicide bombing at a major intersection outside Tel Aviv during rush hour Thursday killed four people and wounded 13, according to Israeli authorities.₁

₂The Popular Front for the Liberation of Palestine claimed responsibility for the terror attack that also killed the suicide bomber.₂

The bomber approached a bus stop and blew himself up, Israeli Police Commissioner Shlomo Aharonishki told The Associated Press.

₃The Israel Defense Forces imposed a full closure on the territories after the suicide attack.₃

In a written statement from Washington, ₄US State Department spokesman Richard Boucher said the United States 'strongly condemns' the 'wanton act of terror.'₄

'The United States reiterates the absolute need for urgent action by the Palestinian Authority to confront terror and violence,' he said.
The assault was the first suicide bombing in Israel since an October 4 attack in Haifa. That incident killed 21 people.

There has been relative calm since the Haifa bombing, but Avi Pazner, a spokesman for Israeli Prime Minister Ariel Sharon, said Israel has foiled about 35 attempted attacks in the past two months.

The similarities that exist in the details of the story (sub1 and sub3 in both) are eclipsed by the outright condemnation of the 'other' in *CNNWorld* without the inclusion of any opposing voices. Consequently, only part of the story is told and the *CNNWorld* listeners are left with a one-sided rendition. The distinction in the coverage is not merely a difference in the text which can be identified or the situational context requiring a diverse treatment of the details; it is a choice by the news agency to exclude mitigating evidence which would lend itself to a more balanced interpretation by listeners and viewers. In other words, the condemnation of one side – the purported 'other' or 'they' – advances an understanding of the 'we' in the story that is akin to the audience.

In a final example of spin and spin control, (12a) and (12b) exhibit examples of all the elements discussed thus far. Sub1 (the leader) and sub4 (the identification of the location) in the respective pieces affirm that the same stories are being told; the similarities, however, end there.

(12a) Al-Manar 12/27/2003
Israel Kills a Palestinian Teenager in Nablus, Wounds Two Peace Activists at the Separation Wall [1]Israeli occupation forces killed a Palestinian youth Saturday and wounded 30 others when the forces opened fire at stone-throwing demonstrators.[1]

[2]Earlier, Israeli occupation troops fired rubber bullets and live rounds at pacifists[2] [3]who were protesting Israel's erection of the separation wall that annexes the West Bank. Some 400 Palestinians and 150 foreign activists, including Israeli pacifists,[3] [4]took part in the protest in the village of Masha, near Qalqiliya.[4]

[5]The occupation forces shot two protesters, an American and an Israeli, as a small group of activists tried to pull down the wall's yellow gate, while others opened a hole with wire cutters. The activists said they were acting on behalf of Palestinian villagers and farmers whose lands have been divided by the wall.[5]

(12b) CNN 12/27/2003
Israeli Troops Wound 2 in Barrier Protest

JERUSALEM (*CNN*) – [1]Israeli troops wounded two demonstrators Friday afternoon in a protest against a barrier under construction along the West Bank, the Israel Defense Forces said.[1]

[3]About 200 protesters began climbing and cutting the fence in an attempt to get to the Israeli side, the IDF said.[3]

₂Israeli soldiers fired warning shots and then opened fire when pro-testers continued to advance, the IDF said.₂

₅An Israeli man was in serious condition. A female foreign tourist was slightly wounded, according to Israeli officials.₅

₄The incident occurred at the Palestinian village of Masha near Qalqilya in the West Bank.₄ Israel's GOC Central Command is investi-gating the incident.

Israel said it is building the barrier to keep terrorists from entering from the West Bank. Palestinian officials have characterized the move as a land grab by the Israelis.

Once again revealing different positioning by the two media sources of the actors involved, *Al-Manar* emphasizes Israeli aggression in sub2 by focusing on firing at individuals characterized as 'pacifists'; *CNNWorld*, on the other hand, presents its different perspective in sub2 by indicating that, after firing 'warning shots', the soldiers had no choice but to open fire when 'protesters continued to advance', suggesting that the response was in reac-tion to a threat. Another stark difference in degree emerges in sub3 with the reporting of numbers: *Al-Manar*'s '400 Palestinians and 150 foreign activists' to *CNNWorld*'s '200 protestors'. Finally, sub5 follows the trend of personalizing the reporting by *Al-Manar* where it reveals something about the identity of two of the protestors who were shot – 'an American and an Israeli' – while *CNNWorld* acknowledges the 'Israeli man', but vaguely refers to a 'foreign female tourist'; the justification for the omission remains elusive, but it is certain that an audience which includes Americans would not have a favorable opinion of Israeli soldiers who shot an American woman, whether her nationality was known in advance or not.

Throughout the examination of the two media sources, then, it is clear that differences abound on multiple levels. They can be identified not only in the texts themselves, which may be an artifact of the distinct situational contexts, but also in the interactions between broadcasters and their respective listening and viewing audiences (e.g. positioning of actors according to each source's depiction of the 'we' and the 'they'). As a result, the descriptions, interpretations and explanations of and for events also emerge as different, leading to separate understandings of the situation and the participants involved by the respective audiences.

Conclusion

Returning to the original questions for the study, it appears that since neither news source can be said to be innocent of propagandizing to a certain extent, it can be confirmed that media sources operating in different parts of the world will tend to present the dominant ideology of their respective regimes. Consonant with this point, the analysis indicates that the media sources reviewed are not exercising unbiased journalism, regardless of whether or not they are allegedly operating within a free and democratic society. Whether they choose to admit it or not, it appears that the capacity to influence the public mindset lends itself to hegemony, regardless of whether or not the source claims to be working on its behalf. Nevertheless, it is unclear whether the polities within which (or from which) the media operate can be said to be directly influencing or duping the news agencies; neither can claims of collusion be made from this level of analysis. What is apparent, though, is that media are largely responsible for creating ideologies or, at the very least, spinning and, in turn, influencing public opinion.

Notes

1. The No Child Left Behind Act of 2001 became a law under former US President George W. Bush in January 2002. Its intention was to mandate educational reform nationwide, especially in the areas of reading and math. Its efforts to increase accountability of schools, however, had some immediate and lasting negative effects which included (1) the depiction of some schools and their teachers as 'failing' and (2) the increased testing of students. In particular, the combined effects have resulted in the closure of schools across the country that have been unable to demonstrate increased student performance at prescribed levels and, in some areas, increased dropout rates, especially among minority student populations.
2. The question regarding the legitimacy of comparing these two sources was raised during a public presentation of the study. While the resources of each news media source are vastly different with varying levels of access to 'on the ground' events in Israel and Palestine – specifically, a question about the extent to which *Al-Manar* would have access to events in Israel, for example – the essence of the contrast between the two is firmly situated in the language use; thus, the spin underscores the nature of the different ideological orientations.
3. Despite the limited access *Al-Manar* might have had to events within Israel, it presented four times the number of pieces on the Intifada as *CNNWorld* during the same time period. While it might be argued that *Al-Manar* has a vested interest in events in the region, it should again be reiterated that the texts obtained from *CNNWorld* originated in its Middle East bureau.
4. 'Intifada' refers to resistance, ostensibly justified, to aggressors or, in the case of the Palestinian Territories, more generally to occupiers. 'Martyr' refers generally to anyone on the side of the identified resistance who is killed during the uprising, whether or not the person is actively engaged in fighting. The translation in Arabic (*shahid*) suggests any type of tragic death. As these words are familiar in the interactional context of the Arab world, it is not surprising that they are used in news broadcasts within the region. Contrastively, the

more global scope of *CNNWorld* might also explain why the terms are not used in its broadcasts.

5. It should be noted that the headlines are not always presented as part of the televised version of the news; therefore, this additional level of analysis available through the online transcripts permits a unique opportunity to gain insight into the news agencies' intentions and messages being conveyed in the various stories.

6. The use of quotations around Israel is relevant and only occurs in *Al-Manar*; it is a political acknowledgment of the difference between the borders of the state of Israel at the time when it was established and the annexation of additional land during the 1967 war, still considered an illegal action by many Arab states. Thus, the reference to present-day Israel and its current borders are signified by the enclosure in quotations.

7. In the analysis of comparable content on the topic during the established time period issued by the two news agencies, it was evident that *CNNWorld* covered the entirety of the story on December 7, 2003 that was reported in two separate pieces by *Al-Manar* on December 6 and 8. While this occurrence is suggestive of the finding that there was a larger number of articles by *Al-Manar* compared to the longer articles by *CNNWorld*, the two-to-one ratio for coverage of the same story was rare and only occurred a couple of times in the entire corpus.

8. Complete transcripts for the broadcasts represented here are available from *Al-Manar* (http://www.almanar.com.lb/) and *CNNWorld* (http://www.cnn.com/WORLD/) respectively, or the author of this chapter.

9. It is equally possible that the information attributed to Israeli police could have been obtained from a wire service rather than through an actual face-to-face interviews; if so, *Al-Manar* would then be responsible for minimizing the possible responsibility of 'a Palestinian operation'.

Part 3

Dialogue

Chapter 10

Dis-covering Peace: Dominant and Counterdiscourse of the Middle East[1]

S. SILBERSTEIN

Introduction

The figure of Palestine enters the popular imagination through domi-nant discourses too often characterized by a resolutely narrow view. Familiar in worldwide media coverage is a Middle East portrayed as an inevitable cauldron, a site of inescapable bloodshed. Eclipsed by these rhetorics of violence, however, are profound counterdiscourses of dia-logue and reconciliation. This chapter begins with a critique of what can pass as dialogue in dominant rhetorics about Palestine, and then explores characteristics of successful dialogue under occupation.

Dominant Discourses: Imagining Palestine

In recent decades, rhetorics of Middle East occupation have centered on Palestine, an icon of grievance and Western domination for some, of ter-rorism for others. There has been a kind of circular logic of occupation in the Middle East, with Palestinians discursively invoked to provide ratio-nales for the actions of others. The circle is particularly evident in dis-courses surrounding Iraq. Saddam Hussein justified his 1991 invasion and occupation of Kuwait in part on the basis of long-standing regional grievances with respect to the Israeli occupation of Palestine. We can see that this played out rhetorically in a series of press conferences held on January 9, 1991 in the wake of the failure of the Geneva Peace Conference (excerpts reproduced below). The press conferences, carried live on CNN, effectively instantiated a public dialogue among Iraqi Foreign Minister

Tariq Aziz and US Secretary of State James Baker in Geneva and President George H.W. Bush in Washington, DC. Within a week the United States would launch 'Operation Desert Storm.'

In his press conference, Aziz presses the issue of 'linkage':

> I told [US Secretary of State James Baker] very clearly and I repeated my idea and explained it at length that what is at stake in our region is peace, security, and stability. What's at stake is the fate of the whole region .... If you are ready to bring about peace to the region – comprehensive, lasting peace to the whole region of the Middle East, we are ready to cooperate ..... I spoke at length about the linkage between the issues in the region. (Tariq Aziz, Press Conference)

But US public policy has been clear: there will be no linkage between Iraq and Palestine:

> We went through a good bit of the history of the personal efforts that I made for fourteen months to bring about a dialogue between Arab – between Palestinians and Israelis .... And we had a full discussion of that issue. A complete discussion of it. I want to make it clear that I made it very clear though that there would be no linkage here of that issue to Iraq's withdrawal from Kuwait. (Baker, Press Conference)

> There will be no linkage. (Bush, Press Conference)

James Baker mocked Iraq's invocation of Palestine to justify occupation: 'I think most people realize that Iraq is trying to use the Palestinian issue to shield its aggression against Kuwait.'

But this invocation of Palestine is not unique on either side, and continues to the present. In May 2008, for instance, on the 60th anniversary of the founding of the state of Israel, Osama bin Laden issued a taped message to 'the Peoples of the West'. Described by CBS: 'Bin Laden began his message by telling listeners that the Palestinian-Israeli conflict has always been the primary cause for friction between the West and the Muslim world' ('Bin Laden', 2008).

Ironically, US policy justifications for its occupation of Iraq often link to Palestine as well. Terrorism enters the American imagination in/as Palestine, and the United States 'War against Terrorism' resonates with the well-publicized Israeli experience. Al Qaeda's powerful entry onto the world stage on September 11, 2001, generated a generalized 'Muslim terrorist', whose founding image was that of the Palestinian suicide bomber. And once terrorism is generalized, anything Middle Eastern can be linked. Ayish (this volume) documents over time the development in film of the stereotypical fundamentalist terrorist. Writing about the effects of the news media, Berlin (this volume) notes that after 9/11 more than 60% of Americans erroneously linked Iraq and Al Qaeda, generating support for the US invasion of Iraq. Like Berlin, Ayish confirms that 'the cumulative effect of such misinformation and stereotypes, often translates into real political and social consequences' (Ayish, this volume: 100).

Thus, while the US government does not necessarily grant linkage of Palestine to the solution of other international problems (does not, e.g. grant linkage to Saddam Hussein), American public discourses often link Palestinian terrorism to any violent act aimed at the non-Muslim world. Palestine invokes other linkages. US government and media discourses have powerfully linked the United States to Israel and its 'Palestinian problem' through a series of rhetorically framed parallels.

In dominant American discourses, the United States and Israel are narrated bringing democracy to the region, often termed a 'tough neighborhood'. Notwithstanding its demographics (its Arab citizens and large population of Sephardic ['Oriental'] Jews) and its location, Israel's identity lies with the West. Israeli novelist and commentator Yitzhak Laor (2008) noted with irony that its soccer teams play in the European league – another manifestation of Israel's role as a Western outpost. With the United States occupation of Iraq, it joins Israel as a Western outpost in that tough neighborhood. Terrorism – often termed a clash of civilizations by George W. Bush – is a shared burden.

Both the United States and Israel narrate themselves as reluctant occupiers, often bristling under the term. If Palestinians would only renounce violence and provide a 'partner for peace', the narration goes, the conflict would be over. Until recently, Israeli Palestinians were often portrayed as 'the only Arabs with a democratic vote'. The United States entries into Afghanistan and Iraq were narrated as liberations; the term *occupation* was not part of the Bush White House lexicon (*whitehouse.gov* web search).

A final link to Palestine is the expertise that Israel brings to US strategies in Iraq and elsewhere. The United States learns from Israel how to deal with terrorists. Former Israeli antiterrorist 'experts' find new careers in the US Homeland Security industry; the former head of the security at Ben Gurion Airport, for example, has a private security firm in Maryland (Machlis, 2009). Policy wonks trumpet Israeli successes. Jonathan B. Tucker's (Monterey Institute, Center for Nonproliferation Studies) 2003 paper, 'Strategies for Countering Terrorism: Lessons from the Israeli Experience' is typical. Tucker accesses a standard discourse of expertise:

> Over the past 50 years, the Israeli government has developed a variety of measures to prevent terrorist attacks or mitigate their effects. Israel has also made a virtue of necessity by creating a cutting-edge security industry that markets counterterrorism technologies, products, and services throughout the world. (Tucker, 2003)

Tucker uses this expertise (accessed by him through a study trip to Israel) to recommend 'Lessons for US Policy.' He does not recommend adopting all Israeli policy, 'it would be unwise to adopt the Israeli policy of assassinating terrorist leaders'. But clearly this bit of Israeli policy did resonate for the Bush-43[2] White House. Early on, Bin Laden was designated 'Wanted – Dead or Alive.' In a final bit of shared expertise, Israel's Palestine strategies presumably inform 'the wall' being erected along the Rio Grande, and in prosecuting the war in Iraq, the United States consulted on Israel's urban warfare experience in the West Bank and Gaza (Associated Press, 2003).

Just as the image of Palestine has served Saddam Hussein and Osama bin Laden through a circularity of logics, Palestine is a link to US policy and strategies as well. For Saddam Hussein in Kuwait, for Bin Laden in New York, or for the United States in Iraq, Palestine is the icon of violence and its responses. In 1991, James Baker mocked Iraq's invocation of Palestine to justify an occupation. It is a sad irony that the United States occupation of Iraq stood on a similar linkage: the erroneous connection of Hussein to Bin Laden and the latter's link to Palestine. The mainstream media have been saturated with these discourses.

Another circularity in rhetorics of the Middle East has been the juxtaposition of peace and war.

Talking Peace, Waging War

This circularity is easily seen in another discursive mirroring, that of the Bush-41 and Saddam Hussein governments. For both, rhetorics of peace justified the necessity of war.[3]

To begin, in the media dialogue, all parties cloaked themselves in the need for peace:

> We would like to have genuine constructive dialogue between us, between our two nations, in order to make peace in the region and between our two nations. (Aziz, Press Conference)

We welcome any and all diplomatic efforts to solve this crisis peace-fully and politically. We want it solved peacefully and politically. (Baker, Press Conference)

Just as the Bush-43 Administration avoided the term *occupation*, his father's avoided another term:

Reporter: Can you tell us ... that if Saddam isn't going to move then we're going to war.

Bush: I'm not going to use that, that phrase. (Bush, Press Conference)

But there is always another, unfortunate alternative to peace:

We prefer a peaceful outcome. However, anything less than full com-pliance with UN Security Council Resolution 678 and its predecessor is unacceptable. (Bush, Letter to Saddam Hussein, January 9, 1991)[4]

In fact, in a familiar rhetorical circularity, without war, there can be no peace:

I've already told you why I think linkage is a bad idea. I think that it doesn't, it will not tend to promote peace in the region, it will tend to be read as a reward for the aggressor, and it would jeopardize future peace in the region. (Baker, Press Conference)

There can be no reward for aggression. (Bush, Letter)

By the last quote above, peace and war have been conflated. If peace can be read as the reward for aggression, then only war can bring peace. War is the only peaceful act. Aziz similarly associates war and peace. For Aziz, peace in the region is brought about through addressing issues relating to the Palestinians. If linkage makes it possible to address these issues, then peace is facilitated by the occupation of Kuwait. Again, as has so often been the case, war conflates with peace.

At the center of these discourses lie imaginings of Palestinians – imag-inings that are used by others on diverse 'sides' to justify bellicose acts across the region and beyond it. Conjured rhetorically when terrorism or war is invoked, in much of the West violent Israeli/Palestinian conflicts are emblematic of terrorism in general and the necessity of war. Tragically, as this volume was under preparation, these images moved beyond the iconic with the horrifying images of Gaza. To listen to the coverage in the mainstream press, one might never know that dominant discourses of violence do not go entirely uncontested.

In fact, there have been growing nongovernmental counterdiscourses in the United States, Israel and Palestine, including joint peace initiatives. Unfortunately, these are dialogues that only rarely make their way into the mainstream media. The next sections give some visibility to a rhetoric that is largely elided in Western coverage of occupation. But it is easily accessible through its presence on the web. Central to this counterdiscourse is a commitment to the position that war does not bring peace. To explore what makes dialogue possible, one organization's counterdiscourse is examined in some detail.

Hegemony is Not Destiny: Counterdiscourses of the Middle East

> May we be drenched with the longing for peace
> that we may give ourselves over
> as the earth to the rain, to the dew,
> until peace overflows our lives
> as living waters overflow the seas
> (Marcia Falk, 1996: 250)

As this volume attests, dialogue itself has come to constitute a counterdiscourse. In North America, one venue of dialogue between Jews and Arabs can be found in the burgeoning peace camp movement.[5] Within Israel and the Palestinian territories, Jewish Israelis and Palestinians dialogue through efforts such as the Bereaved Families Forum (and All for Peace Radio) – discussed in detail below – as well as Combatants for Peace,[6] and the shared Israeli-Palestinian village: Wahat al Salaam/Neve Shalom. In all cases, discourses of social justice and an end to occupation pose stark contrasts to the violent rhetorics that seek to overpower them.

What distinguishes all of these is that they are joint ventures, founded and run by Arabs and Jews that build the cooperation necessary to the establishment of mutual respect. They also highlight or create joint identities. In the case of the Bereaved Families Forum and Combatants for Peace, members share a violent history. In contrast is their recognition of shared humanity, a renunciation of violence, and a recognition of similar goals: education of the public and advocacy for policy transformations. Note, however, that organizations that promote dialogue do not necessarily suggest specific solutions. Working across boundaries, in a dynamic situation, peacemakers do not seek to determine in advance which ultimate outcome (e.g. a binational or two-state solution) should prevail. But peace with justice lies at the center of these dialogues. Finally, organizations building these joint counterdiscourses are NGOs. The website for Camps for Jews and Arabs in North America makes this clear: they are 'not waiting for governments or "experts"'. The remainder of this chapter examines a set of counterdiscourses that reclaim the humanity of those who have lost loved ones as a result of war.

Bereaved Families

Also known as the Bereaved Families Forum, the Parents Circle – Families Forum (PCFF) is a grassroots organization of bereaved Palestinians and Israelis:

> Consisting of several hundreds of bereaved families, half Palestinian and half Israeli, The Families Forum has played a crucial role since its inception in 1995, in spearheading a reconciliation process between Israelis and Palestinians. The Forum members have all lost immediate family members due to the violence in the region.[7] (PCFF website)

The Forum is profiled in the remarkable film *Encounter Point*.

The Bereaved Families Forum is unique in promoting reconciliation while the conflict is ongoing:

> It is, as far as we know, a world precedent that bereaved families, victims from both sides, embark on a joint reconciliation mission while the conflict is still active. (PCFF website)

> The Forum activities are a unique phenomenon, in that they continue during all political circumstances and in spite of all tensions and violence in our region. (PCFF website)

It is also unique in facilitating perhaps the most ambitious initiative. Supported by the European Community, the Families Forum created the infrastructure for hundreds and thousands of Jewish Israelis and Palestinians to dialogue. Its description from the PCFF website is quoted in its entirety here:

> Large numbers of Arabs and Jews are picking up the phone and talking to people 'on the other side' about reconciliation, tolerance and peace thanks to a toll-free telephone service. Over 1,000,000 calls were placed since the project has started. (PCFF website)

> Sammy Waed, a Palestinian, never thought he would become friends with an Israeli soldier, especially one who had occupied his hometown of Ramallah. But using the new hotline, the 20-year-old ended up speaking to Arik, a 23-year-old from Tel Aviv.

'Arik told me how much he hated his army service, because he was in the middle of a civilian population, policing children and causing harm to innocent people,' Waed told New York Daily News special correspondent, Deborah Blachor.

'Before, I thought Israelis didn't care at all when innocent Palestinians suffer and are killed', he said. 'But now I know they do care and I have hope that there can be peace.'

Hello, Peace! (Hello Shalom-Hello Salaam!) was launched in October 2002 by the Parents Circle-Families Forum, a joint group of over 400 bereaved Israeli and Palestinian parents who believe peace is still possible despite having lost a child or loved one in the conflict.

Hello Peace! advertisements appear on billboards and in newspaper ads in Israel and the Palestinian territories.

The power of dialogue is leading to friendships. Callers reconnect with each other after terrorist attacks, making sure their friend is okay. It influences children. One Palestinian asked a Jewish Israeli to speak with his two children. He wanted them to learn that Jews were not monsters.

Callers will hear a voice message: Hello, you have reached Hello Shalom, Hello Salaam. If you wish to talk to an Israeli about reconciliation, tolerance and peace, dial 1; if you wish to talk to a Palestinian about reconciliation, tolerance and peace, dial 2. They can listen to the hundreds of voice messages and decide whom they want to contact, and remain anonymous. They can call as often as they want.

From Israel, Gaza or the West Bank, just dial *6364 from a land line or 054-7900055 from any mobile phone and listen to the instructions.

'It's time to stop the killing and start talking again.'

The Hello Peace Project is financed by the European Community.

What does a Palestinian share in these dialogues? An Israeli Jew? For people in a war zone, what makes dialogue possible? There is a window on these issues through a group of narratives in the 'Personal Stories' section of the same website. Posted there are 11 narratives of bereaved families – four are Palestinian. Examining these narratives, one finds significant similarities and some differences in these courageous statements.

The pain is shared, but the experiences of being occupied/occupier are different. As the website reminds us, this is reconciliation while the violence is ongoing.

Dialogues under Occupation

These activities aim to make the public aware of the enormous tragedy common to both nations, in this bleeding country, which is dear to both.

Nir Yesod, Bereaved Families Forum

What makes dialogue possible? The question has taken on an awful urgency as 2009 arrived with Gaza in flames. It is not an 'academic question', but was posed to me as I worked on this chapter by a young Arab American peace activist, who had come of age in Seattle's Middle East Peace Camp community. The remainder of this chapter explores this fundamental question. It provides the context for the dedication of this chapter to the courageous members of the Bereaved Families Forum.

Because I am an applied linguist, my approach to this question comes through language: How can narratives simultaneously construct and be constructed by possibilities for peace? Implicit in this kind of analysis is the notion that possibilities are created through language as speakers invoke and listeners recognize particular rhetorics/narratives/voices. In sharing profoundly personal stories of loss and transformation, the Bereaved Families narratives make it possible for others to imagine how dialogue can come into being.

In a research climate that stresses large-scale social, cultural and economic forces, it would be easy to forget that change often comes with single individuals taking courageous action. Some members of the Bereaved Families Forum highlight being approached personally by Yitzchak Frankenthal, the group's founder, who had lost his son in 1994. Those members then become emissaries to others. Sometimes seeds are planted. One of the Palestinian members of PCFF describes being invited to a meeting by the group's Israeli General Manager. He 'did not pursue the invitation' until it came from the Palestinian representative. But one also has to be ready to pursue such an invitation. And that takes time. An early PCFF member, Rami Elchanan, son of a Holocaust survivor, who lost his daughter to a suicide bomber, describes this process for him: 'I was no longer the same person, and under the surface a change had started in me so deep I was unconscious of it.'

As in many of the online narratives, Elchanan describes a virtual conversion experience – a moment of amazement – that allows individuals so bereaved at each other's hands to accept an invitation to engage in dialogue:

> And then I saw an amazing spectacle! Something that was completely new to me. I saw Arabs getting off the buses, bereaved Palestinian families: men, women and children, coming towards me, greeting me for peace, hugging me and crying with me...

Later, Osama Abu Ayash meets Rami Elchanan at the home of a relative in Hebron. Again it is amazement at tears that allow individuals to see 'the other' as fully human:

> Later I told my wife about the meeting with Rami and told her that there are Israeli families who suffer and cry when they lose their dear ones. She did not believe me and said they are murderers and don't cry but let the Palestinians cry .... I persuaded my wife to join me.....
> There we met additional bereaved families. My wife was amazed to see Salma the Israeli Druze who lost her brother and two sons who were serving in Zahal and were killed in Lebanon...... When we met at the end of the day, she told me she had spoken to bereaved Israeli families and heard their stories. She felt, for sure, that the pain was the same pain, the suffering the same suffering, and *the tears the same tears with the same salty taste.* I couldn't believe that this was my wife talking in this vein. (Emphasis added)

Tragically, for the bereaved families, what creates the appreciation of shared humanity is their shared pain. As Jalal Khudiari describes it, 'I went to Jerusalem. There were Israeli and Palestinian families. All spoke about pain, and of what we had not gained with violence.' Those renouncing violence in the face of so much fighting are joined by a very particular experience – losing those closest to them. At that moment of loss everything becomes different: 'time stopped' (Litvak); 'I was transferred to another world' (Hirshinzon); 'Your whole life is totally changed forever' (Damelin). (Ayish (this volume) notes that negative stereotypes can be undermined only by such a fundamental shift in context.) For many people, hate triumphs. But what this chapter documents is that endless cycles of mistrust are not inevitable. As Rami Elchanan implores on the Bereaved Families website, 'This is not our destiny!'

One initial perception that seems to make dialogue possible is an awareness of similarities between warring parties. In the words of Osama

Abu Ayash's wife, 'the pain was the same ... the suffering the same suffering'. In the Bereaved Families Forum, Aziz Sarah discovers 'normal human beings, just like me'. For Elchanan, 'our suffering is identical'. And that suffering is sutured into history in very similar ways. These are not random losses. Almost all come at recognizable moments of conflict and oppression: the Holocaust, 1948, Yom Kippur, the Intifadas, Lebanon. Dialogue comes among individuals, suffering individual losses, within a very collective reality, spanning generations. There is no sugar coating. On both sides, many of these losses are 'murders'. Jewish Israeli Ben Kfir documents five generations of captivity and murder in both Europe and Palestine/Israel. Multigenerational Palestinian narratives begin in 1948. This longevity of violence is matched by a very personal attachment to the land. Jewish Israeli Rami Elchanan reports seven generations in Jerusalem. Osama Abu Ayash describes his ill father's efforts to cement the family history:

> My father told me of the pain and bitterness he felt after his father had fallen and the land was occupied by the Jews. He told me about the occupation of all of Palestine, about the '48 war and the '67 war. I was then one year old and he carried me and walked with my mother, my grandmother, and me to the cave, which existed on the land owned by us in the name of Abu Ayash. The cave exists till today.

Not surprisingly, part of a shared historical legacy is the Holocaust. Those familiar with the Israeli/Palestinian conflict will be aware of charges that the Holocaust is manipulated to justify recent Israeli policies (cf. Tom Segev's *The Seventh Million*, Norman Finkelstein's *The Holocaust Industry*, or the speech on Gaza by British MP Gerald Kaufman: www. youtube.com/watch?v=qMGuYjt6CP8). But the voice of the Holocaust speaks more authentically for Bereaved Family members. For several of the Jewish writers, the Holocaust is a more immediate, family affair, linked very much to the present. Rami Elchanan describes his father as 'an Auschwitz graduate'; in calling for international responsibility to stop killing, he speaks as 'the son of a holocaust survivor'. Jalal Khudiari, too, takes a message from the Holocaust that does not parrot the Israeli state uses of it to justify all policies. He describes his religious father inviting him to watch a documentary on Hitler and the Holocaust: 'After the showing, he said to me: 'I want that you learn a thing. When you hate somebody, you cannot reflect, when you cannot reflect, you cannot make a good decision. Hatred can only cause you to make errors ....'

Hatred is not easily overcome. After a friend is killed in the Intifada, Khudiari speaks of his 'hatred of the Jews'. When Elchanan's daughter is killed, he describes 'unlimited anger and an urge for revenge that is stronger than death'. Perhaps what makes these deaths at each other's hands so horrible is the youth(ful innocence) of those lost. Aaron Barnea speaks for all the bereaved when he describes his son, lost: 'in all the splendor of his youthful radiance'.

What changes eventually for these families is their willingness to stop blaming each other and to look critically at the political context in which they find themselves. Arguably more than in the United States, one finds in Israel and Palestine vigorous debate and critique – a kind of debate that, were it more available, could help shape a more informed US policy. Both the Palestinians and Jewish Israelis speak about the 'myths' that they have confronted in order to become peacemakers. For Elchanan, this is the myth that Israel has no partner for peace. Barnea critiques 'the primitive idea that power will overcome all'. Clearly at a certain point these families turn their attention to governments. Barnea again: 'hundreds and thousands of ... lives ... were cut short because the leaders of both sides lack the imagination, courage, daring, vision and responsibility to end this insane conflict.... human lives are being sacrificed with intolerable ease ....' Nir Yesod, who grew up on a kibbutz in northern Israel under Kityusha rockets fired from Lebanon becomes unpersuaded by the reasons given for Israeli incursions into Lebanon: 'This pretentiousness cost much blood.' And Aziz Sarah speaks generically of the 'lies that fuel the conflict'.

The conflict itself becomes the enemy for those willing to engage in dialogue: that 'cancerous bloody conflict' (Elchanan), that 'unnecessary, cruel bloodbath' (Yesod), and 'worthless conflict' (Sarah). In the end, for Barnea, the target of anger shifts: 'As time goes by the heart bleeds, and anger increases in the face of the tragic policies and insensitivity which led to the march of folly, to several unnecessary wars.' There is, then, a convergence as Abu Ayash calls for 'an agreement which honors the national rights of both sides'. While most narratives renounce violence, and many espouse a two-state solution, they do not necessarily presuppose the content of dialogue. How could they? For all the fundamental mutuality that characterizes dialogue, there are also important differences (and different discursive needs) by different parties. Atawneh (this volume) notes that even saying the same thing has different meanings, depending on one's positioning. For example, what is a threat by an occupier becomes a face-saving move by the less powerful. In these narratives, neither side seeks to invoke power, but the differences in positioning are manifested in discursive contrasts.

Dialogic Differences

For several Israelis, it is important to be understood as long-time peace seekers, dissenters from their government's policies. It is a painful position to be in. Aaron Barnea's son, a young Israeli soldier who does not believe in the necessity of entering Lebanon, is killed in Lebanon. He did not want to let down his comrades by not going. He dies wearing a badge reading 'To Leave Lebanon in Peace'. Robi Damelin, a South African Jew who had been active in the antiapartheid movement, lost a son who had not wanted to serve in the occupied territories, where he died. He joined the military, but continued to attend peace demonstrations. He, too, did not want to let down other soldiers and argued that 'if I don't go someone else will and will do terrible things'. Rami Elchanan lost his 14-year-old daughter, heir of peace initiatives, to a suicide bomber:

> [She was] buried next to her late grandfather General (ret.) Prof. and MK (ret.) Matti Peled, the Peace Fighter. The fact that the enemies of peace murdered his granddaughter drew huge attention in Israel and abroad. And as at his funeral, so at hers the mourners represented all the nuances that make up the wonderful mosaic of this unbelievable country.... from the representatives of the settlers in the Occupied Territories to the personal representatives of chairman Yasser Arafat.

For peace-oriented Israeli Jews, some who describe themselves as being relatively untouched by war until it knocks on their door, there is a special narrative that needs to be shared. They hate the wars, but not the Arabs. Although their pain is unspeakable, they do not necessarily speak of revenge. Some Israeli Jews go out of their way to indicate that they did not seek revenge. Roni Hirshinzon becomes enraged when he discovers an extreme right-wing organization using the name and picture of his dead son (a soldier) to indict peace initiatives: 'My son died because there isn't peace. How does anyone allow himself to take my own private pain and use it to stop the peace process?' These parents and their children are people of conscience.

But these are not parallel situations. And the dialogues cannot be entirely parallel. For Palestinians, there has been little opportunity to forget the war. Living under occupation, some Palestinians report torture at the hands of the Israelis. And they lose children throwing stones, not in uniform. As the Bereaved Families Forum reminds us, it is not easy to create dialogues while the conflict is ongoing. The differences in power, privilege and options are immense. One side has a 21st-century military, with both military and economic assistance from the most powerful nation on earth. The economy of the occupied territories is shattered.

For Palestinians in the occupied territories, their primary contact with Israelis comes within the power relations instituted by the military and settlers. As Rafael Reuveny (Israeli-American professor of political economy) describes in a recent issue of *Tikkun:*

> The situation in the Territories has standard colonial attributes, including social segregation; separate laws for settlers and natives; settlers interacting with natives only economically, employing them in menial, low-paying jobs; settlers and other Israelis looking down on natives; and Palestinians having few rights, requiring Israeli permits for daily affairs. As with other colonial societies, there is a high settler-native income inequality in the Territories. Israeli settlers typically live in spacious villas or nice apartments and control disproportionally large shares of local waters and lands, while many Palestinians live in wretched conditions. (Reuveny, 2009: 48)

Additionally, the contrasts in access to education (particularly access to English, in which to make an international case) are extreme (Peled-Elhanan, this volume). And, as outlined above, international rhetorics have naturalized others speaking for Palestine, often obscuring an autonomous voice for Palestinians. In that context, Jewish Israeli Robi Damelin captures one of the most profound challenges in creating dialogue. Describing her entry into the Bereaved Family community she explains: 'It was the beginning of understanding how not to be patronizing; that's a really easy trap to fall into in this kind of work – 'I know what's best for the Palestinians, let me tell them what to do.' Ayish (this volume) notes that negative stereotypes frequently involve condescension. It is all too easy for occupiers to lose track of their own partial understandings and their responsibility for humility, to fail to understand how much they have to learn. This alone can explain why Jewish Israelis in these narratives are not necessarily anxious to advocate a solution for others beyond an end to the violence and the guarantee of human rights.

While acknowledging inequities in power, there is yet another trap to avoid – one cannot assume that every interaction within a joint peace initiative is infused with power in predictable ways. In fact, the goal of these initiatives is to dismantle hierarchical relations. To study these peace ventures is to engage with a 'decolonized imaginary' (Perez, 1999) – a lived process seeking to create oppositional, transformative selves. An analysis that reified power through familiar lenses would fail to see the living reality of peacemaking. These dialogues seek to imagine something quite different from the status quo, creating something even beyond counterdiscourses. Through dialogue, speakers seek to create a counter-public (Warner, 2002), that is, individuals with identities distinct from those accepted uncritically in the current public sphere. To fail to represent these new relationships around the joint struggle for peace would be to do a different kind of violence to the Bereaved Families.

Shared Obligations

Thus, we see that despite terrible loss and very different positions, dialogue becomes possible. Often Forum members come together to work for peace through a compelling sense of obligation to keep others from becoming bereaved, to stop the cycles of violence through dialogue. Unlike the abstract, strategic constructions of peace found in the mainstream press, 'peace' in these instances is the natural and desired state of human affairs – a condition that protects the well-being of individuals.

> Maybe I will never see the world restored to perfect humanity, but I still feel obligated to believe that the tools for peace are not tools of violence and hatred [one does not wage peace with war]. More than this, I feel obligated to use my pain to spread peace, rather than using it to fuel a hatred that would have eventually consumed me. I believe we are all obligated to do our best to create peace, and not wait until it hits home. After all, there is no good war or bad peace. (Aziz Sarah)

> [Through the Bereaved Families Forum] I got a reason to get out of bed in the morning. Since that day on I have dedicated my life to one thing only: to go from ear to ear and from person to person and to shout in a loud voice, to all who are prepared to listen, and also to those whose ears are blocked: This is not our destiny! It is not a decree of fate that cannot be changed!!! Nowhere is it written that we must continue dying and sacrificing our children forever and forever in this difficult horrible holy land. We can and once and for all must stop this crazy vicious circle of violence, murder and retaliation, revenge and punishment. This never-ending cycle, with no purpose. With no winners and only with losers.

> This is the message that, together, my Palestinian brother here beside me and myself are putting across. (With this one-of-a-kind rare

cooperation we are brothers in pain. And you will not find many examples in history where bereaved people, from both sides of the cancerous bloody conflict, holding out hands to one another). And we, the bereaved families, together from the depth of our mutual pain, are saying to you today: Our blood is the same red color, our suffering is identical, and all of us have the exact same bitter tears. So, if we, who have paid the highest price possible, can carry on a dialog, then everyone can! (Rami Elchanan)

the work I'm doing, which is almost the reason I get up in the morning, actually. It's something I feel almost duty-bound to be doing; it's not a favor that I'm doing for anyone else but a personal mission almost. I know this works. I believe removing the stigma from each side and getting to know the person on the other side allows for a removal of fear, and a way to understand that a long-term reconciliation process is possible. (Robi Damelin)

I felt that I had a mission, a national duty. The release of land is not done only with rifles. (Jalal Khudiari)

It is important that these counterdiscourses and dialogues be made visible, that they disrupt the hegemonic discourses that constitute violence as inevitable. As uncommon as these dialogues are, they are not unique: Judea Pearl, father of Daniel Pearl, the journalist killed by al Qaeda in Pakistan in 2002, has been holding public dialogues with Akbar Ahmed, chair of Islamic Studies at American University. In the wake of the Gaza incursion, Ahmed used an appearance on CNN to call for a 'wider dialogue' (War, 2009):

[as] for example [with] Judea Pearl and myself. His son is killed brutally in Karachi. And yet, Judea and I have become great friends. We have constant dialogues. We have huge audiences turning up.

And that's changing how people – the dynamic of how Jews and Muslims relate to each other. This needs to happen much more vigorously in the Middle East. And the leaders on both sides need to be looking at each other through a human frame, not seeing each other as potential enemies, as potential people to be targeted and blown up.

Yet each time the violence escalates, one wonders how individuals on either side of these terrible lines can possibly (re)engage. But it is far more dangerous to ratify the familiar silencing – the suppression of dialogues under occupation. In calling out for dialogue, it is the bereaved who should have the final word:

> Sixty years ago when my (grandparents?) forefathers were sent to the crematoriums in Europe, the free and civilized world stood aloof and did not lift a finger to save them. Today, too, sixty years later while these two mad nations are mercilessly butchering one another, the world again looks the other way and does nothing to put a stop to the killing and this is a shame! And this is a crime!!! All I have left is to beseech you not to behave that way. Do not stand aloof. Be involved and concerned because we are talking about your future and ours. Not everyone must think the same. It is possible and necessary to argue .... To have the ability to listen and the ability to talk to each other. We must be prepared to listen to 'the other'. Because if we will not know how to listen to the other's story we won't be able to understand the source of his pain and we should not expect the other to understand our own pain.

Here is where it begins and here it will end. (Rami Elchanan)

Notes

1. This chapter is dedicated, with humility, to those who wage peace in the face of horror, particularly the members of the Bereaved Families Forum.
2. Bush 43 refers to George W. Bush, the 43rd president of the United States. Bush 41 refers to his father, George H.W. Bush.
3. An earlier version of this observation appears in Silberstein *et al.* (1998).
4. This version of the letter was made available by the *Seattle Times*.
5. My entry into dialogue comes as a founding member of Seattle's Middle East Peace Camp for Children, founded in the wake of September 11, 2001.
6. 'Started jointly by Palestinians and Israelis, who have taken an active part in the cycle of violence; Israelis as soldiers in the Israeli army (IDF) and Palestinians as part of the violent struggle for Palestinian freedom' (website).
7. Here and elsewhere in the chapter, all of the quotes from the Bereaved Families are taken from the PCFF website.

Chapter 11

An Israeli-Palestinian Partnership: Can We Find a Joint Language? And Should We?

M. ZAK

Encounters in Israel: From Interpersonal to Intergroup Dialogue

In the 1980s, the School for Peace (SFP), a joint Jewish-Palestinian center for political education, conducted dialogue programs between Jewish and Palestinian citizens of Israel. We based the programs on the interpersonal relations paradigm (for more on the SFP approach, see Halabi, 2004). We sought ways to break down stereotypes and to encourage participants to empathize and identify with the other. We soon realized that the psychological nature of this approach enabled participants to evade the tough questions that we wanted to address. Workshops on the interpersonal level were capable of leaving issues of conflict outside of the discussion, contributing little to the participants' insight into the broader nature of Jewish-Palestinian relations in Israeli society. The risk of such an approach was that it may have served the status quo rather than challenge it. In the SFP youth encounters, we saw that while Jewish participants tended to be more content with workshops based on the interpersonal paradigm, the Palestinian participants in general and the Palestinian staff in particular were less satisfied with them. Though Palestinian participants at the SFP did not complain out loud, they were often late for activities or skipped them altogether. They tended to make more trouble than the Jewish participants during free time. Jewish participants complained that the Palestinians were too passive in the discussion sessions, not fully cooperating in the tasks that they were given. This was perceived as having to do with Arab culture rather than as a structural or ideological flaw in the workshop.[1]

Through the years, we realized that our approach to dialogue workshops enabled the Jewish participants to feel that they held the cultural high ground. They came out of these programs with a strong feeling that they were more advanced, cultured, modern, liberal and progressive (Halabi, this volume; Halabi & Zak, 2007).

At that early stage we were not aware that we, the Jewish staff members of the School for Peace, were not all that different. Although we sympathized with the Palestinians in the political discussion, we did not speak Arabic and we tended to share Jews' perception of the Palestinian participants' patterns of participation in the dialogue as a reflection of some kind of cultural deficiency.

Thanks to insight and pressure that came primarily from the Palestinian staff members, the SFP began to focus on intergroup rather than interpersonal dynamics. We wanted participants to use the opportunity to confront what we saw as the most difficult issues of the encounter. We started introducing political discussion in the opening stages of the workshop. Through trial and error we found that the field of social psychology helped us to make the connection between group dynamics on the microlevel and intergroup power relations on the macrolevel. We began to define our goals and to develop our methodology accordingly. We wanted participants to gain insight into majority–minority group power relations by identifying how they played out in the dialogue group.

Though much time has passed, the intergroup work is still regarded as innovative. In their survey of dialogue work around the world, a South African research team recently wrote: 'The School for Peace approach is surprising and contrary to much of what we have been taught about dialogue. What attracts us to it is its emphasis on authenticity and facing up to reality, and developing a process that is not imported from a different context, but truly applicable to Israel' (Mapping Dialogue, 2006: 48).

For years we faced resistance, particularly from Jewish participants, donors and academics who preferred the interpersonal approach. We often came across people who may have been prepared to adopt a discourse of power relations, but who are not necessarily prepared to accept that those relations are asymmetrical. Despite the opposition, we have maintained our focus on the intergroup rather than on the interpersonal encounter, and we have done so with the recognition that relations between Jews and Palestinians, as majority and minority groups, are not symmetrical. We work with the conviction that an understanding of these power relations is the key to raising awareness of the conflict.

Cross-Border Work and Its Influence on the SFP Model

In 1994, less than a year after the signing of the Oslo Accords, the SFP began to conduct dialogue work between Palestinians from the Occupied Territories and Jewish-Israeli citizens. We began by applying the same approach that we used when we worked on the conflict with Palestinians and Jews within Israel. Time passed, the military occupation continued, the Palestinians revolted twice, and unfortunately the situation got worse. Our approach, however, changed very little. We thought that since ours was the most radical and political educational approach in Israel, it must be adequate to encounter work across the border.

In the initial years, the Palestinians from the OccupiedTerritories participated enthusiastically and almost obediently in SFP facilitator-training courses. They readily adopted our approach. We started cooperating with them in different programs and they were grateful for the opportunity to earn a living from the encounters. It took time for us to realize that the examination of majority–minority group power relations was not the issue in working across the border. The Palestinians who came from the OccupiedTerritories were not interested in social psychology. They wanted less empathy and more solidarity, or at least discussion about what can be done in order to move Israelis to end the military occupation. It took us time to understand that if dialogue was not explicitly aimed at advancing political change, the Palestinians had no use for it.

The Palestinians in these encounters were suspicious of all Israelis, especially those who professed good will. For example, in a workshop between university professors, the Palestinians demanded that the Israelis first declare their opposition to the occupation as a condition for any future academic cooperation. Many of the Israelis claimed that such a condition was childish and defeated the possible academic benefits from the encounter. They failed to see any connection between academic work and politics. We reflected upon these differences and challenged the Israelis for their fear to take a political stand. But we did not yet change the structure of the meetings in order to meet a political agenda. It was as if in a situation of occupied and occupier, there could be two legitimate perspectives – for and against.

The Palestinians who came to meet Israelis wanted to state their political claims, believing with some naiveté that once the Israelis heard how they lived, how much they suffered and what they wanted, they would join the struggle to end military occupation. In the early years, the Palestinian participants tried to be nice, polite and friendly. The Israeli Jews came in order to get to know the Palestinians and to hear their side of the story. They also wanted to be acknowledged as good conscientious Jews, differentiating themselves from the rest of the Israelis. After hearing the Palestinians' stories the Jews usually shared their own moral dilemmas, which generally reflected a lot of mainstream Jewish perspectives. They spoke at length about the tension between their fear and their security needs and how bad they felt by the suffering of the Palestinians that they met. Most of the Israelis managed to detach themselves, as if someone else was the cause for the suffering of the Palestinians. They believed that with all of the wrong-doing, Israelis were still more cultured, liberal and morally advanced. They wanted to make sure that they maintained control, because the alternative seemed to them much worse. They viewed the idea of sharing power as a euphemism which really meant giving up all power. Memmi (1965) summed up these dynamics in his discussion on colonialism when he wrote that there are neither good nor bad colonialists. There are colonialists. Some may express their objections, but in their day-to-day reality they do what they condemn, for all of their actions serve to perpetuate oppression.

When facing the occupier, the occupied has little tolerance for pseudo complexities. Some things are clear, and presenting the situation using moral dilemmas as the point of reference is a method that the occupier uses to take the higher moral ground while preserving the status quo. We, the Israeli staff (of Jews and Palestinians), were quick to challenge the Jewish participants for their beliefs and behavior in the workshops. We were not immediately aware how similar we were in our own behavior and attitudes.

Occupier and Occupied: How Well We Worked Together

In the first years that we conducted encounters across the border, we initiated them alone, without a Palestinian partner organization. Later, after training some Palestinians to facilitate dialogue groups, a number of graduates opened an organization in the West Bank and began to conduct joint projects with the SFP. The Palestinian organization was in charge of recruiting the Palestinian participants; we recruited the Israeli participants and the program was developed jointly by the staffs of both of our organizations. At first, we conducted the dialogue work in English; later, we used Hebrew and Arabic with the Palestinian facilitators doubling as translators.[2]

All through those first years we were aware of the unequal relations between our organizations. We were uncomfortable with them, but we did very little to change the structure or the basic assumptions of our work. And since we had the experience, the connections and the know-how in grant-writing, the fundraising was done almost completely by the SFP staff. We received the funding and paid the Palestinian organization for its work. The relations that developed between our Israeli and their Palestinian organizations bore similarity to the colonial relations between Israelis and Palestinians at large. Rather than recognizing the power that came with funding, we complained that we did all the work. Another thing that remained in our hands was the educational approach used to conduct the encounter programs. It was the approach developed by the SFP and adopted, with very minor changes, by the Palestinian organization.

The intifada

In the wake of the second Palestinian uprising, in October 2000, most Israeli NGOs that did educational work stopped cross-border work altogether. We continued to work with three Palestinian NGOs. At one point, one of the organizations boycotted us as a part of the struggle against *Tatbiee* or normalization. The others who still worked with us insisted on making changes in the program. They introduced films with footage of what was really going on in the West Bank, including footage of daily invasions with tanks, door-to-door inspections of residents, imprisonments and torture. The local Israeli media, which is the main source of information for most Jews, did not show such pictures. Our partners also asked to add lectures where they described their life and struggle, rather than using all the time for open, dynamic group process. They insisted that we add a translator to each dialogue group and not depend only on Palestinian facilitators who spoke Hebrew as well as Arabic. We accepted these demands as valuable input and improvement in the program and methodology. We did not yet see them as signs of resistance. It is important to note that the Palestinians did not ask to change anything in the distribution of budgets, which was what really would have changed the power relations. Their total economic dependency on the Israeli NGO gave them no leverage to negotiate economic terms.

It was around this time that I began to notice ways that we imposed our approach. In the opening session of one of our joint training courses, all the Israeli participants introduced themselves as psychologists, students of social psychology or social workers. The Palestinians came from diverse backgrounds. Among them was a pharmacist, a youth worker, the head of the ex-prisoners organization, a graphic designer and a lawyer. After the Israelis introduced themselves, one of the Palestinians said, 'I see that you are all psychologists. What is the connection between psychology and the struggle to end occupation?' It took us five years to ask the same question. The truth of the matter is that there is a connection between psychology and the struggle. Psychology has a negative impact on the dialogue. It personalizes it, amplifying the importance of feelings at the expense of discussion of history, values, facts and rights. I will give one example.

Even when we focused on intergroup dialogue, there was great intimacy in the small-group discussions. Participants were encouraged to speak from their heart, relating more to the 'here and now' rather than to the historical context of the conflict. Palestinians generally described details of their life under occupation, believing that if the Israelis only knew the truth, they would do something against the occupation. Unfortunately, it was not ignorance but a desire to maintain control that motivated the Israelis. We did not encourage discussions about the historical reasons for the conflict, and we even saw participants who dwelt on history as being 'boring' and 'lecturing'. We encouraged those who 'spoke from their heart' about their daily life and about how they felt within the group. When Palestinians told stories about their hardships and suffering, they evoked great sadness and empathy for their distress. This reaction was human and important, but if it remained at the level of empathy, there was a risk that it enabled the Israelis to 'forget' that they were not only the listeners, but also the perpetrators. They may have come out of the sessions feeling sensitive and humane, a few came out criticizing themselves as privileged or racist and even fewer did something about it. It is important to realize that while most of the Israelis thought that coming to encounters was already in itself a form of activism, the Palestinians had much higher and apparently unrealistic expectations from them. The Palestinians' role models were women like Tali Fahima and Rachel Corrie. Tali Fahima was an Israeli woman who crossed the border, became a human shield to a Palestinian freedom fighter, and imprisoned for two years for 'aiding the enemy'. Rachel Corrie was an American member of the International Solidarity Movement who was killed by the Israeli army as she tried to stop a bulldozer from destroying a Palestinian home.

By 2004, we ended one partnership because the Palestinian NGO did not conform to the foundations' and our administrative requirements. We ended the second partnership because we did not regard the staff as being professional enough, even though they had undergone our own facilitator-training courses. The staff of that organization was highly motivated to bring participants to meet and influence Israelis, despite the criticism that they endured from their own society, and despite the risk of being imprisoned or even shot by soldiers as they crossed illegally into Israel in order to conduct dialogue. They were willing to do a great deal in order to continue their cooperation with us which, in addition to serving their political goals, was also a valuable source of income in their besieged city. But it was hard to work with them. Sometimes they were aggressive, short tempered and not altogether focused on the facilitation task. We were critical of their work ethics. In retrospect, I could say that they were posttraumatic. One minute they were besieged and hunted by the army and the next minute, when we sat together in the workshop setting, they were expected to perform as professionals. We were operating in two different worlds: Our working conditions were peaceful while they were operating in a war zone. It pains me to say that with all our awareness of asymmetrical power relations, we were blind to the power that we had and the insensitivity that we displayed in this case. We weighed every aspect of our partnership very seriously, but in the end we had our professional standards and they did not meet them. This leads me to the examination of the problematic term 'professionalism', the role it plays and the importance that we attribute to it. It took a new partnership to make us aware of our manipulative use of professionalism.

The Long Road to a More Equal Partnership

I tried to demonstrate that even in relationships between well-intentioned organizations working to promote peace between the two peoples, the Israelis still maintained control. This posed serious questions about the role that projects of this nature had in creating change. In 2004, we entered a new partnership with the Center for Conflict Resolution and Reconciliation (CCRR). The CCRR is a Palestinian NGO committed to an alternative approach to conflict transformation. In this case, our partners' firm resistance may have moved us a step toward liberation from our colonialist patterns (Freire, 1985).

From 2004 to 2006, the CCRR and the SFP worked together on a project targeting Palestinian and Israeli media people from both sides of the border. Funded by the European Union, the program consisted of six four-day dialogue workshops that were to address tensions between the participants' national and professional identities. In the ceremonial opening session, I introduced myself as follows:

> My name is Michal. I am the coordinator of the Media & Conflict project. I am a member of Neve Shalom/Wahat al-Salam and a member of the management team at the School for Peace. My field of expertise

is the role of language in encounters between Palestinians and Jews and I have been doing encounter work for twenty years.

The director of the Palestinian organization introduced himself differently:

> My name is Noah Salameh. I am a refugee from the village of Zakariah. I grew up in the Dehaishe refugee camp and I live in Bethlehem. I was in an Israeli jail for fifteen years and I have worked in the field of encounters for the last fifteen years. Five years ago, we established the CCRR and I am the director of the organization.

The story of our partnership lies in the difference between these two introductions. I could have mentioned that my grandfather established the Israeli navy. I could have said that I myself was a soldier in the Israeli army, but that my daughters are conscientious objectors. I could have introduced my Mizrahi Jewish identity by mentioning my mother's Algerian origins.[3] I could have said many things, but I didn't. I chose to be 'professional'.

Our relations were friendly and cooperative as we prepared the grant proposal together. The atmosphere changed after we received the funding and began to work out the details of the program. The projects began with preparatory meetings between the managerial staffs of each organization. In our previous cooperative projects with Palestinian organizations, most of the meetings that included the Jewish staff of the SFP took place in Israel. This time the management of the Palestinian organization made it clear that they would not come to Israel without permits from the Israeli army. They were not prepared to risk imprisonment. We went to Bethlehem, also without permits from the Israeli army, but in our case it was an illegal act that did not risk serious consequences.

In our discussion on politics and occupation, we found that we were very much in agreement. Our language was direct and precise. We tried not to use vague terms such as 'peace', 'peace education' or 'coexistence'. We shied away from empty slogans such as 'we are all victims', and we avoided terms such as 'reconciliation' and 'forgiveness', recognizing them as processes that could take place only after a solution to the conflict was agreed upon. This was helpful for cooperation between the organizations.

The tension rose when we began to address the organizations' respective philosophies and the goals that we wished to pursue. We presented our educational approach explaining to them how our work was influenced by revolutionary thinkers like Paulo Freire and Franz Fanon who gave voice to the oppressed. But our new partners were not impressed by our professional experience or by the books that we had published. The CCRR management had something else in mind though it was not clear to us what it was. I felt that the Palestinians were testing the Jews on our management staff, trying to decide how willing we would be to work cooperatively rather than fall into the familiar patterns of occupier and occupied. We, on the other hand, tested the Palestinians' level of professionalism, which was where we felt strong. We left the first meeting angrily and puzzled. We decided that only the Palestinians from the SFP management would participate in the second meeting, hoping that without the Jews the atmosphere would be more productive. We were wrong. The same patterns developed. Our staff insisted that we were bringing the proper tried-and-tested approach, while the CCRR staff resisted our claims in what seemed an unreasonable and stubborn manner. At that time we did not understand that the CCRR wanted to create a new approach to encounter work.

After the meetings on the managerial level, we conducted a meeting that included the management and the two teams of facilitators who would work on the media project. This time we met in Jordan. It was the first time that we held a program with Jews in an Arab country. The sense of being an outsider in Jordan is not like the sense of being an outsider in Turkey, for example, where we usually conduct work with Palestinians from across the border. I was concerned for my and my Jewish colleagues' security in Jordan, and I was preoccupied with our sense of strangeness in an Arab country. I assumed that the Palestinians felt more at home. I had not noticed that the Palestinians did not necessarily feel welcomed by the Jordanians. In fact, during each of our subsequent trips to Jordan with the project participants, the Israelis were being welcomed with open arms at the border while the Palestinians, who cross the border at a different crossing, were periodically taken for strict questioning by the Jordanian police, in addition to what the Palestinians had to go through beforehand with the Israeli border police. After our arrival at the hotel with the staff, Noah Salameh, the CCRR director, took me aside a moment before we were to begin the meeting, and said that it was not okay that on the announcement board in the lobby the hotel had posted the information that the *School for Peace* group was meeting in the hall downstairs. I promptly went to the reception and asked them to change the group's name to the Media Project group. At the reception, they explained that the SFP is the name on the reservation from the travel agent, but that of course there would be no problem changing the wording on the notice board. Had I, in the past workshops in Turkey, simply not noticed the signs in the lobby? Had the previous partners simply remained silent about it? Was the partner this time just being petty? These worrisome thoughts were repeatedly running through my head. But it would take more than one remark for us to understand that what we were used to would not work this time.

So what is professionalism?

The meeting between the teams was cautious, revolving around a seemingly hopeless attempt to create a base of trust. All the Israelis had met with Palestinians in the past and had worked as facilitators at encounters. All the Palestinians had met Israelis in the past, most likely as soldiers and armed settlers, but for some, this would be their first encounter in a workshop format. Some of them had never facilitated meetings with Israelis. As opposed to the previous teams of facilitators who had worked with us, this Palestinian team had not undergone an SFP training course. In the past, this had simplified the joint work in many respects. However, in retrospect, we now see that our control of the methodology also kept us from reexamining our approach, seeking out a common language and creating a joint model that responds to the different social and political reality of our new target groups.

At no point during that first meeting in Jordan did anyone explicitly ask, 'What is professionalism?' but that may have been the underlying topic of the meeting. 'Who decides what the important parameters of professionalism are and what kind of experience in our field is regarded as relevant? Is an Israeli who has trained in the field and facilitated 10 workshops better acquainted with dialogue about the conflict than a Palestinian who has spent two years in an Israeli prison? And if the Palestinian had spent 10 years in prison?' A narrow view of the term professionalism naturally produces one answer, whereas perhaps we should reconsider whether political and social activities are to be measured only by academic–professional standards. We should be taking note of who it is that sets the standards and why it is that we restrict ourselves to the social psychology discipline – a discipline that allows us to overlook the historical and cultural context of the conflict.

My staff found it difficult to get used to the partnership this time. In a uninational forum, first time in Jordan, I was criticized angrily for being overly submissive to the Palestinian director. Some thought that perhaps this had to do with the Palestinian being a man, or that I was compensating for the violent behavior of the Israelis in the West Bank and Gaza. They accused me of altering the usual SFP workshop setting. For example, we generally facilitated in pairs, with the facilitators sitting across from one another in the circle whereas the Palestinians in the CCRR were accustomed to sitting side by side. In this workshop we sat side by side. The Jewish staff perceived change, even in seating arrangements, as a threat to everything that we stood for.

The CCRR team initiated additional changes in the media project as it progressed. One major change was that they introduced more plenary sessions into the program. They said that working in the plenary forum functions like a national assembly or like the village square, where one could speak out publicly and where, in the natural way of things, people who were stronger could express themselves to promote the needs of the group. It was, of course, less personal and intimate, and therefore it represented the relations between Israelis and Palestinians at this stage in a much more accurate way. The Jewish-Israeli participants preferred the intimacy of the smaller forums. They felt safe there. The question was why had we let them feel safe all those years and who benefited from that? (CWS, 2000).

Throughout the course of the project, the SFP team had trouble adapting itself to the joint work. Our team asked for more time in the small groups, instead of the plenary sessions, and there was uneasiness about cofacilitating. The Israelis felt that the Palestinians intervened 'personally' rather than 'professionally' (remember how we introduced ourselves). The Palestinian facilitators did not look at the dynamics between the groups in the 'here and now', and they freely expressed their point of view in the group regarding the political and historical content. The Israeli facilitators expressed their point of view about the dynamics in the group and for some reason we regarded this kind of intervention as professional, whereas we saw intervention regarding questions of history and politics as unprofessional and personal. In short, they did not do things our way. The feedback that we received in interviews that we later conducted (Halabi, 2006) showed that the participants made no distinction between one kind of intervention or another. We appeared to be the only ones concerned about defining proper and improper intervention.

As I noted, both sides had a similar reading of the political reality from the outset. We saw this as a necessary precondition for long-term cooperation. It was obviously more important than agreeing about seating arrangements. Now we know that although these were important preconditions, they represented only the shallow surface of our relations. More significant were the deep-seated beliefs and assumptions that we Jewish and Palestinian Israelis had, and the structures that we formed in order to maintain our sense of superiority. We thought and acted as if we were more developed, more reliable and more professional. We actually thought that we could teach the occupied about what they needed and what was good for them. This racist mindset was extremely difficult to expose and even harder to change because the dominant group's style of thinking, acting, speaking and behaving were generally the socially accepted or privileged ways of doing things. We had been so radical in our own society that we lost sight of the fact that this time we, as the occupiers, were the dominant group. In the words of Scheurich (1993), we lost sight of how much our intellectual productions are enacted by our identity.

Awareness and compassion

Though our terminology was clear, critical and assertive when we discussed the political situation, we, the Israeli team and the Palestinian team, spoke a different language when we defined the aims of our workshops. We at the SFP had always thought that we were being realistic by recognizing the limitations of educational work and by speaking in terms of 'promoting greater awareness about the conflict'. The Palestinian partner wanted to create change among the Israelis and motivate them to take action. They were critical of our terminology, especially of our repeated use of the word 'awareness'. Our minimalist goals were influenced by our position of privilege. The social forces that had acted upon us had led us to formulate our goals carefully in order to gain legitimacy in Israeli society and to avoid alienating funding sources. In the process, we had betrayed our role as educators who set out to challenge the status quo. It is clear to me that our role should be to support the oppressed in their struggle by expressing confidence in their abilities and in the justice of their cause. The oppressed do not need us to express our compassion. Post colonialist writers seem to capture this most successfully. As Fanon wrote, 'They approached the Algerians with the terribly paternalistic air to sympathize with their sufferings. In any struggling people this kind of "help" arouses an immediate and instinctive rejection, because they feel that it is the "pacifist" form of the old colonialism and they feel that it damages the innermost source of their fighting power – their faith in their own strength, their confidence in their ultimate superiority over the imperialist enemy' (Fanon, 1994: 11).

During the partnership with the CCRR, we worked with about 150 Israeli and Palestinian journalists. As in the relations between our NGOs, the dynamics between the participants reflect the colonialist relations between our two groups. We found the same disparity between Israelis and Palestinians in terms of what motivates people to attend joint workshops. The Israelis in the media project came to listen, to meet the other, to do some networking and learn about the situation. Most of them did not come with a concrete political agenda. During the course of the dialogue, they also seemed to be out to prove that as journalists they were more professional than the Palestinians.

The Palestinian participants' main motivation was to make their voices heard in the hope that they would influence the Israelis, encouraging them to take action to bring about change. They were also motivated by a desire to improve the personal and professional image that Israelis have of them. The Palestinians struggled with a dilemma that had no parallel on the Jewish side. They were concerned by questions about the signifi-cance of their very participation in the workshops. The encounter itself could have been construed as a betrayal of their brothers and sisters who have paid with their lives in this struggle (Halabi, 2006).

Throughout our partnership we tried, unknowingly, to maintain con-trol by setting the standard of who and what was professional. Instead of recognizing the resistance in our partners' behavior, we regarded them as inflexible and ungrateful. The occupied, as we can learn from Fanon (1994), tried to make their voices heard, change the status quo and human-ize themselves.

Can We Balance the Unbalanced?

Jad (2004) identified a tendency of NGO leaders, empowered by high levels of education and professional qualifications, to patronize the groups of people who they would be expected to serve. The attempt of our Palestinian and Israeli NGOs to cooperate brings additional questions of power relations to the surface. Initially we were inclined to overlook or ignore the asymmetrical relations between our organizations and bet-ween the project participants. In this case we had to constantly turn the Israelis' attention to ways in which privilege and power influence their perspectives. The banality of discussion about us all being human beings, or about being two groups who are suffering and have similar claims for security and independence, can ultimately serve the reality of oppression by not explicitly naming it. I believe that the way to counter this tendency is to change the goals and structure of encounters. Instead of declaring that we bring together two conflicting groups, we should declare that we bring Israeli and Palestinian groups together in order to find ways to put an end to the occupation.

Within the discipline of social psychology, our intergroup approach is still relatively political and radical. But today, my colleagues and I recog-nize that an encounter model with such a heavy focus on group dynamics is not only insufficient, but can even be reactionary. We had already been aware that our work does not necessarily change the Jewish participants' perception of their own group as being more humane. But until now our inclination has been to try to improve the way that we implement our existing model, rather than to question some of the very premises upon which it is built. Friere (1985) stresses that educational work must not pretend to be neutral. When he speaks of education as 'praxis', he refers to a continuous process that combines action, reflection and reevaluation.

This story began with us trying to impose our model of intervention, but the model proved to be serving our side in a way that does not necessarily encourage change in the deep mindset of the Jews. I am especially afraid of the real possibility that the members of the oppressing group will not necessarily change their self-perception as being more humane, cultured, liberal and peaceful. A display of empathy alone might only serve to reinforce that perception (Halabi & Zak, 2007). If, from the outset, we had created our model in dialogue with our Palestinian partners, we might have guided our work by a call for solidarity rather than a call for empathy and compassion.

I want to conclude with some words from my partner Noah Salameh:

> Our first struggle with Israeli organizations is based on the fact that many of them think that Palestinians are still weak and that they are helping us by adopting us instead of being real equal partners. This makes our job more difficult as we have to achieve this balance in a completely unbalanced situation. We have to prove our professionalism and our ability to administer a project, not only to the donors but also to our partners. [...] For me it is an educational process to talk about the Palestinian issue and about our suffering. I am not only a facilitator or a coordinator. I am also a messenger. In this project I learned a new Hebrew word, which I will never forget: *hitnas'ut*, meaning arrogance. I felt that the Israeli staff was patronizing us and trying to prove that we are less experienced, less professional and even less developed. This put me in a challenging position for the whole project. I became very careful about measuring things, especially during the first months, until confidence was built between us as coordinators. Now that the project is over, my opinion is that Palestinians who want to work jointly with Israelis need to be strong, professional and careful, or else not do joint work at all. (Salameh & Zak, 2006: 6)

Paradoxically, in the past we preferred to work with nice, easy going partners who underwent our training programs, used our model and spoke our language. We pushed away strong, stubborn partners for various reasons that we thought were justified, not realizing that in the process we were perpetuating colonialist relations.

In light of the changes that our work has undergone over the years, and in light of critical examination in our work and of our work, I have no illusions about the latest solutions that we have reached. The story will not end here. As Friere wrote: 'The act of knowing involves a dialectical movement that goes from action to reflection and from reflection upon action to a new action' (Friere, 1985: 50). We need to continue to discover who our work serves and how the structures can better create solidarity and liberation. We need to be open to the possibility that encounters can be counterproductive, and we should never rest and feel good about ourselves as long as oppression continues.

Notes

1. Maoz described similar patterns of interaction between Jewish and Arab teachers who took part in encounters conducted by a different organization:

   The Jewish teachers tended to take more active stands and had a greater impact on the proceedings of the encounter, they talked more, took more leadership roles, decided what would be done and how, brought new directions for discussion and activity, and had a greater effect on the nature and quality of the shared educational work. Parallel with the dominance of the members of the Jewish majority, a tendency towards passivity or lack of involvement was evident among members of the minority. The Arab teachers tended to show up late for meetings or not arrive at all, to have only part of the group show up, or to cancel or postpone meetings without prior notice. They also tended not to prepare or to prepare only partially their allocated tasks between encounters, not to carry out their part of the joint educational work or to do it with a minimal investment of effort ... This pattern appeared ... when the groups dealt with neutral [...] subjects [...] however, a second [...] pattern of Arab dominance or power emerged at encounters dealing directly with the 'hot' issues connected to the Jewish-Arab political conflict. (Maoz, 2000: 266–267)

2. Language is the most concrete resource in dialogue groups and the choice of one language over another is the most tangible manifestation of the groups' identity and power (for more on the role of language in the encounters, see Zak, in Avnon, 2006; Zak & Halabi in Halabi 2004; Halabi & Zak, 2007).

3. Mizrahi Jews are those Jews who came from Arab countries. Closer to Arab culture and mentality, the Mizrahi Jews face discrimination by the dominant European Jewish establishment in Israel.

Chapter 12

Postcolonialism and the Jewish Palestinian Encounter

R. HALABI

Introduction

In this chapter, I will look at encounters between Jews and Palestinians in Israel in a critical way. I will also suggest a different and totally new option to understand these encounters. Whereas most of the relevant research hitherto has analyzed the situation through a psychological prism, devoid of political context or historical depth, I propose a new option herein: to frame our analysis of the Jewish-Arab encounter in the context of the literature of postcolonialism.

In contemplating human nature, philosophers have always sought to understand the reasons for hatred and aggression toward others. After World War II, this question seemed yet more acute, and many social psychologists studied the reasons for conflicts between groups and various ways of resolving them. This study recognizes two principal responses: one under the heading of 'a real conflict'; the second under the heading of 'social identity theory'.

A number of scholars are responsible for the first response, notably Sherif *et al.* (1961), who argued that the source of prejudice and hatred of the other is competition over scarce resources. Consequently, if we resolve the competition for resources and encourage cooperation between participants, we can root out prejudice and hatred. The second response is more pessimistic; the primary exponent in this group is Tajfel (1978). He argues that some of our individual identity actually involves our affiliation with groups, and since human beings have a basic need for a positive self-image, they will generally tend to favor their own group while devaluing others. This phenomenon creates an imminent structural conflict between the various groups.

Alongside the research dealing with human nature and the reasons for conflicts between groups, there is also a fairly rich body of empirical research into ways of addressing and resolving these conflicts. One of the first well-articulated theories is the contact hypotheses theory originated by Allport (1954); the assumption was that the best way to reduce tensions, prejudice and hatred between groups in conflict is to bring people from the various groups into unmediated personal contact with one another under circumstances that enable positive and effective interaction (Ben-Ari, 2004).

Many studies have examined the contact hypotheses theory, attempting to ascertain the effectiveness of planned encounters between groups in conflict. The research compared participant attitudes before and after the encounter (Cook, 1984; Pettigrew, 1998). Some of the researchers claimed that this model is not effective (Hewstone & Brown, 1986; Mackie & Smith, 1998). Others claimed that the model is effective, with the provision that certain conditions for the encounter were met; these were elaborated elsewhere by Allport (Pettigrew & Tropp, 2000). Even among observers who are persuaded that the model achieves its aim of reducing prejudice and moderating the negative approach of participants toward the other group, many have expressed reservations about the ability of participants to generalize from the specific experience of the encounter to the broader reality (Hamilton & Bishop, 1976; Weber & Crocker, 1983).

At the start of the 1970s when planned encounters began to take place between Palestinians and Jews in Israel, organizations that were initiating and arranging such encounters adopted the contact hypotheses theory imported from the United States. Naturally enough, the studies done of these encounters also looked at changes in participant attitudes and the degree to which stereotypes appeared to have been moderated following the encounter (Amir, 1976; Beezman, 1978). As time went by, professionals who took part in organizing these encounters – particularly Arab professionals – became uncomfortable with the use of this model, and efforts were made to find an alternative approach to encounters between groups in conflict (Abu-Nimer, 2004; Halabi, 2004; Maoz, 2004).

Abu-Nimer (2004) describes the changes and divides the progression into three periods. The first, from 1950 to 1970, he calls the 'coexistence' era, dictated by the Israeli establishment. The second period, roughly from 1970 to 1990, saw the introduction of coexistence encounter models imported from the United States; the declared aim of these sessions was to reduce stereotypes. The third period began around 1990 with the emergence of a new model for encounters whereby the organizers placed the issues in conflict squarely at the center of the discussion. Maoz (2004) surveyed the activities of most of the organizations engaged in Arab-Jewish encounter work at the time and reached conclusions similar to those of Abu-Nimer, but she referred to the early period as the 'coexistence' era, and to the later programs as 'confrontational' in approach.

Maoz and Abu-Nimer noted that this new model, focusing squarely on the conflict, was developed at the School for Peace. This approach is explicitly deemed 'political' and addresses the encounter between two groups in conflict rather than between individuals. The approach sees the conflict as being between two national identities and looks at the relationship between the groups in terms of power. Encounter organizers employing this model are aiming for greater awareness among the parties to the conflict and want to help participants to reconstruct their identities accordingly (Halabi, 2004; Halabi & Sonnenschein, 2004).

The changes taking place in the encounters in the field were reflected in the research being conducted about them. The early 1990s saw a transition: the earlier research based on the contact approach with its investigation of participant attitudes before and after the encounter, aiming to pinpoint the changes they had undergone, was supplanted by research dealing mainly with the processes that participants underwent during the encounter itself, the dilemmas involved in the encounters, the types of discourse that developed and their significance (Bekerman & Horenczyk, 2004; Herzt-Lazarowitz, 2004; Kelman, 1998; Maoz, 2000). All of these researchers are Jewish and none of them pause to wonder at, or argue about, the necessity for such encounters but focus rather on the dilemmas that emerge from them; this may be related to their being members of the majority group, for whom a change in the existing situation is not a burning issue (cf. Zak, this volume). In contrast, other researchers, most of them Arabs, which may not be coincidental, have expressed reservations about holding such encounters, at least in the current format, citing mainly the asymmetrical conditions under which they are conducted. Some even wonder whom the encounters in fact serve and what use they are to Arabs in Israel (Abu-Nimer, 1999; Halabi, 2004; Rouhana & Korper, 1997; R. Suleiman, 2004).

In conclusion, when we exam the development of the whole field of Jewish-Arab encounters in Israel, as well as the accompanying research, we see that all of the work has been conducted within the discipline of social psychology. The first period rested on theories of contact, as noted; that work addressed the reduction of prejudice and ignored the external reality. The next period was a transition featuring the adoption of motifs from Tajfel's social identity theory with all its incarnations and ramifications; this dealt with awareness and the construction of identity under circumstances of an asymmetrical, majority–minority group reality.

The two approaches presented here do not fully explain what happens in today's encounters and perhaps did not completely explain what was being observed in the past, either. This is particularly true of the contact model, but even the newer model that does address majority–minority power asymmetries cannot explain the reality, because it does not encompass the political context or the historical dimension. There is, however, a third option: to try to understand the Jewish-Arab encounter and analyze it with the aid of the literature of postcolonialism. This literature emphasizes the historical and cultural dimensions and can elucidate the complexities of the conflict. We may find our way via this literature to a better understanding of the essence of the encounter. I will use it to try to answer the questions I have posed in the summary of the literature. What is the focus of this encounter? What happens to national identities in this encounter? To what degree does history shape these identities and influence the encounter outcomes? How much can what happens in the encounter help us to understand the conflict and the options for its future resolution?

The concept of postcolonialism is an inclusive one that embraces the attempt to describe all the cultures influenced by colonialism from its inception through our own time. The concept is the most appropriate one to use in dealing with cultures and with cross-cultural criticism, two areas which in recent years have become popular subjects for scholarly investigation. Postcolonialism deals with social phenomena as manifest during the period when the West ruled over other peoples of the world and also deals with the influence of that era on the period after liberation from colonial rule (Ashcroft *et al.*, 1989).

Colonialism is first and foremost the control of land and natural resources, and also control of the discourse, control of a native people's thought and will. Colonialism is, above all, cultural control, with the underlying moral justification that such control is a humane act meant to improve the situation of the natives, by enabling people without culture to become part of civilization. The aim of this control is to humanize the savage, to insure that native peoples join the West and receive the benefit of a superior culture (Cesaire, 2000; Said, 1993; Wa Thiong'o, 2005).

The colonialist treats the natives as lacking in values, or even as animals requiring domestication (cf. Atawneh, this volume). For the colonialist, this perspective provides justification to behave as he likes toward the native people, treating them in the best case as slaves or, in the worst case, ignoring them completely, negating them, and making them invisible. The colonialist alienates the natives from their own culture and language, and tries to make them forget their history; he tries to persuade them to disparage their own culture, to disparage what they are – and in this way strips them of any power of resistance (Cesaire, 2000; Fanon, 1963; Memmi, 1965; Wa Thiong'o, 2005).

These cultural conceptions are sometimes accepted by the natives and become part of their lives and their identity. The natives accept the colonialist's definition of their own people's values and culture, internalizing the discourse as framed and elaborated by those who rule over them. This espousal of the situation leads to an acceptance of the colonial situation; the natives may even think that, given their shortcomings in ability, values and will, perhaps they are indeed meant to be ruled over. The situation appears to be their inevitable destiny; they refrain from struggling against it. They sometimes entirely lose their voice and the colonialist speaks for them, shaping their identity as he wishes (Fanon, 1967; Said, 1978; Wa Thiong'o, 2005).

Since the colonialist, along with power and weapons, also uses the discourse as a means to justify his rule, it follows that language has an important place in the colonial experience. The imposition of the colonialist's language, mainly English, which gradually has become the language of colonialism, and the corresponding marginalization of local languages were common practice in colonial educational systems. This is how the colonial ruler took over the culture and even the thinking of the natives. And it was all done with the active participation of intellectual authors who, in fact, provided the value structure to rationalize and maintain colonialism in the long term (Ashcroft *et al.*, 1989; Ayish, this volume; Said, 1993; Wa Thiong'o, 2005).

Said (1993) and Chomsky (2004) argue that colonialism lives on in our time, if somewhat different in appearance. Nowadays, we see less of the classic model of physical conquest and rule by colonialist armies and weaponry. In the global world, there is no need for this type of control; the West, led by the United States, rules the world by economic and political means, with the media playing a central role in this new colonialism (cf. Berlin, this volume).

The findings of research that we conducted on Palestinian-Jewish dialogue groups at the School for Peace aligns with what is reported in the postcolonialist literature (Fanon, 1963, 1967, 1994; Memmi, 1965; Said, 1978, 1993). When we look at the discourse of the participants, we see that they experience and perceive the situation as colonial in nature. This is the clearest perception emerging from the Palestinian participants' reports but also, if to a lesser extent, from the Jewish participants' reports. The Palestinian participants feel that they do not exist in the public sphere, that their voice is not heard and that the Jews do not acknowledge them as a national group. When they do acknowledge them, they label them as terrorists and primitives. Hence their first goal in the encounter is to tell their story so that they can put themselves on the map, clear their name and prove themselves as human as anyone else (Halabi, 2004; Halabi & Zak, 2007; Zak, this volume).

Meanwhile, the Jewish participants, or at least some of them, report that they are surprised to discover at the workshop that the Arabs are as human as they are. This means that hitherto their concept was that the Arabs are not human, or at least that the Arabs are not human in the same way that they, the Jews, are. But even when the Arab succeeds in entering the Jewish consciousness, the Jews ascribe to him a primitive, failing culture and treat him as someone who needs to be redeemed from his own culture and brought into the light (i.e. blessed with the enlightened and liberal Jewish-Western culture instead (Halabi & Zak, 2007).

These phenomena, as noted earlier, are familiar in the postcolonialist literature. This literature holds that native, conquered groups have no existence and no voice beyond that created for them by the Orientalist and the colonialist. The group is transparent, as if they are tools, the existence of which in this world rests solely on the degree they are needed by the colonialist (Fanon, 1963; Said, 1978). Sometimes there is an illusion that the Palestinian group has a strong voice, because in recent years the Palestinians participate in the discussion and speak up quite a lot, but this cannot be interpreted as having a voice in the public sphere; it is best to compare it, in the words of Alaothmi (1997) to the singing of a bird in its cage.

Said describes the silence and the absence of the Orient:

> What these widely diffused notions of the Orient depended on was the almost total absence in contemporary Western culture of the Orient as a genuinely felt and experienced force [...] To the extent the Western scholars were aware of contemporary Orientals or Oriental movements of thought and culture, these were perceived either as silent shadows to be animated by the Orientalist, brought into reality by him. Or as a kind of cultural and intellectual proletariat useful for the orientalist's grander interpretative activity, necessary for his performance as superior judge, learned man, powerful cultural will [...] The Orient is all absence. (Said, 1978: 208)

Fanon gives a sharp description of the way the native is viewed:

> The native is declared insensible to ethics; he represents not only the absence of values, but also the negation of values. He is, let us dare to

admit, the enemy of values, and in this sense he is the absolute evil [...] At times this Manichaeism goes to its logical conclusion and dehumanizes the native, or to speak plainly, it turns him into an animal. (Fanon, 1963: 41–42)

These descriptions dealing with the colonial situation of the conqueror and the conquered portray in the best possible way what Arab participants reported, even though the situation in Israel is not strictly comparable to these descriptions of the colonial situation in the literature. The participants reported that they try, in the meeting, with all their strength, to make their presence felt, to exist, to be acknowledged, while simultaneously working to prove that they are not terrorists, that they are human beings just like the Jews. On the other hand, the Jews seem to change the way they perceive the Arabs on the stereotyped level: They declare in the meetings that they acknowledge and even identify with the suffering of the Arabs. But if we look more closely, we will see that when they discuss topics that touch on cultural differences, and cultural identity, there is almost no change. They are rigid in the way they see the Arab culture; they label it as traditional and even primitive and they expect the Arabs to change, develop and become like them (Halabi & Zak, 2007; Zak, this volume).

This is a surprising and rather serious finding. Colonialism came about when one state or a group of people conquered another on its territory. In the situation we are trying to analyze, there are two peoples in the same state, which even describes itself as democratic. But if we try to understand these findings within the historical context, the picture can become much clearer and more comprehensible. The State of Israel was founded with colonialist, Western conceptions. The Zionist movement is a product of the Western culture out of which colonialism arose in the 19th century. The Zionist movement, however, arose as a result of the fact that that same West excluded the Jews, but evidently the sense of Western superiority at the heart of the colonialist phenomenon was internalized as part of the Zionist ethos (Masalha, 1992; Pappe, 2007; Shenhav, 2003).

One of these Zionist conceptions is the notion of making the wilderness bloom and redeeming the land (Wong & Nasser, this volume). In other words, as the slogan has it, a people without a land came to a land without people. From the outset, Zionism nullified the Palestinians, and later on began to relate to them as natives. The basic attitude of the Israeli establishment toward these natives is to treat them like overgrown, backward children who must be managed; savages to be rescued from their barbarism and violence, who must be brought out of their darkness and into the light (Shenhav, 2003).

The Zionist movement and later the leaders of the state did not come to this new space in order to become part of it, but rather to conquer it, to try to domesticate the natives living in it. These are the formative attitudes that shape the identity of Jews (in Israel) and are difficult to counter or to change (Shenhav, 2003). Likewise in the broader reality, they have not changed significantly over the years, so it is no wonder that they underpin the discourse of the Arab and Jewish participants in the encounters we studied.

This is a racist concept that exalts the hegemonic group and treats the culture of the subject group as inferior and primitive. To begin with, the Palestinians accepted this concept and its diminishing of their self-worth, and related to Jewish-Western culture as an ideal that should be aspired to. Over the years they regained a measure of composure and rooted out the internalized oppression so that today, as demonstrated in prior studies (Halabi & Sonnenschein, 2004; Rabinowitz & Abubakr, 2002), the Palestinians do not accept the concept that the Jews and the establishment have of them; they challenge the Jewish discourse and lay bare its true face. The preceding situation was deemed ideal, at least from the Jewish standpoint, and some see the current situation as problematical and blame the Palestinians for being 'extremists'. My opinion is that the preceding situation was grotesque and inhuman, and that now, thanks to these changes stemming from the great effort and energy that Palestinians have invested, we are on the threshold of an altered and more humane situation.

Fanon (1967) writes in his book *Black Skin, White Masks* that a condition for escaping from this inhuman situation is the acknowledgment of the other, an acknowledgment that liberates a person and makes him human; it enables him to connect with himself and thence to the universal. A person who is not acknowledged is forced to fight and to risk himself in order to obtain this acknowledgment and thus becomes an existential threat to the other. I believe that we still have a long road to travel until mutual acknowledgment is forthcoming – or, more precisely, until the Jews acknowledge the Palestinians as a people entitled to self-determination as a political entity. Meanwhile, apparently, the two peoples will go on suffering and a lot of blood will be shed along the way.

Considering the above analysis, a change in the structure of the dialogue encounters between Palestinians and Jews is suggested, but first and foremost, the basic concepts that guide their understanding and engagement must change. The first practical change that derives from the conceptual change is changing the setting from dialogue which is based mainly on meetings in small groups of up to 16 participants to dialogue in large groups. Sitting in a small group creates an atmosphere of intimacy and friendliness and it invites psychological interventions and interpretations. It prohibits discussions about the conflict in an upfront manner, and it especially emphasizes talking about the 'here and now' instead of talking about history.

I believe that history, similar to culture, is key to any discussion about the conflict; it is impossible to talk about the future without acknowledging the past and trying to reach agreements about the past. Most approaches to dialogue see the historical discussion as unnecessary or superfluous, and more than that it is seen as obstructing the dialogue process. There is a notion in these encounters that the message to participants is that the conflict started as they walked into the room, as if the participants themselves caused the conflict. In order to better deal with these obstacles, I suggest that the encounter will take place in large groups or at least will alternate between the different forums, with a stress on the larger forums. I also suggest that the dialogue takes place in the shape of negotiations and not in the shape of dynamic group discussions. It is possible and preferable to conduct the negotiations around a table, with each group sitting on either side. We know that any sitting arrangement transmits a message to the participants, and sitting around a negotiations table sends a more realistic and productive message in my opinion.

The second and most important change is in the type of interventions that the directors and the facilitators use when they help conduct the dialogue. I suggest that we abandon interventions that derive from the psychological field and that we adopt knowledge from the field of social science, and especially postcolonial theories and theories from the discipline of critical pedagogy. The psychological field can talk about power structures between groups, but even that which is the most radical concept in the field does not connect the power structures to a historical, cultural or political context. The discussion on power is based on clinical and laboratory experiments that are detached from any real life reality. The postcolonial literature, as we have seen, relates to concrete realities, to history, to culture and to political processes.

The conflict between Israelis and Palestinians is mainly about land; it is influenced by deep historical roots, and by cultural and economic parameters which are translated into political and military power relations. It is impossible to understand the conflict by looking through the prisms of theories that developed in social labs, as good as these theories may be. Social psychology, as I already mentioned, focuses on power relations between groups, but it does not relate to the cultural dimension; therefore, a key word is missing from its dictionary, and this word is racism.

The role of the facilitators in this approach that I propose is different from what we are used to. The facilitators should declare that they are not objective or neutral; they should declare their agenda to the group. 'Fairness' is a better term than 'objectivity'. It is impossible to be objective. Objectivity, as Fanon wrote (cited in Said, 1993) always works against the weak, because it is the strong who defines the term objective, its meaning and its limits. We can see that facilitators who declare that they are objective and neutral really deceive the participants and work in the service of the majority group (Freire, 1995). The facilitator should highlight the different contents that come up in the group discussion, especially the historical content. The group's dynamics and other processes can be helpful in order to help the dialogue develop, but not as a body of knowledge per se. For example, if the dialogue negotiations break down, one possibility for helping the group out is to analyze the process that the group is going through in order to understand the reasons or the behaviors that brought the group to that dead end in the hope that this intervention will enable the group to continue in their negotiations in a productive way. When that happens, we can go back to the negotiation process and put aside the dynamic analysis.

Focusing on the dynamics is a choice which sets aside other focuses, such as on history or politics and in the process it dulls the conflict, and serves the Jewish group, because the focus on the dynamics leads the groups to a process that we can all anticipate: a process where the Jewish participants identify with the Palestinians, with their pain and miserable lives, and they do so as if they are UN observers and have no part in the situation, and that weakens the Palestinians and distorts the dialogue. According to Fanon, the identification of the colonial with the natives sets the revolution and the liberation back:

> They approached the Algerians with the terribly paternalistic air to sympathize with their sufferings. In any struggling people this kind of 'help' arouses an immediate and instinctive rejection, because they feel that it is the 'pacifist' form of the old colonialism and they feel that it damages the innermost source of their fighting power-their faith in their own strength, their confidence in their ultimate superiority over the imperialist enemy. (Fanon, 1994: 11)

To facilitate an encounter in the approach that I propose, the facilitators have to be knowledgeable in the history of the conflict and in postcolonial literature. This is different from what we see today, when facilitators are only knowledgeable in understanding group dynamics, dealing with feelings, and are especially skilled in reflecting what is happening in the 'here and now'.

To summarize, I want to emphasize that the encounters that take place between Palestinians and Jews have very little impact on our reality. Our reality is influenced by military struggle which is accompanied by political processes. A change in the situation will come through political processes that will take place alongside a change in the power balance between the two sides, and even that desired change must be backed by a more fundamental change in the international power balance. In addition, I want to stress that the encounters that take place between Jews from Israel and Palestinians from the Palestinian Authority are not at all obvious in a situation of a still bloody conflict, when the Palestinian side is imprisoned behind an apartheid fence, and the road reaching the location of the encounter is in itself a road through hell. And if such encounters do take place, due to money that is allocated for such programs by the Europeans and the United States, they should be conducted in a manner that will fulfill the needs of both groups, but mainly to the needs of the oppressed and occupied group. The Palestinians must be able to make their voices heard in these encounters, even if it is muffled, as if from the depth of a dungeon. The Jews must be able to cope with their colonial concepts and with their racism. In presenting this new approach to running encounters between groups in conflict, the goal is not that the encounters should attempt to duplicate reality only by fulfilling the needs of the powerful group and by helping maintain the situation as is. Instead, the goal is to challenge the existing situation and open an option for a different kind of dialogue. Until now, the Jewish side is winning the war, and winning the peace as well, by controlling the discourse and the terminology in the encounters between Jews and Palestinians.

Chapter 13

Checkpoint: Turning Discourse into Dialogue

S.J. KENT, R. SIBII and A.R. NAPOLEONE

Introduction

In September 2007, roughly 2 months before converging on a campus in East Jerusalem, Palestine, several of the authors who have contributed to this book were among the 60 or so American, British, Palestinian, and Israeli scholars and activists anticipating the logistical details of traveling to the second *Dialogue under Occupation* (DUO) conference. A boundary-setting exercise occurred via e-mail, foreshadowing the scope and relevance of what the conference could achieve. Not that we recognized the group-level significance of the interaction at the time! Mainly it was uncomfortable – emotional accusations and rationalizing arguments flew through internet space for a few hours until the matter was deemed concluded. There was, however, something salacious enough about the correspondence to catch our attention even though we were not yet clear on the extent of possible lessons. Indeed, the metaphor of a checkpoint was not recognized until a year and a half later during the presentation of a detailed textual analysis in Bogotá, Colombia at DUO III (Sibii & Napoleone, 2009). The process of ideological analysis, combined with Kent and Sibii's encounters (after DUO II) with three unannounced Israeli checkpoints on the Palestinian road between Qabbatya and Bethlehem, were all necessary to achieve the mix of distance and familiarity in order to realize a comprehensive application of Fairclough's (1992) three-dimensional theory of critical discourse, in which every utterance is simultaneously an act, an instance of discursive practice, and an instance of social practice.

In the pages that follow, we present selected communication acts from an e-mail episode deemed (by its interlocutors during the interaction) to be a simple misunderstanding triggered by carelessness. Some of the interlocutors themselves recognize, during the exchange, that with these acts they are enacting a specific discursive practice (Fairclough's second tier), which they label 'acute linguistic analysis'. Finally, we make the leap to illustrate how the claim 'THERE IS NO CHECKPOINT' (rendered in capitals by one of the e-mail interlocutors) enacted the Israeli social practice of 'checking' Palestinians at random times and unannounced places (Fairclough's third level of CDA). On the basis of this analysis, we claim the interaction as an interpersonal reenactment of institutional discourse.

The Constitutive Force of Language

American philosopher Kenneth Burke (1968) argued that every selection of speech is also a deselection: we say *this* instead of *that*; we offer descriptions with *these* terms instead of *those*. Each selection accomplishes a certain depiction of reality, and also a deflection of reality. British cognitive psychologist Michael Billig (1999) goes even further, examining how processes of deselection accumulate into norms in a habitual manner: from learning not to say certain things (via sanctions), to forgetting that there are other things that could be said (successful socialization), to forgetting that one forgot – the psychological state of repression. Another way of referring to the effects of what we tend not to notice is the notion of trained incapacity (Wais, 2005).

When we teach students how to deconstruct media in all its forms, we must also show them how to build alternative interpretations that generate desired meaningfulness. The counterpart to deconstructive analysis is 'constitutive thinking'. Commerson (2009) draws on Saussure, Hall and Foucault in an illustration of how to establish a basis for the notion of expressing oneself constitutively: to use language in such a way that social understandings and common sense are reformed. The writing in this chapter also aims to practice constitutive thinking – the coconstruction of new definitions for familiar terms, and thus, by extension, new social realities – by examining some trends in the conference talk of an assortment of people who have now gathered three times for an academic conference called *Dialogue under Occupation* (Chicago, USA 2006, Abu Dis, East Jerusalem [West Bank] 2007 and Bogotá, Colombia 2009). The appeal of the conference was – and is – the notion of dialogue. Dialogue, according to Isaacs, 'seeks to address the problem of fragmentation not by rearranging the physical components of a conversation but by uncovering and shifting the organic underlying structures that produce it' (Isaacs, 1999: 20).

Two key terms are inscribed in the conference title, *dialogue* and *occupation*; a third, *discourse*, is added in the extended description and structure of four conference tracks. As discursive events, the first two DUO conferences succeed in foregrounding a range of tensions: peace-building versus militarization; the relations between international and sovereign law; uses of film, news reporting, photography, the internet and social interaction as media for contests of occupation; and colonial versus indigenous language education policies. Recognizing the tensions between and among the frames that presenters bring to their topics enables an exploration of how presenters and participants oriented to the key terms in the conference call, first in Chicago, USA (2006), and second, how these tensions were continued or absent from the conference in East Jerusalem, Palestine (2007).

Our view is firmly grounded in the constructivist paradigm, insofar as the following analysis of DUO-spawned e-mail messages assumes a view of communication as not just an informational conveyor belt, but also a generator of social 'reality'. We rely on Carey's (1992/1989) 'Communication as Culture' text for a succinct explanation of this crucial distinction. According to Carey, two models of communication (the 'transmission' model and the 'ritual' model) have long existed, side by side (although in different power ratios), in American society and elsewhere. Like all other models that have acquired a high degree of salience in a culture, they have become self-fulfilling prophecies (i.e. both 'symbols of' and 'symbols for' reality).

The first of these models, the 'transmission model', is a perspective based on the assumption that communication's foremost purpose is the transmission of information across space for the purpose of influencing the attitudes and behaviors of other people. Individuals whose outlook on communication is shaped by this model will equate successful communication with the correct decoding, on the part of a receiver, of messages that have been previously encoded by a sender. From this perspective, the DUO e-mail communication would be significant only insofar as it facilitated some sort of obvious, quick, mutual understanding between people. The second model described by Carey, the 'cultural/ritual model', conceives of communication as a type of communion, a coming together of sorts whose purpose is not to exchange raw data, but rather to create and confirm cultural values, beliefs, norms, expectations, assumptions, social roles, and so on. From this perspective, writes Carey, communication is a 'symbolic process' with a crucial role in the 'construction and maintenance of an ordered, meaningful, cultural world that can serve as a control and container for human action' (Carey 1992/1989: 18–19). Individuals whose outlook on communication is shaped by this second model will equate successful communication with the creation of a community over time, and the maintenance of its cohesion and of its relevance in people's lives.

Working from the perspective of the ritual model of communication, we see language use as the premier human technology for creating institutions, codifying and prioritizing values, beliefs, and norms associated with cultures and communities, and for the creation of an entire array of identities and group memberships through the constant negotiation of various aspects of our selfhood with others. 'If I had to single out a primary function of human language', writes Gee, 'it would be not one, but the following two: to scaffold the performance of social activities (whether play or work or both) and to scaffold human affiliation within cultures and social groups and institutions' (Gee, 1999: 1). We engage Gee's second type of scaffold in our foundational textual analysis. To which 'social group' did the e-mails' authors gain affiliation as a result of their sometimes explicit, often implicit negotiation of subject positions? How can the associated intragroup identifications inform us about intergroup dynamics? From this base, we then interrogate Gee's first type of scaffold: Was the online DUO communication successful in the 'cultural/ritual' sense? If so, what social activities were performed, and how can they continue to be relevant to our lives? If, on the other hand, the e-mails under study here failed to lead to the creation of a cohesive overall group identity (inclusive regardless of discrete social group identifications), how can we continue to *communicate* ourselves into a more viable community?

Sticking through 'the Storm' to build Group Resilience

The following excerpts are taken from an e-mail exchange that occurred within the DUO community in the break between the first two conferences: before the second conference took place in East Jerusalem and after the inaugural conference had occurred in Chicago. A clash occurred between a young, female, Palestinian graduate student and three authoritative figures (males, with established reputations: Palestinian, Israeli and American) over a particularly loaded choice of words alluding to the status of East Jerusalem. We analyze a cluster of six e-mails, most of them sent in rapid succession over the duration of 1 day. The heated exchange amounts to a discursive treasure, as one can find in these e-mails anything from identity claims and negotiations to competing views about the functions and consequences of language use. Specifically for our purposes in this chapter, the episode serves simultaneously as an instance of group dynamics indicative of a crucial stage of group development and – on the basis of that recognition – as an opportunity to practice shifting monologic discourse into dialogue.

Although we had not yet met for the second DUO conference, the e-mail correspondence shows that group dynamics were well underway. Indeed, one can imagine a temporal layering of the stages of group development, in which the participants of each conference compose a group in real time that proceeds, in its own specific fashion, through the usual stages of group development. A longer developmental process occurs simultaneously from conference to conference, such that at some point in the future, long-term and/or repeat participants in DUO conferences can look back and identify some rough parameters for stages of group development as they unfold over the years. The challenge of turning monologic discourse into dialogue involves recognizing a group's stage of development by the qualities of interaction at a given time. We offer here a discourse diagnostic in which we frame and present the communication acts, discursive practice and social practice of conference participants and planners as indicative of group member roles typical for the 'storming' stage of group development.

Tuckman (1965) describes a four-stage model of group development labeled forming, storming, norming and performing. His rubric was adopted and illustrated by Weber (1982), delineating interpersonal issues, group behavioral patterns, leadership issues and group task/issues as areas with distinctive dynamics in each stage. Schein (1982) offers explicit guidelines about the kinds of dynamical, communicative acts one typically observes in these areas during each stage of group development. All of these psychological theorists draw on the change theory proposed by Lewin (1948) involving three stages of unfreezing, change and freezing. In this chapter, we will analyze the e-mail correspondence in the context of group developmental stages to show how discourse practices (evident in specific communicative acts) tend to keep long-term group dynamics frozen by reenacting intergroup dynamics established as normative intra-group social practice. Hopefully, the role we take up in offering this analysis is productive and functional for the purpose DUO is defining for itself.

From the viewpoint of group relations theory, what matters most is that all roles are interchangeable; they are not necessarily fixed by national, religious or gender identifications. Despite the correspondences we name between the kind of role an individual takes up in a group and the generalized characteristics stereotypically attributed to (one or more of) their identities, there are no hard-and-fast rules. Instead, whatever rules are operating (in social reality) can be apperceived in the ways that group members respond to each other. What we understand from the discourse of 'acute linguistic analysis' and subsequent attempts at repair that emerge in the e-mail correspondence is that, in fact, *there is a relevant checkpoint* – a discursive one, and it is imposed before we ever meet in person. The social practices governing the social dynamics and discursive practices of the DUO II conference parallel those governing official interactions between Israelis and Palestinians (nonconstructive quasiengagement, with Americans and others looking on); and – crucially, from a group development point of view – these practices cohere synchronically with the discursive and social norms that unfolded at the first DUO conference, despite the fact that three of the four protagonists in the e-mail exchange were not present in Chicago the year before.

There are identifiable group dynamics whose emergence can signal the stage of group development relevant to the constitution of the group in that moment of time and space. In the case explored here, we identify certain types of communicative acts (Austin, 1962) that are commonly enacted by individuals taking up particular roles in order to contain, limit, or suppress the tensions inherent in the group developmental stage of storming. These tactical moves are communicative acts, which (in this case) are readily categorizable as gendered, agist and classist. Yet engaging *only* in one or more of these necessary critiques is to reinforce hegemonic discourses and *avoid* turning to actual dialogue. The deployment of our own acute linguistic analysis is strategic in the sense that we aim not to end the analysis with categorical identifications but to invite a commencement of conversation premised upon the recognition of complicity in discourses that are reliant upon such categorizations. From here, we can try – collectively – to stretch and otherwise reshape the boundaries of those categories, laying groundwork for potential future movement from dialogue to action.

We propose that: *to dialogue* is to collectively change the meanings of the present and – by doing so – collaboratively invoke new meanings for the future. To collectively change the meanings of the present means to recognize *and interrupt* one's own role in enacting familiar dynamics, accept the interventions of others when they recognize your role (as habit or pattern) in the enactment of familiar discourses, and to experiment with alternative ways of talking about the issue, problem or task (cf. Halabi, this volume; Zak, this volume). Acknowledgment of how not only our own words but our very selves (through the imposition/enactment of certain roles in particular groups at specific times) are *used* by discourse – by language itself – to continue to speak antagonism into being must be accompanied by efforts in interaction to act out of/away from historical trajectories through collaboratively risking communicative actions that have the potential to lead us into new relationships.

Such admission and recognition requires a level of courage that moves beyond reenacting established discourses of critique into creative unknown zones of relating through communicative moves that refuse to let go of the integrity of the Other. The storming phase of group development involves the struggle of members of a group in deciding whether to engage the challenge of accepting actual Otherness or refuse it. Storming cannot occur until after groups initially form, but its timing and persistence is always unpredictable. In the case of DUO, convened so 'that scholars and professionals in applied linguistics and related fields might come together to present, discuss, and dialogue in areas of the world experiencing occupation' (Wong *et al.*, 2008: 165), it is not a surprise that elements of storming emerged during the first conference, between conferences, and at the very start of the second conference.

We Are All Guilty Here: Enacting an E-mail Checkpoint

As is typical with obvious conflict, most of us remained silent while the e-mail drama unfolded. It would not be unfair to describe us as bystanders. From a group relations view, what happens when a person speaks out in a difficult situation is that they represent not only themselves but reflect an aspect of the overall group's dynamics. During the storming phase of group development, it is common for anyone who asserts leadership to be shot down or fail to draw adequate support in order to persist. Whatever the bystanders felt or thought during the interaction, we left it to the four protagonists to resolve. Nor, at the time, was there any public protest of the outcome.

Not surprisingly, given the uncertainty initially surrounding the identity of DUO II's participants, Jonathan Schwab,[1] DUO's main organizer, opts for as inclusive a vocative as possible in his opening e-mail: 'Greetings everyone!' The term 'everyone' does not possess any obvious connotations for either one of the groups of people potentially interested in the conference and, as such, does not divulge Jonathan's own expectations of (and preferences for) a particular DUO community identity.

> *E-mail 1*: (Received at 13:08 on September 11, 2007. Sent by Jonathan Schwab)
>
> Greetings everyone!
>
> Thanks to Dr. Emilio Scola and employees of Peace Now, I have some good news to share:
>
> THERE IS NO CHECKPOINT to pass through in getting from Israel (including East Jerusalem) in order to get to the campus in Abu Dis. There is a wall, to be sure. But it must be bypassed, not crossed. The way to bypass it is very simple ...

The use of passive voice is described by Pinker (2007) as a means of conveying moral judgments. The phrase, 'There is a wall', purports to tell us nothing more about the checkpoint than the fact that it is there, a natural fact of life (i.e. an 'existence'), and both wall and checkpoint exist without anyone's agency. The erasure of agency is an achievement of language use, a linguistic realization. There are different ways to 'bypass' the wall, and these means are contingent upon identity:

> For Israeli citizens, unless there is some special alert, nobody will check you. Also, since Abu Dis is in Area 'B', no violation (by an Israeli) of any Israeli law is involved in going there.

Only Israeli citizens are addressed, leaving us to guess that there must have been specific questions or concerns expressed by Israelis to warrant such an announcement. However, the silence regarding other groups attending the conference – notably, Palestinians – is loud. Palestinians can be checked under any kind of alert. Despite the singling out of Israeli citizens, Jonathan expresses the hope that 'this information helps everyone', and moves on to information about the website and conference program before closing. Three days later comes Amira Husayni's challenge.

> *E-mail 2*: (Received at 12:18 on September 14. Sent by Amira Husayni)
>
> Thank you Jonathan [...]
>
> I really appreciate your efforts, but would also like to express my disappointment concerning two main issues:
>
> 1. Unfortunately, the updates miss information relevant to Palestinian participants (I mean Palestinians with West Bank and maybe Gaza ID cards) ...

Amira does not waste any time identifying the target of her critique, as she opens with the organizer's first name, a sign of familiarity between a graduate student and a professor that is accepted in many American university departments, but not so much in Europe, where Amira studies. Perhaps Amira simply intended to address Jonathan, an American professor, in a manner that he would be accustomed to. Or perhaps she simply wanted to establish a relationship of equality (from participant to participant, or academic to academic). Whatever her reasons for using the vocative 'Jonathan', Amira is clearly aware that this manner of direct interpellation would be far too offensive to Jonathan if it were to accompany her specific critiques of his language use. Thus, while she credits him explicitly for helping out with the directions to the conference site, she does not identify him as an agent when verbalizing her complaint, shifting the blame from a confrontational 'you' to a formally agent-less object, 'the updates'. The discursive practice established so far is to elide human agency: checkpoints, walls, and updates are of the same existential class – they simply happen – and are therefore morally neutralized.

> 2. In the last update, I read 'THERE IS NO CHECKPOINT to pass through in getting from Israel (including East Jerusalem) in order to get to the campus in Abu Dis' well, I do not know what to say, but East Jerusalem is not part of Israel.

Interestingly, Amira does not take issue with the checkpoint statement. Her attention is to asserting the national claim of Palestine, which has already been linguistically weakened by omission and now seems erased by the apparent inclusion of East Jerusalem in Israel. Within an hour and a half, Amira receives a response from Emilio Scola, an Israeli professor.

> 1. I was requested only to provide information on how to reach Abu Dis from Israel or/and/including from East Jerusalem.

With his e-mail lacking any salutation whatsoever, Emilio does not make any efforts to soften his defense or his rebuttal, further on characterizing Amira's self-described 'frustrate[ion] that such a mistake comes from the organizers of a conference on Discourse Under Occupation'as (just) a performance of 'acute linguistic analysis':

> The acute linguistic analysis of the phrase in parenthesis prefigures a sharp conference. However, the phrase in question does not logically imply, semantically presuppose or pragmatically implicate that *the conference* considers East Jerusalem a legitimate part of Israel. At most you can blame me for my in your eyes careless phrasing.

Emilio's dismantling of Amira's concern continues the discursive practice of agency elision already underway – his identity as an Isreali is unnamed. Further, he employs two additional rhetorical tactics characteristic of academization: (1) recourse to jargon and (2) a three-pronged counterattack that is reminiscent of the prescriptions of formal parliamentary debate. Emilio relegates Amira to an inferior position in relation to his own, possibly also in relation to the audience's assumed position, and dismisses his own culpability as, at worst, innocent carelessness. The discursive practice enacted with this e-mail continues the elision of agency and arguably displays a social practice in which Israelis' complicity in any infringement of Palestinian autonomy can only be considered a minor matter. It is difficult not to read Emilio's closing statement for its attitudinal value:

> Looking forward for an *interesting and fruitful* conference.

The asterisks that enclose 'interesting and fruitful' are a common way for online writers to compensate for the absence of nonverbal cues, such as intonation and face expression (Benwell & Stokoe, 2006). They serve to emphasize the two adjectives, thus indicating to the reader the existence of a subtext that, we propose, is anything but flattering to Amira.

Amira responds nearly immediately, only 14 minutes later.

E-mail 4: (Received at 13:56 on September 14. Sent by Amira Husayni)

Dear Professor Scola,
I would like first to clarify that I did not intend my message to blame you (or any of the organisers). It was just meant to draw attention to two issues that caused disappointment to me, as a Palestinian partici-pant in the conference. On the contrary, it's in fact because I really appreciate your efforts, that I find it a pity to let a careless phrasing cause misunderstandings.

Having been positioned as the junior partner in the (already) asym-metrical power relationship with Emilio, Amira moves quickly to restate her case by embracing Emilio's admission of carelessness. She then pro-ceeds with an attempt to establish some sort of an ideological founda-tion for this discussion, in particular, but also for the entire conference:

> the conference organisers do not want to assume any position regard-ing the status of East Jerusalem. That's fair enough as common ground for the conference.

At this point, Amira has actually named the essential problem of pur-pose for the DUO conferences. As it is for any and all groups in the early stages of group development, members/participants need to know if the collective goal(s) of the group are consonant with individual goals. But Amira is now caught up in the discursive practice of 'acute linguistic anal-ysis', which coopts her resistance to the social practice of eliding Israeli collusion with the military occupation of Palestine.

She proposes a better phrasing that would make the nonposition of conference organizers clear, such that 'happy Palestinians' (like herself, which she had identified in her first e-mail) can attend. She ends her email with a tongue-in-cheek coopting of Emilio's condescending language:

> Looking forward to the conference and the even more acute analsysis [sic] and discussions!

Two hours after Amira's e-mail, Emilio fires off his second response. As with his first one, the opening lines of this message do the work of informing the audience of his formal role within the conference.

> *E-mail 5*: (Received at 15:42 on September 14. Sent by Emilio Scola)

> Thank you very much for your clarification, dear co-participant (I am just one participant, not an organiser of the conference).

Even though Amira tried to convey her understanding that Emilio is not an organizer, he still feels it necessary to clarify the issue. That suggests he does place a significant amount of strategic importance to his official role within the DUO hierarchy. While he seems very much secure in the capital that his professional credentials award him, he does wish to retain the ability to choose his battles: he is not an organizer so he can legitimately stop participating in this discussion any time he sees fit (he is 'just' a participant). Citizenship remains unnamed, presumably a nonissue. Also Emilio seems to want his audience to understand that he does work with an assumption of equality between 'dear' DUO participants: he is *'just one* participant' (as in, 'one among many others just like me'). Nonetheless, while some common ground may exist, he continues the discursive practice of giving lessons in linguistics.

> We basically agree that it is not *an assumption* of the conference that the status of East Jerusalem is this or that. We still disagree, though, about the linguistic analysis.

Social practice is again reenacted: 'this or that' stands in for the names of nation states. In the face of 'acute linguistic analysis,' such elisions are quite significant: what has been secured is there is no assumption about the status of Palestine which can be attributed to the DUO conference. In fact, Emilio proposes a ban on words that might raise sensitive issues:

> I admit that, under the extreme conditions of sensitivity in which we live here, it would be better to ban words such as 'include' that may, even remotely, suggest annexation and similar things.

It is in the next-to-last sentence of the e-mail, however, that Emilio abandons any trace of a conciliatory tone. After addressing the use of 'including' in Jonathan's original e-mail, Emilio writes:

Let us leave the other linguistic aspect of this to our discussions in Jerusalem. See you soon.

This is an unambiguous move to terminate the conversation – a move that is predicated on every power resource that the institutional setting has awarded to him and that he has claimed for himself. The objection raised by Amira was not legitimate in the first place, he seems to be saying, and now this discussion is over.

However, barely minutes after Emilio's last e-mail, the first of two more e-mails on the topic arrive. Jawad Mansour, a Palestinian professor who holds a high rank within the host university's administration is one of the local organizers of the conference. His e-mail is brief (an opening saluta-tion, four sentences and a sign-off). He begins with 'Dear Colleagues', thus appearing to position everybody involved in the discussion (Jonathan, Amira, Emilio, himself and the silent DUO participants who have been receiving all of these e-mails) as professional scholars. But the very first sentence of his e-mail – undoubtedly the most explicitly accusatory state-ment in the entire exchange – seems to be excluding Amira from that community of equals:

E-mail 6: (Received at 15:47 on September 14. Sent by Jawad Mansour)

Dear Colleagues,
Apparently Ms Amira Husayni misunderstood your e mail … (origi-nal ellipsis).

The juxtaposition of 'Dear Colleagues' and 'Ms Amira Husayni' and '*your* e-mail' indicates that he is not addressing Amira, to whom he appar-ently has nothing to say. He clearly sees no merit in Amira's arguments since he declares that she has 'misunderstood' the 'colleagues' e-mail. The ellipsis following this statement implies that there's more that he could say about the situation, but that he has chosen not to share any more observations on that score at this time.

We Palestinians are becoming oversensitive about all issues due to the hopelessness of the plitical [sic] situation to the degree of alienating our friends.

The sense of finality permeating his message indicates that Jawad, like Emilio before him, intends his e-mail to put an end to this conversation.

The timing and content cause one to wonder if he was writing simultaneously with Emilio or if he had just read Emilio's e-mail and was concerned with further escalation. At any rate, he joins with Emilio in the discursive and social practice(s) of sexism, classism and agism. As another established academic male, the gender accusation of oversensitivity echoes Emilio's suggestion of a ban in order to avoid confrontations from young persistent women. Rather than recognizing the hopefulness of Amira's desire to correct misunderstandings, Jawad projects his own – and other Palestinians' – despair onto Amira. The group developmental storm of defining a common, conference-wide purpose has been effectively ended, at least for now. About 90 minutes later, one more e-mail arrives, written by the first speaker in the entire series, Jonathan.

> *E-mail 7*: (Received at 17:27 on September 14. Sent by Jonathan Schwab)
>
> Dear friends,
> Please do not allow my carelessness in phrasing to imply anything other than an outsider's attempt to facilitate transit …

Social practice, discursive practice and communicative act are clearly merged: the outsider (and main conference authority figure) who triggered the episode absolves everyone of blame, taking the judgment of carelessness upon himself. Jonathan reiterates the

> deepest desire to have the conference hosted in the West Bank and to provide a venue where scholars from all parts of the world can come together in a welcoming environment to open a dialogue and discuss ways to better understand the issues and promote paths to resolution of conflicts. I have much to learn from all of you and I look forward to being given that opportunity. […] I look forward to speaking with all of you in November when we are together.

The opportunity presented by this rare confluence of academic activists was so unprecedented that participants had no basis for acting into the potential of this new frame (Halabi, this volume; Zak, this volume). Instead, we adhered to the form and structure of any other academic conference: monologic discourses in competition, not dialogue, characterized prominent communicative acts relating to the DUO conferences. And yet, the excess of tensions spilled over – unable to be contained.[2] A conflict over (in one case) the role of bilingual or mother tongue education in language policies (emergent at DUO I) may not have been a surprise, given that the four themed strands of the conference (labeled 'discourses') were created from three types of language planning reconceived and reconfigured to include a focus on the people involved in occupied lands and their reactions to corpus planning, status planning and peacemaking (Wong *et al.*, 2008: 166). Other emergent conflicts from the first conference (roughly considered as part of the 'forming' stage in a long-term view of group developmental processes) prefigured the contentious ground of communicating with each other in East Jerusalem.

Although the dynamical tensions of DUO I are not detailed here, it was in the wake of DUO I's success that Palestinian, American and Israeli academics (among others) chose to meet together under the DUO II banner in a land under military occupation. Nasser and Assaf (2008) assert that many participants from the first DUO conference were looking forward to the chance 'to enter the dialogue in a more authentic way due to the political and social realities surrounding the [upcoming] conference site', (Nasser & Assaf, 2008: 247), and Wong *et al.* report after DUO II that 'being witness is a life-changing experience' (Wong *et al.*, 2008: 168).

DUO II: Straight into the Storm

One British participant asked, 'Can we just celebrate that we're actually here?' It was the end of the first day of the conference. The campus had been quiet all day: we seemed to be the only people present. Shooting between Hamas and Fatah fighters had led to the temporary closing of the campus and an intensive, nearly all-night effort to keep students of the two political movements talking instead of fighting with each other. While faculty- and administrator-facilitated dialogue occurred with students off-campus, conference participants *in situ* were missing another potential turning point.

'Do you have the transparency and the courage to speak out loud?' The challenge came as soon as Dr Dajani,[3] the Acting President of the host university, asked members of the audience for questions directed to the opening panelists. 'Very difficult questions you are asking!' Dr Dajani responded in his role as panel moderator to Dr Safadi, one of the university faculty members, drawing some laughter from the audience. 'What did you mean', Dr Safadi wanted to know, 'by "dialogue" in the title of the conference?' No answer was forthcoming.[4] Instead, the next person with a question turned our attention back to the panelists with what she characterized as 'a small question'. Just as the discursive practice of acute linguistic analysis prevented an uptake of dialogue in the e-mail exchange a few months before, the discursive and social practices of academic conferencing channeled us away from the tensions evidenced by the emergent conflict. Nonetheless, the question was posed: the long-term storming stage of group development (already begun at DUO I) emerging at the first

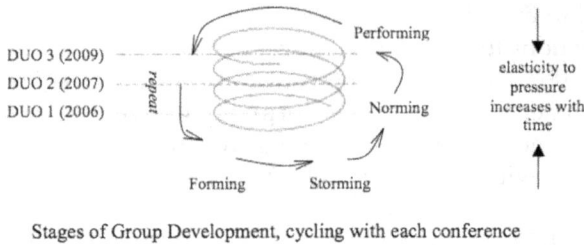

Stages of Group Development, cycling with each conference

Figure 13.1 Group resilience to tensional dynamics

possible instant in DUO II, while most attendees were absorbed with the behaviors typical of the short-term first stage of 'forming' (review Figure 13.1).

However, just as the social practice of postponement enacted by the e-mail protagonists deferred the substance of dialogue (i.e. of jointly reconstructing different meanings than originally understood/intended) from that time and space (prior to the conference) to this present, here-and-now location, the combined communicative acts of the panel modera-tor and conference participants diverted us again from engaging in real time the core problem of the relationship between talk and occupation. By turning us back to the usual conference format, we (everyone in the audi-torium at that time) agreed implicitly – at least in that moment, in that place – to define neither our intentions nor our terms.

We had barely been together for an hour, and the format was formal. Broaching differences or deviating from institutionalized norms of genre-specific behavior could not have happened effectively in this short-term forming stage of group developmental processes, and certainly not within the typical academic normative structure. Singling out this instance and the cooperative interactions involved in silencing the chance for dialogue is, therefore, a descriptive maneuver intended by the authors to fore-ground our focus on role enactments for the group-as-a-whole, shifting analysis away from particular individuals as uniquely autonomous agents who are presumed to be disconnected from each other. In this group-based view, individuals enact roles that serve purposes of the entire group through utterances that are representative of the dynamical tensions embodied in perceptions and attitudes of various subsets of members.

Contrary to the global scope and historical breadth of presentations at DUO I, the program for DUO II was sharply contained, reflecting the pain-ful and frustrating local and immediate realities of the place where we met, with its dense overlays of recent and historical strife. Despite the explicit variety of DUO I, the discourse diagnostic presented so far is also premised upon the unexpected emergence of conflict between peace activists and military personnel at DUO I (see blogposts at reflexivity.us). While DUO I included many presentations on figurative and literal occupations worldwide and over several decades, DUO II was confined to on-the-ground-now realities of the Israeli-Palestinian conflict. The discursive restriction may have intensified dimensions of group dynamics and stages of development: the entrenched features of discourse that maintain one monological center became more discernable, highlighting attempts at dialogue, such as the questions posed by Dr Safadi, which become more marked.

Considering DUO as a social process trafficking in symbols is consistent with the theories of group relations and group development utilized in this chapter thus far. The applied critical discourse analysis we present here selectively extracts elements of language use (actual communicative acts) and mines them for continuities in both discursive and social practices. While there are other maps through the same terrain, we propose that our map provides a coherent reading of the most crucial issues that have emerged in the conference group's dynamics. Throughout DUO I and DUO II, the original framing of language policy clearly asserted itself over the unwanted tangent of the military's role in ending occupation and contributing constructively to building peaceful interrelationships.

Reframing: From Monocentricizing Discourses to Generative Dialogue

The negative effects of particular instances of interpersonal communication (such as the e-mail exchange and participation in academic conferences) can only be assessed and comprehended through a holistic analysis of their use in context. Working in intercultural collaborations on entrenched problems can lead to the discovery of communicative moves that enable shifts away from ritualistic discourses to new rituals of dialogue that constitute possibilities for coordinated, collaborative action. For instance, experimenting with specifically polycentric maneuvers (that diverge from the monocentric habits of established patterns of discourse) could lead to discoveries that unfreeze dialectical tensions, situating participants in processes of mutual change. This was modeled in a DUO II presentation on the pedagogy of teaching a joint history of the region, during which Peled-Elhanan and her copanelists articulated their own microsocial, interactive creation of new interrelations. Hagar described finding the willingness to give up the need to tell certain things which have always seemed to require telling. Kahanoff developed a willingness to include parts of stories and histories with which she has moral problems. Peled-Elhanan became willing to give up retelling her parents' story, musing that this discursive shift became 'possible because we [the intercultural team] share the same idea about the history of the conflict, about the vision of the future and we act together to transform reality' (Peled-Elhanan, 2007, conference presentation).

Sharing an idea about the future returns us to stages of group development. It is inevitable that a diverse group of people with mixed identifications on both the oppressor and oppressed sides of an occupation dynamic will engage each other on the basis of different frames. Difference is produced automatically as everyone seeks to orient relative to each other while maintaining reference to personally, professionally and culturally salient identities. These maneuverings manifest themselves in group member roles that emerge in interaction: each role-type serves a particular functional (or dysfunctional) purpose for the group-as-a-whole. With reflection, we can explore the efficacy of role enactments at specific moments to the group's overall progress toward tangible, common goals. In this way, instances of overt conflict such as the e-mail checkpoint can be transformed into levers for dialogue rather than barriers to connection. Recognizing how personal language use (in any and all settings, e.g. professional or activist, formal or casual) reflects one's own particular position in relation to larger 'group-constituted' framings of 'reality' is a skill that can be cultivated for practical use in reconciling all our destinies.

Notes

1. The e-mail interlocutors' names mentioned in this article are all pseudonyms.
2. Blogposts detailing group-level conflicts enacted at DUO I and DUO II are posted at www.reflexivity.us, search for Series: Dialogue Under Occupation.
3. Actual names.
4. A violation of the implicit social and cultural order, Dr Safadi's 'voice' could not be assimilated at that time and place. Blommaert explains that voice is 'the capacity for semiotic mobility' (Blommaert, 2005: 69), which means being able to make sense within the situation's hierarchical order of reference (its indexicality) well enough to achieve functional goals or otherwise generate uptake. Dr Safadi's 'voice' was insensible in the given indexical order of an academic conference, which enables only questions relevant to the immediate panel rather than to the higher order of context or mission of the entire conference.

Chapter 14

Where is the Hope? A Call for Action

S. WONG, I. NASSER and L.N. BERLIN

> As we attempt to analyze dialogue as a human phenomenon, we dis-
> cover something which is the essence of dialogue itself: the *word*. But
> the word is more than just an instrument which makes dialogue pos-
> sible; accordingly, we must seek its constitutive elements. Within the
> word we find two dimensions, reflection and action, in such radical
> interaction that if one is sacrificed – even in part – the other immedi-
> ately suffers. There is no true word that is not at the same time a
> praxis. Thus, to speak a true word is to transform the world. (Freire,
> 1998a: 68)

Dialogue is surely central to this book, but without a direction, dialogue is empty. Unless the notion of dialogue is given adequate philosophical and political grounding, it does not rise above the existence of
talk (Kent *et al.*, this volume). And unless dialogue is accompanied by
action, it is empty and ineffectual. As Freire points out, praxis includes
action (practice) and reflection: 'When a word is deprived of its dimension
of action, reflection automatically suffers as well; and the word is changed
into idle chatter, into *verbalism*, into an alienated and alienating "blah"'
(Freire, 1970: 75–76). In these final pages, we highlight and reflect on the
political, philosophical and ethical considerations that the authors of this
volume have put forward.

After over 60 years of the Israeli-Palestinian conflict, one might reason-
ably ask if there is *any* way out of the impasse that has come to define it.
Atawneh (this volume: 168) opens his chapter with a quote from Israeli
filmmaker and peace activist, Ron David, 'The Arab-Israeli conflict makes
smart people dumb, sensitive people brutal, and open-minded people pigheaded fanatics' (Ron David, 1993: 2).

The chapters in Part 1 – Education – offer multiple ways of theorizing the relation between language, power and dialogue in diverse contexts: a bilingual school in Israel (Schlam-Salman & Bekerman, this volume); Israeli textbooks in Israel (Peled-Elhanan, this volume); and the adaptation of a learner-centered pedagogical model from the United States in Israel, Hebron and al-Quds (East Jerusalem) (Deeb & Weinstein, this volume). Shakhshir (this volume) provides a historical, sociocultural analysis of Palestinian education. Histories of indigenous voices from the ground up and the margins offer an anti-colonial counter narrative to the dominant Zionist narrative of the establishment of the state of Israel as 'a land *without people* for a people without land' (Peled-Elhanan, this volume: 121). The struggle of Palestinians including Bedouins and Druze who were colonialized by Britain before the establishment of the State of Israel for inclusion into textbooks and the educational curriculum has parallels with the Native American, Native Hawaiian (Sai, 2006), and Chicano studies projects in the United States (Acuña, 2000), indigenous peoples struggles in Bolivia (Postero, 2005), and New Zealand (Smith, 2006). Counternarratives of indigenous peoples assert that the land was not devoid of people, but that indigenous people inhabited the land long before the Western conquerors, European plantations and colonial settlements enslaved local peoples (Anzaldúa, 1990; Solórzano & Yosso, 2009).

Schlam-Salman and Bekerman (this volume) offer important questions for consideration in the search for a discourse of resolution and liberatory educational initiatives within indigenous struggles: Can the use of a third language, such as English (i.e. neither Hebrew nor Arabic) be a medium for emancipation? How do language users construct systems of meaning to challenge and reinforce the status quo? What would it take to replace the Arab and Jewish binary? Representing the diverse voices of Palestinians (Muslims, Christians and Druze) in textbooks and school curricula is an important area for change as is the development of bilingual schools and defense of the rights of Palestinian students in education. Fundamentally, the issue of representation is a political question that cannot be accomplished in the discourse of enactment alone through imposed reforms in educational institutions separate from addressing political inequality inherent at all levels of government and civil society.

Linguistic Inequality and Language Hegemony

A central concern running through a number of chapters in Part 1 – Education – is linguistic inequality and language hegemony. We note, with the rise and fall of empires, change in the medium of instruction in schools with the introduction of Turkish language instruction under the Ottoman Empire (1516–1917) and English language instruction under the British mandate (1917–1948).[1] With the establishment of the state of Israel, Hebrew changed from being a classical, 'dead' language (like Latin, spoken mainly for religious purposes) to being revitalized as an official language that now dominates domains of use in the discourses of enactment, transaction and reaction in Israel. The growth of Hebrew was accompanied by eventual suppression of all other languages, even those of European Jews, such as German and Yiddish (Shohamy, 2008). As Schlam-Salman and Bekerman (this volume: 51) point out, today within the state of Israel, there is a language hierarchy 'in which Hebrew emerges as the dominant language and Arabic has little representative power'.

The Polarized Binary: Arab and Jew

One discursive practice that has been described in a number of chapters (Schlam-Salman & Bekerman, this volume; Peled-Elhanan, this volume) is the polarized binary between Arab and Jew. The term 'Arab', (rather than 'Palestinian') may serve to essentialize, silence and suppress Palestinian rights and Palestinian identity.

The blurring of Palestinian, Arab and Muslim identities as one stereotypical 'other' is found not only in Israeli schools, but also in US contexts as well (Ayish, this volume). A number of chapters from Part 2 – Media – show the influence of stereotypes in US popular culture, in Hollywood movies and in the news media which reinforce the confusion between race and religion, Arab and Muslim:

> Such broad labels are often used interchangeably – and erroneously – and reflect an inaccurate but popular perception among many Americans (and perpetuated in popular culture) that Arab Americans – irrespective of their ethnicity, national origin or religious affiliation – are the same [...] And because of the negative stereotypes associated with these two groups [Arabs and Muslims] Palestinians often experience a double indignity: They are overtly disparaged in popular culture, while also being disparaged by their association with Arabs/ Muslims (i.e. when an Arab or Muslim, for example, commits an act of violence Palestinians are likely to be implicitly [if not explicitly] associated with this act. (Ayish, this volume: 140)

The media stereotyping of Islam and Arabs is further linked with radicalism and terrorism. Unfortunately this has led to racial profiling, guilt by association and laws, such as the US Patriot Act of 2001, with serious ramifications leading to the violation of civil rights and civil liberties of anyone who might question US military involvement or seek a change in US foreign policy. Of particular concern is the culminating effect of *dehu-manizing* stereotypes so that the victim is seen as deserving inhumane treatment (Atawneh, this volume; El-Bilawi, this volume). Furthermore, after every major event that involved or purported to involve Muslims, hate crimes against minority Arab and Muslim communities in the United States and those who are mistaken for them (e.g. Sikhs, Native Americans and Latinos) have been on the increase (Ayish, this volume: 141; Salaita, 2005; Wong & Motha, 2007).

The Law of Return and the Unrealized Right of Return

An important corrective to the Arab and Jewish essentialist binary is to defend the human rights of all in the state of Israel and in the Palestinian occupied territories. Currently, through the Israeli law known as the 'Law of Return' (Bennis, 2007: 17), Jewish immigration from anywhere in the world is encouraged. Citizenship for Jewish citizens includes privileges, such as state-financed language classes, housing, job placement and medical and welfare benefits. While all Jewish people have the right to immigrate to Israel, this right is denied to those who are not Jewish (Muslim, Christian, Druze and others) who were displaced by the establishment of the state of Israel in 1947–1948 and the Six-Day War of 1967. Although the Right of Return for Palestinians has been established by international law through the United Nations Resolution 194 (institutionalizing the Right to Return) and the Universal Declaration of Human Rights which provides the right of all refugees to return to their homes, this right has never been recognized by the State of Israel (United Nations Report of the Human Rights, UNRHRC, 2009).

Media Representation

Dehumanization of the Palestinian as 'other' is also rooted in the discourse of transaction as practiced in the mainstream media, if not only in its overt choice of covering one side of a story over another, then in its covert inculcation of a particular ideological perspective that remains largely unchecked and unquestioned by the general public (Berlin, this volume; El-Bilawi, this volume). Until news media return to the practice of holding governments accountable for their actions and not merely acting in complicity with them, hope for change appears bleak.

When Edward Said wrote *Covering Islam: How the Media and the Experts Determine How We See the Rest of the World* (1997, 2nd edition), he challenged intellectuals to look critically at the media in relationship to representation, knowledge and power. Said, a Palestinian Christian, wrote:

> In the fifteen years since *Covering Islam* appeared there has been an intense focus on Muslims and Islam in the American and Western media, most of it characterized by a more highly exaggerated stereotyping and belligerent hostility than what I had previously described in my book. Indeed Islam's role in hijackings and terrorism, descriptions of the way in which overtly Muslim countries like Iran threaten 'us' and our way of life, and speculations about the latest conspiracy to blow up buildings, sabotage commercial airlines and poison water supplies seem to play increasingly on Western consciousness. (Said, 1997: xi)

Many of the authors in this book employ a critical discourse analysis to examine how ideology is instantiated through various popular and news media. Atawneh analyzed the discursive position of Palestinians in a corpus of press statements by both Israeli political leaders and Palestinian political leaders to justify, mediate, reproduce or resist oppression. Representation of Palestinians as 'beasts walking on two legs' and 'cockroaches' enabled the Israelis to justify killing (Atawneh, this volume: 116). The aim of war propaganda is to unite the nation and to rally support from the domestic population as well as third parties to justify attacks on the enemy (Lakoff, 2000).

'Palestine' has been evoked as a rhetorical justification for wars involving other countries in the Middle East (Silberstein, this volume). After the September 11th attacks on the World Trade Center and the Pentagon more than 60% of Americans believed that Iraq was linked to Al Qaeda, providing support for the US invasion and occupation of Iraq (Berlin, this volume). Silberstein also takes up the problem of the way Palestinians are constructed, 'American public discourses often link Palestinian terrorism to any violent act aimed at the non-Muslim world. [...] US government and media discourses have powerfully linked the US to Israel and its "Palestinian problem" through a series of rhetorically framed parallels' (Silberstein, this volume: 248). The US and Israel are both seen as 'bringing democracy to the region' and they both view themselves as 'reluctant occupiers'. For example, when US military troops entered Afghanistan and later Iraq, their deployments were described as 'liberations' not 'occupations'.

Atawneh (this volume) pointed out the huge disparity between the media coverage of casualties of noncombatants. During the period from 2000 to 2009, 1487 Palestinian children and 123 Israeli children were killed yet Palestinian injuries and fatalities are underreported.

El-Bilawi utilizes media framing, narrative theory, news decontextualization and dramatization to analyze how US public opinion was shaped and altered to support Israeli's blockade of the Gaza and to ignore Palestinian reports of the attack which began on December 26, 2008:

> The Israeli offensive has resulted in nearly 1000 Palestinian deaths with more than 4000 additional wounded and inflicted incalculable damage to homes, hospitals, schools and businesses in the Gaza Strip. In contrast [...] 10 Israeli soldiers and 4 civilians have been killed. Despite the inequities, however, most of the mainstream media have given equal or greater coverage to the casualties and views of the Israeli side than the Palestinian side. (El-Bilawi, this volume: 190)

As Ayish points out, 'Of course some Palestinians, Arabs and Muslims have committed horrible acts of violence. The problem is that the 'picture in our heads' of these individuals or groups has come to represent 10 million Palestinians, 300 million Arabs and 1.5 billion Muslims' (Ayish, this volume: 153). In analyzing the complex reasons why dehumanizing Palestinian stereotypes persist, Ayish sees curriculum and dialogue as a way to critique media stereotypes. He argues for a comprehensive shift in thinking that is necessary for meaningful and sustained change in people's perceptions of Palestinians.

Counterdiscourses

Silberstein's chapter presents significant Palestinian and Jewish Israeli grassroots organizations that are committed to dialogue to end the violence. Combatants for Peace is comprised of former soldiers of the Israeli army (IDF) and Palestinians who participated in armed struggle for freedom. Wahat al Salaam/Neve Shalom is a shared Israeli-Palestinian village. In North America there is a peace camp movement involving Palestinian and Jewish children and youth. These perspectives are rarely covered in the mainstream news media in the United States and serve as an important counterdiscourse to the representation of Palestinians as being violent and the source of 'the problem'. The Bereaved Families Forum (also known as the Parents Circle – Families Forum) is a grassroots organization of over four hundred families – half Palestinian and half Israeli – who have lost immediate family members due to violence in the region. Silberstein puts forward the question: 'How can narratives simultaneously construct and be constructed by possibilities for peace? In sharing profoundly personal stories of loss and transformation, the Bereaved Families narratives make it possible for others to imagine how dialogue can come into being' (Silberstein, this volume: 181). In the encounter between grieving families, one by one they share their initial anger and desire for revenge and their determination to direct their anger toward the senseless policies that lead to war and violence.

Differences in Power and Privilege

Running throughout this volume is the theme that the two 'sides' of the conflict are not equal in power, nor parallel in situation. The differences in power, privilege and options are immense. One side has a 21st-century military power with military and economic assistance from the United States, the most powerful country in the world (Silberstein, this volume). The other side is occupied, under a system of apartheid (Carter, 2006) The Palestinians may lose a child throwing a stone; the Israeli may lose a child in uniform. The Palestinian may have been tortured or have a family member in prison.

In Part 3 – Dialogue – authors continue to struggle with the issue of 'power'. For example, Zak poses the problem of Israeli-Palestinian dialogues that 'reflect the power structure between occupied and occupier [and even asks whether] partnerships with such a huge gap in power should even take place' (Zak, this volume: 269). She points out inequality in dialogue encounters between Palestinians and Jews. Differences in power result in Israeli participants tending to be critical of Palestinians for not being professional enough while Palestinians, who come to the table to enlist support for change, become frustrated with the individual and psychological dimension of the dialogue, and see little change in the misery and oppression they face. The different sides enter dialogue with different aims, those with privilege want 'awareness' and want to express their 'compassion' while those who are oppressed want the Israelis to express solidarity. They hope that Israelis will stand up to the bulldozers like young American Rachel Corrie who was killed by a bulldozer when she stood in front of a Palestinian home scheduled for demolition (Kline, 2003). In addition, the notion of dialogue encounters pose a huge concern for Palestinians because by participating in dialogues with the Israelis that emphasized reconciliation at the expense of justice or an end to the suffering, they might be perceived as betraying those who had been killed or are in prison and even contributing to the 'normalization' of occupation.

Halabi also presents the problem of dialogues that are focused on the psychological and eschew discussions of power and history; as such, the discourse of reaction appears to take the form of a circular dialogue rather than being allowed to emerge into a discourse of resolution. He proposes postcolonial frameworks that address the history of the oppression between colonizer and colonized, rather than facilitators who see conflict resolution as group dynamics between small groups of people. If encounters take place, they should be conducted in a manner that will fulfill the needs of both groups, but mainly attend to the needs of the oppressed and occupied group.

> The Palestinians must be able to make their voices heard in these encounters, even if it is muffled, as if from the depth of a dungeon. The Jews must be able to cope with their colonial concepts and with their racism [...] the goal is to challenge the existing situation and open an option for a different kind of dialogue. Until now the Jewish side is winning the war and winning the peace as well, by controlling the discourse and the terminology in the encounters between Jews and Palestinians. (Halabi, this volume: 307)

Ultimately, until we can push past our own self-imposed limitations of talking about talk (i.e. dialogue for dialogue-sake), taking on the challenge to not merely understand the powerful frameworks of dialogue and their potential for conflict resolution (cf. Kent *et al.*, this volume), but also to move dialogue in the direction of action in order to achieve the eradication of occupation.

> It is our task as progressive educators to take advantage of [the] tradition of struggle, of resistance, and 'work it'. It is a task that, to be sure, is a perverted one from the purely idealistic outlook, as well as from the mechanistic, dogmatic, authoritarian viewpoint that converts education into pure 'communication', the sheer transmission of neutral content. (Freire, 1998b: 108)

By reading this volume, we are called upon to act; study should not leave us in a permanent state of stagnation, but empower us to effect change in our world.

Note

1. Public and mandatory education under the Ottoman Empire (1516–1917) predated establishment of public and mandatory education in Western Europe. After the defeat of the Ottoman Empire, Palestine was demarcated with specific borders and turned over to Great Britain to rule as a Mandate territory under the League of Nations. In Palestinian education under the British mandate (1917–1948) one can see the parallels between Palestinian educators' long standing struggle to establish schools in the context of a broader anticolonial struggle for independence, democratic rights and national liberation and the struggles to establish education in other British colonial contexts in Asia, Africa and the Caribbean (i.e. India, Kenya, Hong Kong and semifeudal, semicolonial China during the same period).

References

Abraham, N. (1995) Arab Americans. In R.J. Veroli, J. Gallens, A. Sheets and R.V. Young (eds) *Gale Encyclopedia of Multicultural America* (Vol. 1) (pp. 84–98). New York: Gale Research Inc.

Abraham, S.Y. and Abraham, N. (1981) *The Arab World and Arab-Americans: Understanding a Neglected Minority.* Detroit: Wayne State University Center for Urban Studies.

Abramowtiz, M. (2008, December) Israeli Airstrikes on Gaza Strip Imperil Obama's Peace Chances. *The Washington Post.* Retrieved from http://www.washingtonpost.com/wp-dyn/content/article/2008/12/27/AR2008122700962.html

Abu-Nimer, M. (1999) *Dialogue, Conflict, Resolution and Change: Arab-Jewish Encounters in Israel.* Albany, NY: SUNY Press.

Abu-Nimer, M. (2004) Coexistence and Arab-Jewish encounters in Israel: Potential and challenges. *Journal of Social Issues* 60, 405–422.

Acuña, R.F. (2000) *Occupied America: A History of Chicanos* (4th edn). New York: Longman.

ADC (2009) *Report on Hate Crimes and Discrimination Against Arab Americans (2003–2009).* Washington: ADC Research Institute.

Aden, H. Ashkenazi, V. Alperson, B. (2001) Being Citizens in Israel – A Jewish Democratic State. Maalot Publishers and The Ministry of Education, Jerusalem.

Agamben, G. (1987) *Homo Sacer: Sovereign Power and Bare Life.* Meridian: Crossing Aesthetics.

Ahmed, K.N. (1998) Voices from within the invisible minority: A phenomenological study of school and social experiences of Arab American students. Unpublished doctoral dissertation, State University of New York at Buffalo.

Aharony, Y. and Sagi, T. (2002) *The Geography of the Land of Israel. A Geography Textbook for Grades 11–12.* Tel Aviv: Lilach Publishers.

Aharony, Y. and Sagi, T. (2003). *The Geography of the Land of Israel. A Geography Textbook for Grades 11–12.* Tel Aviv: Lilach Publishers.

Aikhenvald, A. (2004) *Evidentiality.* Oxford: Oxford University Press.

Alaothmi, A. (1997) *The Woman and the Language.* Beirut: Arab Cultural Center (Arabic).

Alatom, B.E. (1997) Orientalist stereotyping in modern American popular culture. Unpublished doctoral dissertation, The University of Texas, Arlington.

Alavi, K. (2001) At risk of prejudice: Teaching tolerance about Muslim Americans. *Social Education* 63, 67–81.

Al-Czar, S. (1989) Education under the shadow of the Intifada, University Graduate Union, Research Center, (Hebron), pp. 43–47.

Al-Haj, M. (2002) Multiculturalism in deeply divided societies: The Israeli case. *International Journal of Intercultural Relations* 26, 169–183.

Al-Haq (1989) Israel's War against education in the occupied west bank; A penalty for the future. Al-Haq Law, Rammalah.

Al-Haq (1990) A nation under siege; Annual report on human rights in the occupied Palestinian territories. Al-Haq Law, Rammalah, 453.

Allport, G.W. (1954) *The Nature of Prejudice*. Cambridge, MA: Addison-Wesley.

Amara, M. (2002) The place of Arabic in Israel. *International Journal of the Sociology of Language* 158, 53–68.

Amara, M. (2005) *Yad Le yad assoc Bilingual Schools*. (Hand in Hand Association- in Hebrew). "Tel Aviv" The Hebrew Arabic Education Centre, Dvir publishers.

Amer, M. (2009) Telling it like it is: The delegitimation of the second Palestinian Intifada in Thomas Friedman's discourse. *Discourse & Society* 20, 5–31.

American Muslim Council (1993) *American Attitudes Toward Islam: A Nationwide Poll*. Conducted by the John Zogby Group International, Inc. Washington: American Muslim Council.

Amir, Y. (1976) The role of intergroup contact in change of prejudice and ethnic relations. In P.A. Katz (ed.) *Toward the Elimination of Racism* (pp. 245–308). New York: Pergamon.

Anderson, B. (1991) *Imagined Communities: Reflections on the Origin and Spread of Nationalism*. London: Verso.

A.N.S.W.E.R. Coalition (2009) Friday protest in Los Angeles against Gaza assault. On WWW at http://uscsjp.wordpress.com. Accessed 10.01.09.

Antoun, R.T. (1994) Sojourners abroad: Migration for higher education in a post-peasant Muslim society. In A.S. Ahmed and H. Donna (eds) *Islam, Globalization and Postmodernity* (pp. 161–189). New York: Routledge.

Anzaldúa, G. (1990) *Making Face, Making Soul: Creative and Critical Perspectives by Feminists of Color*. San Francisco, CA: Aunt Lute Books.

Arman, A. (2009) Media bias and distortion fuels war in the Middle East. Global research. On WWW at http://globalresearch.ca/index. Accessed 20.12.08.

Ashcroft, B., Griffiths, G. and Tiffin, H. (1989) *The Empire Writes Back: Theory and Practice in Post-Colonial Literatures*. London: Routledge.

Associated Press (2003) U.S. employs Israeli tactics in Iraq: Urban warfare methods adapted. On WWW at http://www.msn.com. Accessed 26.11.09.

Aswad, B.C. (1993) Arab Americans: Those who followed Columbus (1992 Presidential Address). *Middle East Studies Association Bulletin* 27, 5–23.

Atawneh, A.M. (2009) The discourse of war in the Middle East: Analysis of media reporting. *Journal of Pragmatics* 41, 263–278.

Austin, J.L. (1962) In J.O. Urmson and M. Sbisa (eds) *How to do Things with Words: The William James Lectures Delivered at Harvard University in 1955*. Oxford: Clarendon.

Avieli-Tabibian, K. (2001) *The Age of Horror and Hope (Chapters in History for Grades 10–12)*. Tel Aviv: The Centre of Educational Technologies Publishers.

Ayish, N. (2006) Stereotypes, popular culture, and school curriculum: How Arab American Muslim high school students perceive and cope with being the 'other'. In D.A. Zabel (ed.) *Arabs in the Americas: Interdisciplinary Essays on the Arab Diaspora* (pp. 79–116). New York: Peter Lang Publishers.

Ayish, N. (2008) *Stereotypes and Arab American Muslim High School Students: A Misunderstood Group*. Saarbrücken, Germany: VDM Verlag Dr. Müller.

Bakhtin, M.M. (1981) *The Dialogic Imagination: Four Essays* (M. Holoquist, trans.). Austin: University of Texas Press.

Bakhtin, M.M. (1986) *Speech Genres and Other Late Essays* (V.W. McGee, trans.). Austin: University of Texas Press.

Bandura, A. (2006) Toward a psychology of human agency. *Perspectives on Psychological Science* 1, 164–180.

Bar-Gal, Y. (1993a) *Moledet and Geography in a Hundred years of Zionist Education.* Tel Aviv: Am Oved Publishers.

Bar-Gal, Y. (1993b) Boundaries as a topic in geographic education: The case of Israel. *Political Geography* 12, 421–435.

Bar-Gal, Y. (1996) Ideological propaganda in maps and geographical education. In J. van der Schee and H. Trimp (eds) *Innovation in Geographical Education* (pp. 67–79). The Hague: Netherlands Geographical Studies, IGU, Commission on Geographical Education.

Bar-Gal, Y. (2000) Values and ideologies in place descriptions: The Israeli case. In *Erdkunde*, archive for *Scientific Geography* 54, 168–176.

Barlow, E. (ed.) (1994) *Evaluation of Secondary Level Textbooks for Coverage of the Middle East.* Ann Arbor, MI: Middle East Studies Association/Middle East Outreach Council.

Bar-Navi, E. (1998) *The 20th Century – A History of the People of Israel in the Last Generation (for Grades 10–12).* Tel Aviv: Sifrei Tel Aviv Publishers.

Bar-Navi, E. and Nave, E. (1999) *Modern Times Part II: The History of the People of Israel (for Grades 10–12).* Tel Aviv: Sifrei Tel Aviv Publishers.

Barthes, R. (1980) La chambre claire. In *Oeuvres Completes* (Vol. 5). Paris: Editions du Seuil.

Barzak, I. (2009, January) Israel Wants International Truce Monitors. *The Daily News.* Retrieved from http://www.thedailynewsegypt.com/article.aspx?ArticleID=18893.

Bauml, Y. (2002) The military government on the Israeli Arabs and its cancellation, 1948–1968. In *Hamizrach Hachadash (The New Orient)* (In Hebrew), Israel, Tel Aviv (Vol. 43, pp. 133–156).

Bayoumi, M. (2001) How does it feel to be a problem? *Amerasia Journal* 27, 69–77.

Bayoumi, M. and Rubin, A. (2000) *The Edward Said Reader.* New York: Vintage Books.

Beasley, B. and Standley, T. (2002) Shirts vs. skins: Clothing as an indicator of gender role stereotyping in video games. *Mass Communication & Society* 5, 279–293.

Beezman, A. (1978) Similarity in status, status level and reduction of stereotypes following an encounter between national groups. PhD dissertation, Department of Psychology, Bar-Ilan University, Hebrew.

Behdad, A. (2005) *A Forgetful Nation: On Immigration and Cultural Identity in the United States.* Durham: Duke University Press.

Bekerman, Z. (2005) Complex contexts and ideologies: Bilingual education in conflict-ridden areas. *Journal of Language, Identity, and Education* 4, 1–20.

Bekerman, Z. and Horenczyk, G. (2004) Arab-Jewish bilingual coeducation in Israel: A long-term approach to intergroup conflict resolution. *Journal of Social Issues* 60, 389–404.

Bell, A. (1991) *The Language of News Media.* Oxford: Blackwell Publishing.

Ben-Ari, R. (2004) Coping with the Jewish-Arab conflict: A comparison among three models. *Journal of Social Issues* 60, 307–323.

244   *Examining Education, Media, and Dialogue under Occupation*

Bennis, P. (2007) *Understanding the Palestinian-Israeli Conflict*. Northampton: Olive Branch Press.

Benwell, B. and Stokoe, E. (2006) *Discourse and Identity*. Edinburgh: Edinburgh University Press.

Berlin, L.N. (2005) Media manipulation. In A. Betten and M. Dannerer (eds) *Dialogue Analysis IX. Dialogue in Literature and the Media: Selected Papers from the 9th IADA Conference, Salzburg 2003 – Part II: Media* (pp. 173–182). Tübingen: Max Niemeyer Verlag.

Berlin, L.N. (2007) Cooperative conflict and evasive language: The case of the 9–11 Commission hearings. In A. Fetzer (ed.) *Context and Appropriateness: Micro Meets Macro* (pp. 176–215). Amsterdam: John Benjamins.

Berlin, L.N. (2008) 'I think, therefore …': Commitment in political testimony. *Journal of Language and Social Psychology* 27, 372–383.

Bhatia, A. (2009) The discourse of terrorism. *Journal of Pragmatics* 41, 279–289.

Billig, M. (1999) *Freudian Repression: Conversation Creating the Unconscious*. Cambridge: Cambridge University Press.

Billig, M. (2001) Discursive, rhetorical and ideological messages. In M. Wetherell, S. Taylor and S. Yates (eds) *Discourse Theory and Practice: A Reader* (pp. 210–221). London: Sage Publications.

Bin Laden (2008) Palestinian cause prompted 9/11. *CBS News*. On WWW at http://www.cbs.com. Accessed 15.1.09.

Bleier, R. (2006) *Webster Tarpley and Rogue Networks*. The invisible government is not separate from the Bush, Rove, Cheney and Rumsfeld clique. On WWW at http://desip.igc.org/WebsterT.html.

Blommaert, J. (2005) *Discourse*. Cambridge: Cambridge University Press.

Bodenhausen, G.V. and Wyer, R.S. (1985) Effect of stereotypes on decision making and information-processing strategies. *Journal of Experimental Social Psychology* 48, 267–282.

Boggs, S.W. (1947) Cartohypnosis. *Scientific Monthly* 64, 469–476.

Brekle, H.E. (1989) War with words. In R. Wodak (ed.) *Language, Power, and Ideology: Studies in Political Discourse* (pp. 81–91). Amsterdam: John Benjamins Publishing.

Brockway, E.M. (2007) The portrayal or the Middle East in secondary school U.S. textbooks. Unpublished thesis for Master of Public Administration. Bowling Green State University, Bowling Green.

Bronner, E. (2008). Israel Rejects Cease-Fire, but offers Gaza Aid. *The New York Times*. Retrieved from http://www.nytimes.com/2009/01/01/world/middleeast/01mideast.html

Burke, K. (1968) *Counter-Statement*. Berkeley: University of California Press.

Burr, V. (1995) *An Introduction to Social Constructionism*. London: Routledge.

Burr, V. (2003) *Social Constructionism*. London: Routledge.

Busselle, R. and Crandall, H. (2002) Television viewing and perceptions about race differences in socioeconomic success. *Journal of Broadcasting & Electronic Media* 46, 265–282.

BZU (1989) The Crimination of Education: Academic Freedom & Human Rights at Birzeit University During the Palestinian Uprising, Public Relation Office, Birzeit University, December, 1989.

Caldas-Coulthard, C.R. (2003) Cross-cultural representation of 'otherness' in media discourse. In G. Weiss and R. Wodak (eds) *Critical Discourse Analysis: Theory and Interdisciplinarity* (pp. 272–296). Hampshire: Palgrave Macmillan Ltd.

Carey, J.W. (1992:1989) *Communication as Culture: Essays on Media and Society* (2nd edn). New York: Routledge.

Carter, J. (2006) *Palestine Peace not Apartheid*. New York: Simon & Schuster.

Cesaire, A. (2000) *Discourse on Colonialism*. New York: Monthly Review Press.

Chetrit, S. (2004) *The Oriental Struggle in Israel*. Am Oved Publisher.

Chomsky, N. (2004) *Hegemony or Survival: America's Quest for Global Dominance*. New York: Owl Books.

Chouliaraki, L. and Fairclough, N. (1999) *Discourse in Late Modernity: Rethinking Critical Discourse Analysis*. Edinburgh: Edinburgh University Press.

Chuh, K. (2005) Edward Said in counterpoint. *Amerasia Journal* 31, 22–24.

Cochran-Smith, M. and Lytle, S.L. (2009) *Inquiry as Stance: Practitioner for the Next Generation*. New York: Teachers College Press.

Coffin, C. (1997) An investigation into secondary school history. In F. Christie and J.R. Martin (eds) *Genres and the Institutions* (pp.161–196). London: Continuum.

Cohen, A., Adoni, H. and Bantz, C.R. (1990) *Social Conflict and Television News*. Newbury Park, CA: Sage.

Cohen, S. (1989) Education as crime. *The Jerusalem Post* May 18.

Commerson, R. (2009) Redefining deaf. On WWW at http://www.mosinternational.com/movie.html. Accessed 29.6.09.

Cook, S.W. (1984) Cooperative interaction in multiethnic contexts. In N. Miller and M. Brewer (eds) *Groups in Contact: The Psychology of Desegregation* (pp. 155–185). New York: Academic Press.

Creveld, V.M. (2003) The Observer Guardian, The War Game, a controversial view of the current crisis in the Middle East, 21 September 2003; the original interview appeared in the Dutch weekly magazine: Elsevier, 2002, no. 17, p. 52–53 (April 27th, 2002).

Crystal, D. (2003) *English as a Global Language* (2nd edn). New York: Cambridge University Press.

CWS (2000) *Political Perspectives of Challenging White Supremacy Workshops*. San Francisco: The Tides Center.

David, R. (1993) *Arabs and Israel, for Beginners*. New York: Writers and Readers Publishing Inc., Beginners Documentary Comic Books.

Davies, L. (2004) *Education and Conflict: Complexity and Chaos*. London: RoutledgeFalmer.

Demo, D. (2001) *Discourse Analysis for Language Teachers (Report No. EDO-FL-01-07)*. Washington: Center for Applied Linguistics, ERIC Clearinghouse on Languages and Linguistics.

Dershowitz, A. (2003) *The Case for Israel*. Hoboken, NJ: John Wiley & Sons, Inc.

Devine, P. (1989) Stereotypes and prejudice: Their automatic and controlled components. *Journal of Personality and Social Psychology* 56, 5–18.

Domka, E., Urbach, H. and Goldberg, Z. (2009) *Nationality: Building a State in the Middle East*. Jerusalem: Zalman Shazar Centre.

Dovidio, J. and Gaertner, S. (1986) *Prejudice, Discrimination, and Racism*. New York: Academic Press.

Durkin, K. and Judge, J. (2001) Effects of language and social behavior on children's reactions to foreign people in television. *British Journal of Developmental Psychology* 19, 597–612.

Edge, J. (ed.) (2006) *(Re)Locating TESOL in an Age of Empire*. London: Palgrave/Macmillan.

Ehlich, K. (ed.) (1989) *Sprache im Faschismus (Language under Fascism)*. Frankfurt: Suhrkamp.

Eldar, Tz. and Yafe, L. (1998) *From Conservatism to Progress (A History Textbook for Grade 8)*. Tel Aviv: Maalot Publishers.

Erikson, E. (1968) *Identity: Youth and Crisis*. New York: Norton.

Erlanger, S. (2008, December). An Egyptian Boarder Town's Commerce, Conducted via Tunnels, Comes to Halt. *The New York Times*. Retrieved from http://www.nytimes.com/2009/01/01/world/middleeast/01rafah.html?_r = 1.

Esposito, J.L. (1988) *Islam: The Straight Path*. Oxford: Oxford University Press.

Esposito, J.L. (1996) American perceptions of Islam and Arabs. *The Diplomat* 1, 10–11.

Essed, Ph. (1991) *Understanding Everyday Racism. An Interdisciplinary Theory. Sage Series on Race and Ethnic Relations* (Vol. 2). London: Sage Publications.

FAIR (2002). In U.S. Media, Palestinian Attack, Israel Retaliates. Retrieved from www.fair.org/activism/network-retaliation.html.

Fairclough, N. (1989) *Language and Power*. London: Longman.

Fairclough, N. (1992) *Discourse and Social Change*. Cambrige, MA: Polity Press.

Fairclough, N. (1993) Critical discourse analysis and the marketization of public discourse: The universities. *Discourse & Society* 4, 133–168.

Fairclough, N. (1995) *Critical Discourse Analysis: The Critical Study of Language*. London: Longman.

Fairclough, N. (2001) The dialectics of discourse. *Textus* 14, 231–242.

Fairclough, N. (2005) Peripheral vision – Discourse analysis in organization studies: The case of critical realism. *Organization Studies* 26, 915–939.

Fairclough, N. and Wodak, R. (1997) Critical discourse analysis. In T. van Dijk (ed.) *Introduction to Discourse Analysis* (pp. 258–284). London: Sage.

Falk, M. (1996) *Blessing of Peace. The Book of Blessings*. San Francisco: HarperCollins.

Fanon, F. (1963) *The Wretched of the Earth*. New York: Grove Press.

Fanon, F. (1967) *Black Skin, White Mask*. New York: Grove Press.

Fanon, F. (1994) *A Dying Colonialism*. New York: Grove Press.

Fein, S. and Spencer, S.J. (1997) Prejudice as self-image maintenance: Affirming the self through negative evaluations of others. *Journal of Personality and Social Psychology* 73, 31–44.

Fine, Tz., Segev, M. and Lavi, R. (2002) Israel – The Man and the Space- Selected Chapters Geography. Tel Aviv. The Center for educational Technologies Pub.

Finkelstein, N.G. (2003) *The Holocaust Industry: Reflections on the Exploitation of Jewish Suffering* (2nd edn). London: Verso.

Firer, R. (1985) *The Agents of Zionist Education*. Tel Aviv: Hakibutz HaMeuhad and Sifriyat Poalim.

Firer, R. (2004) The presentation of the Israeli-Palestinian conflict in Israeli history and civics textbooks. In R. Firer and S. Adwan (eds) *The Israeli-Palestinian Conflict in Israeli History and Civics Textbooks of Both Nations*. Hannover: Georg-Eckert-Institute für Internationale Schulbuchforschung Verlag Hahnsche Buchhandlung.

Fishman, J.A. (1956) An examination of the process and function of social stereo-typing. *Journal of Social Psychology* 43, 27–64.

Freire, P. (1970) *Pedagogy of the Oppressed* (M. Bergman Ramos, trans.). New York: Herder & Herder.

Freire, P. (1985) *The Politics of Education*. New York: Bergin & Garvey Publishers.

Freire, P. (1995) A dialogue: Culture, language, and race. *Harvard Educational Review* 65, 377–402.

Freire, P. (1998a) *Pedagogy of the Oppressed*. New York: Continuum.

Freire, P. (1998b) *Pedagogy of Hope: Reliving Pedagogy of the Oppressed*. New York: Continuum.

Gairola, R. (2005) Queering orientalism: Sexual otherness and Asian American studies. *Amerasia Journal* 31, 27–30.

Gates, H.G.J. (1986) Writing 'race' and the difference it makes. In H.G. Gates (ed.) *Race, Writing, and Difference*. Chicago: The University of Chicago Press.

Gee, J.P. (1999) *An Introduction to Discourse Analysis: Theory and Method*. New York: Routledge.

Geertz, C. (1973) *The Interpretation of Cultures*. New York: Basic Books.

Giddens, A. (1979) *Central Problems in Social Theory*. Berkeley: University of California Press.

Goffman, E. (1981) *Forms of Talk*. Philadelphia: University of Pennsylvania.

Gonzáles, N., Moll, L.C. and Amanti, C. (eds) (2005) *Funds of Knowledge: Theorizing Practices in Households, Communities, and Classrooms*. Mahwah, NJ: Lawrence Erlbaum Associates.

Gordon, N. (2008) From colonialization to separation: Exploring the structure of Israel's occupation. *Third World Quarterly* 29, 25–44.

Gramsci, A., Hoare, Q. and Smith, G.N. (1971) *Selections from the Prison Notebooks of Antonio Gramsci*. New York: International Publishers.

Greenberg, B.S. and Brand, J. (1994) Minorities and the mass media: 1970s to 1990s. In J. Bryant and D. Zillmann (eds) *Media Effects: Advances in Theory and Research* (pp. 273–314). Hove, NJ: Lawrence Erlbaum Associates.

Greenberg, B.S. and Collette, L. (1997) The changing faces on TV: A demographic analysis of network television's new seasons, 1966–1992. *Journal of Broadcasting and Electronic Media* 41, 1–13.

Grice, H.P. (1969) Utterer's meaning and intentions. *The Philosophical Review* 78, 147–177.

Grice, H.P. (1975) Logic and conversation. In P. Cole and J. Morgan (eds) *Syntax and Semantics, 3: Speech Acts*. New York: Academic Press.

Gutierrez, K. and Stone, L. (2000) Synchronic and diachronic dimensions of social practice: An emerging methodology for cultural-historical perspectives on literacy learning. In C. Lee and P. Smagorinsky (eds) *Vygotskian Perspectives on Literacy Research: Constructing Meaning Through Collaborative Inquiry* (pp. 150–164). Cambridge: Cambridge University Press.

Habermas, J. (1970) Towards a theory of communicative competence. *Inquiry* 13, 360–375.

Habermas, J. (1971) *Knowledge and Human Interests*. Boston: Beacon Press.

Haddad, Y.Y. (1991a) American foreign policy in the Middle East and its impact on the identity of Arab Muslims in the United States. In Y.Y. Haddad (ed.) *The Muslims of America* (pp. 217–235). New York: Oxford University Press.

Haddad, Y.Y. (1991b) *The Muslims of America*. New York: Oxford University Press.

Haddad, Y.Y. and Smith, J.I. (eds) (2002) *Muslim Minorities in the West: Visible and Invisible*. Walnut Creek, CA: AltaMira Press.

Haider, J. and Rodriguez, L. (1995) Power and ideology in different discursive practices. In C. Schaffner and A.L. Wenden (eds) *Language and Peace* (pp. 119–135). Dartmouth: England.

Halabi, R. (ed.) (2004) *Israeli and Palestinian Identities in Dialogue*. New Brunswick, NJ: Rutgers University Press.

Halabi, R. (2006) *Citizens of Equal Duties: Druze Identity and the Jewish State*. Tel Aviv: Hakibbutz Hameuchad. (In Hebrew).

Halabi, R. and Sonnenschein, N. (2004) The Jewish-Palestinian encounter in time of crisis. *Journal of Social Issues* 60, 373–389.

Halabi, R. and Zak, M. (2007) *Palestinian-Jewish Youth Encounters at the School for Peace*. Jerusalem: The School for Peace Research Center.

Hale, S. (2005) Edward Said – Accidental feminist: Orientalism and Middle East women's studies. *Amerasia Journal* 31, 1–5.

Hallaj, M. (1980) Mission of Palestinian higher education. In E.A. Nakhleh (ed.) *A Palestine Agenda for West Bank and Gaza*. Washington, DC: American Enterprise Institute.

Halliday, M.A.K. (1978) *Language as Social Semiotic*. Lonon: Edward Arnold.

Hamilton, D.L. and Bishop, G.D. (1976) Attitudinal and behavioral effects of initial integration of white suburban neighborhoods. *Journal of Social Issues* 32, 47–67.

Hashemite Kingdom of Jordan, Department of Statistics (1951–1665). *Statistical Yearbook*. On WWW at http://www.dos.gov.jo/home. March 20th, 2011.

HDR (2005) Human Development Report of Palestine 2004. Birzeit University, Palestine.

Heller, M. (ed.) (2007) *Bilingualism: A Social Approach*. Hampshire: Palgrave Macmillan.

Henrikson, A.K. (1994) The power and politics of maps. In G.J. Demko and W.B. Wood (eds) *Reordering the World: Geopolitical Perspective on the 21st Century* (pp. 50–70). San Francisco: Westview Press.

Hertz-Lazarowitz, R. (2004) Existence and coexistence in Acre: The power of educational activism. *Journal of Social Issues* 60, 357–373.

Hewstone, M. and Brown, R. (1986) Contact is not enough: An intergroup perspective on the 'contact hypothesis'. In M. Hewstone and R. Brown (eds) *Contact and Conflict in Intergroup Encounters* (pp. 1–44). Cambridge: Basil Blackwell.

Hicks, D. (1980) Images of the world: An introduction to bias in teaching materials. *Accidental Paper no. 2*. Center for Multicultural Education. London: Institute of Education.

Holly, W. (1989) Credibility and political language. In R. Wodak (ed.) *Language, Power, and Ideology: Studies in Political Discourse* (pp. 115–137). Amsterdam: John Benjamins Publishing.

Hymes, D.H. (1966) Two types of linguistic relativity. In W. Bright (ed.) *Sociolinguistics* (pp. 114–167). The Hague: Mouton.

Hymes, D.H. (1971) *On Communicative Competence*. Philadelphia: University of Pennsylvania Press.

If Americans Knew (2004) Media report cards. In *If Americans Knew*. On WWW at http://www.ifamericansknew.org/media/report_cards.html. Accessed 10.01.09.

Inbar, Sh. (2004) *50 Years of Wars and Hopes*. Tel Aviv: Lilach Publishers.

Isaacs, W. (1999) *Dialogue: The Art of Thinking Together*. New York: Random House.

Jabareen, Y. (2006) Law and education: Critical perspectives on Arab Palestinian education in Israel. *American Behavioral Scientist* 49, 1052–1074.

Jad, I. (2004) The NGOization of arab women's movements. In A. Cornwall, E. Harrison and A. Whitehead (eds) *Feminisms in Development: Contradictions, Contestations and Challenges* (pp. 177–190). London, New York: Zed Books Ltd.

Jerusalem Media (1989) *Palestinian Education; A Threat to Israel's Security*. The Jerusalem Media and Communication Center, Jerusalem.

Johnson, P. and Tailor, M. (1990) *The Israeli Occupied Territories (Palestine) Academic Freedom* (pp. 73–104). Geneva: World University Service.

Karayanni, M.M. (2007) Multiculture me no more! On multicultural qualifications and the Palestinian-Arab minority of Israel. *Diogenes* 54, 39–58.

Katz, D. and Braly, K. (1933) Racial stereotypes of one hundred college students. *Journal of Abnormal and Social Psychology* 28, 280–290.

Kaufman, G. (2009) UK Jewish MP: Israel acting like Nazis in Gaza. On WWW at http://www.youtube.com/watch?v=qMGuYjt6CP8. Accessed 18.1.09.

Kelman, H.C. (1998) Social-psychological contributions to peacemaking and peace-building in the Middle East. *Applied Psychology: An International Review* 47, 5–28.

Khan, M.A.M. (1998) Muslim and identity politics in America. In Y.Y. Haddad and J.L. Esposito (eds) *Muslims on the Americanization Path?* (pp. 87–104). Atlanta: Scholars Press.

Kline, N. (2003) 'On rescuing private lynch and forgetting Rachel Corrie'. *The Washington Report on Middle East Affairs* 22 (6), 27.

Kramarae, C., Schulz, M. and O'Barr, W.M. (1984) *Language and Power*. London: Sage Publications.

Kreshner, I. and El-Khodary, T. (2009) Escalation Feared as Israel, Continuing Boming, Lets Foreigners Leave Gaza. *The New York Times*. Retrieved from http://www.nytimes.com/2009/01/03/world/middleeast/03mideast.html.

Kress, G.R. (1989) *Linguistic Processes in Sociocultural Practice*. Oxford: Oxford University Press.

Kress, G.R. (2003) *Literacy in the New Media Age*. London: Routledge.

Kress, G.R. and Van Leeuwen, T. (1996) *Reading Images: The Grammar of Visual Design*. London: Routledge.

Kunda, Z. and Oleson, K.C. (1995) Maintaining stereotypes in the face of disconfirmation: Constructing grounds for subtyping deviants. *Journal of Personality and Social Psychology* 68, 565–579.

La Capra, D. (2001) *Writing Shoa, Writing Trauma*. Baltimore, MD: Johns Hopkins University Press.

Lakoff, G. (2004) *Don't Think of an Elephant! Know Your Values and Frame the Debate*. White River Junction, VT: Chelsea Green Publishing.

Lakoff, R.T. (1990) *Talking Power: The Politics of Language*. San Francisco: Basic Books.

Lakoff, R.T. (2000) *The Language War*. Berkeley, CA: University of California Press.

Lantolf, J. (2000) *Sociocultural Theory and Second Language Learning*. Oxford: Oxford University Press.

Lantolf, J. and Appel, G. (eds) (1996) *Vygotskian Approaches to Second Language Research*. Norwood, NJ: Ablex Publishing Corporation.

Laor, Y. (2008) *The Place Where Even Jews Can be as White as Paul Newman*. Seattle, WA: Jesse and John Danz Lecturer.

Lederman, J. (1992) *Battle Lines: The American Media and the Intifada*. New York: Holt & Co.

Lee, C. (2000) Signifying in the zone of proximal development. In C. Lee and P. Smogorinsky (eds) *Vygotskian Perspectives on Literacy Research: Constructing Meaning through Collaborative Inquiry* (pp. 191–225). Cambridge: Cambridge University Press.

Lemke, J. (1998) Metamedia literacy: Transforming meaning and media. In D. Reinking, L. Labbo, M. McKenna and R. Kiefer (eds) *Handbook of Literacy and Technology: Transformations in a Post-Typographic World* (pp. 283–301). Hillsdale, NJ: Lawrence Erlbaum Associates.

Lewin, K. (1948) *Resolving Social Conflicts: Selected Papers on Group Dynamics*. New York: Harper & Row.

Lin, A. and Luke, A. (2006) Coloniality, postcoloniality and TESOL. *Critical Inquiry in Language Studies* 3, 2–3.

Lippmann, W. (1922) *Public Opinion*. New York: Harcourt, Brace, and Co.

Livingston, S. (1996) *Beyond the CNN Effect: An Examination of Media Effects According to Type of Intervention*. Cambridge, MA: Shorenstein Center on Press, Politics and Public Policy, Kennedy School of Government, Harvard University.

Luke, A. (1995) Text and discourse in education: An introduction to critical discourse analysis. *Review of Research in Education* 21, 3–48.

Luke, A. (1997) Theory and practice in critical science discourse. In L. Saha (ed.) *International Encyclopedia of the Sociology of Education*. On WWW at http://www.gseis.ucla.edu/courses/ed253a/Luke/SAHA6.html. Accessed 6.12.08.

Machlis, D. (2009) US gets Israeli security for Super Bowl. *Jerusalem Post*. On WWW at http://www.jpost.com. Accessed 4.2.07.

Mackie, D. and Smith, E.R. (1998) Intergroup relations: Insights from a theoretically integrative approach. *Psychological Review* 105, 499–529.

Malloy, W. (2009) A Florida terrorism suspect's legal odyssey. On WWW at http://www.time.com/time/nation/article/0,8599,1885855,00.html#ixzz0aFVciQCl. Accessed 18.03.09.

Maoz, I. (2000) Power relations in intergroup encounters: A case study of Jewish-Arab encounters in Israel. *International Journal of Intercultural Relations* 24, 259–277.

Maoz, I. (2004) Coexistence is in the eye of the beholder: Evaluating intergroup encounter interventions between Jews and Arab in Israel. *Journal of Social Issues* 60, 403–418.

Mapping Dialogue (2006) *A Research Project Profiling Dialogue Tools and Processes for Social Change*. Johannesburg: Pioneers of Change Associates (Commissioned by the GTZ and the Mandela Foundation).

Masalha, N. (1992) *Expulsion of the Palestinians: The Concept of 'Transfer' in Zionist Political Thought 1882–1948*. Washington: Institute for Palestine Studies.

Mazen, A. (2005) Little Jihad is Over, Big Jihad Starts (Israel National News). January 10.

Mazzetti, M. (2008, December) Striking Deep into Israel, Hamas Employs an Upgraded Arsenal. *The New York Times*. Retrieved from http://www.nytimes.com/2009/01/01/world/middleeast/01rockets.html.

Mearsheimer, J.J. and Walt, S.M. (2007) *The Israel Lobby and U.S. Foreign Policy*. New York: Farrar, Straus and Giroux.

Memmi, A. (1965) *The Colonizer and the Colonized*. Boston: Beacon Press.

Menz, F. (1989) Manipulation strategies in newspapers: A program for critical linguistics. In R. Wodak (ed.) *Language, Power, and Ideology: Studies in Political Discourse* (pp. 227–247). Amsterdam: John Benjamins Publishing.

Miller, A. (1982) *In the Eye of the Beholder.* New York: Praeger Publishers.

Moll, L. (ed.) (1990) *Vygotsky and Education: Instructional Implications and Applications of Sociohistorical Psychology.* Cambridge: Cambridge University Press.

Moraes, M. (1996) *Bilingual Education: A Dialogue with the Bakhtin Circle.* Albany: State University of New York Press.

Morgan, H. (2008) American school textbooks: How they portrayed the middle east from 1898–1994. In N.J. Wessley (ed.) *American Educational History Journal* 35, 315–330.

Mullen, B., Rozell, D. and Johnson, C. (2000) Ethnophaulisms for ethnic immigrant groups: Cognitive representation of 'the minority' and 'the foreigner'. *Group Process and Intergroup Relations* 3, 5–24.

Myers-Scotton, C. (1997) Code-switching. In F. Coulmas (ed.) *The Handbook of Sociolinguistics* (pp. 217–237). Oxford: Blackwell Publishers Inc.

Myre, G. (2003) Israeli army bulldozer kills American protesting in Gaza. *New York Times* March 17.

Naber, N. (2000) Ambiguous insiders: An investigation of Arab American invisibility. *Ethnic and Racial Studies* 23, 37–61.

Nasser, I. and Assaf, M. (2008) Dialogue under occupation. *International Feminist Journal of Politics* 10, 247–255.

Nathanson, A., Wilson, B.J., McGee, J. and Sebastian, M. (2002) Counteracting the effects of female stereotypes on television via active mediation. *Journal of Communication* 52, 922–937.

Nave, E., Vered, N. and Shahar, D. (2009) *Nationality in Israel and the Nations: Building a State in the Middle East.* Tel Aviv: Rehes Publishers.

Neisser, E. (1994) Hate speech in the new South Africa: Constitutional considerations for a land recovering from decades of racial repression and violence. *South African Journal of Human Rights* 10, 336–356.

Nieto, S. (2000) *Affirming Diversity: The Sociopolitical Context of Multicultural Education.* New York: Longman.

Nieto, S., Schaller, M. and Conway, L.G. III (2001) From cognition to culture: The origins of stereotypes that really matter. In G.B. Moskowitz (ed.) *Cognitive Social Psychology: The Princeton Symposium on theLegacy and Future of Social Cognition* (pp. 163–176). Mahwah, NJ: Lawrence Erlbaum Associates.

Nora, P. (1999) *Rethinking France: Les Lieux de mémoire Volume 1: The State.* Chicago: University of Chicago Press.

Olshtain, E. and Nissim-Amitai, F. (2004a) Being trilingual or multilingual – Is there a price to pay? In C. Hoffman and J. Ytsma (eds) *Trilingualism in Family, School and Community* (pp. 30–50). Clevedon: Multilingual Matters.

Olshtain, E. and Nissim-Amitai, F. (2004b) Curriculum decision-making in a multilingual context. *International Journal of Multilingualism* 1, 53–64.

Orfalea, G. (1988) *Before the Flames: A Quest for the History of Arab Americans.* Austin: University of Texas Press.

Pappe, I. (2007) *The Ethnic Cleansing of Palestine.* Oxford: Oneworld Publications.

Peled-Elhanan, N. (2006) The presentation of Palestinians in Israeli schoolbooks of History and Geography, 1998–2003. Paper presented at the Dialogue Under Occupation Conference (DUO II), Al Quds University, Abu Dis, Palestine.

Peled-Elhanan, N. (2010) Legitimation of massacres in Israeli schoolbooks. *Discourse and Society* 21, 377–404.

Pennsylvania Department of Education (2006) On WWW at http://www/education.state.pa.us/learnerslivesascurriculum. Accessed 28.5.11.

Perez, E. (1999) *The Decolonial Imaginary: Writing Chicanas into History (Theories of Representation and Difference).* Bloomington: Indiana University Press.

Pettigrew, T.F. (1998) Intergroup contact theory. *Annual Review of Psychology* 49, 65–85.

Pettigrew, T.F. and Tropp, L. (2000) Does intergroup contact reduce prejudice? Recent meta-analytic findings. In S. Oskamp (ed.) *Reducing Prejudice and Discrimination* (pp. 93–114). Mahwah, NJ: Erlbaum.

Phan, L.H. (2005) Toward a critical notion of appropriation of English as an international language. In P. Robertson, P. Dash and J. Jung (eds) *English Language Learning in the Asian Context* (2nd edn). Hong Kong: The Asian EFL Journal Press.

Phinney, J.S. (1995) Ethnic identity and self-esteem: A review and integration. In A.M. Padilla (ed.) *Hispanic Psychology: Critical Issues in Theory and Research* (pp. 57–70). Thousand Oaks, CA: Sage.

Pinker, S. (2007) *The Stuff of Thought: Language as a Window into Human Nature.* New York: Penguin Books.

Piterberg, G. (2001) Erasures. *New Left Review* (Vol. 10) (pp. 31–46). London: New Left Review LTD.

PNA, Ministry of Education (2004) *Expansion & Annexation Wall and Its Impact on the Educational Process (Palestine).* On WWW at http://www.mohe.gov.ps/reports. Retrieved on December 2009.

PNA, Ministry of Education (2006a) *Summary of Educational Statistics in Palestine 2005–2006 (Rammalah, Palestine).* On WWW at www.miftah.org/Doc/Factsheets/Other/assessment15.pdf. Retrieved on December 2009.

PNA, Ministry of Education (2006b) *The Effect of the Israeli Occupation on the Palestinian Education from (28/9/2000–25/8/2006) (Rammalah, Palestine).* On WWW at www.miftah.org/Doc/Factsheets/Other/assessment15.pdf. Retrieved on December 2009.

PNA, Palestinian Information Center (2006) The Israeli aggression on the Palestinian Education Sector 28/9/2000–12/4/2006 (State Information Center).

Podeh, E. (2002) *The Arab Israeli Conflict in Israeli History Textbooks, 1948–2000.* London: Bergin and Garvey.

Postero, N. (2005) Indigenous responses to neoliberalism: A look at the Bolivian Uprising of 2003. *Political and Legal Anthropology Review* 28, 78–92.

Pulcini, T. (1993) Trends in research on Arab Americans. *Journal of American Ethnic History* 12, 27–60.

Quasthoff, U.M. (1989) Social prejudice as a source of power: Towards the functional ambivalence of stereotypes. In R. Wodak (ed.) *Language, Power, and Ideology: Studies in Political Discourse* (pp. 181–196). Amsterdam: John Benjamins Publishing.

Rabinowitz, D. (2001) Natives with jackets and degrees. Othering, objectification and the role of Palestinians in the co-existence field in Israel. *Social Anthropology* 9, 65–80. Copyright 2001 European Association of Social Anthropologists.

Rabinowitz, D. and Abubakr, K. (2002) *The Stand-Tall Generation.* Jerusalem: Keter (Hebrew).

Rap, E. and Fine, Tz. (1996/1998) *People in Space (A Geography Textbook for 9th Grade).* Tel Aviv: The Centre for Educational Technologies Publishers.

Reisigl, M. and Wodak, R. (2001) *Discourse and Discrimination: Rhetoric of Racism and Anti-Semitism.* London: Routledge.

Reuveny, R. (2009) Healing and reality in the Israeli-Palestinian conflict. *Tikkun* 77, 46–50.

Rouhana, N. (1997) *Identities in Conflict: Palestinian Citizens in Ethnic Jewish State.* New Haven, CT: Yale University Press.

Rouhana, N. (2006) Zionism's encounter with the Palestinians: The dynamics of force, fear, and extremism. In R.I. Rotberg (ed.) *Israeli and Palestinian Narratives of Conflict* (pp. 115–141). Bloomington: Indiana University Press.

Rouhana, N. and Korper, S. (1997) Power asymmetry and goals of unofficial third party interrelations in protracted intergroup conflict. *Peace and Conflict: Journal of Psychology* 3, 1–17.

Rudd, P.W. (2004) Weapons of mass destruction: The unshared referents of Bush's rhetoric. *Pragmatics* 14, 499–525.

Shakhshir, K. (1990) Understanding the feeling of the Palestinian children toward their national cause. *Arab Journal for Humanities* 38, 138–157.

Shakhshir, K. (1994) *The Education System in the West Bank and Gaza Strip.* Geneva: UNCTAD.

Shakhshir, K. (1996) *Women and Education in Palestine.* Palestine: The Palestinian Women Union Publication.

Shakhshir, K. (2003) *Evaluation of the Palestinian New Curricula.* Palestine: Social, Political and Economic Research Forum.

Shakhshir, K., Abu-Dagga, S. and Mohamad, R. (2006) *Policies to Improve the Quality of the Teaching Profession in Palestine.* Palestine: MAS Publication.

Shaath, N. (1972) High level Palestinian manpower. *Journal of Palestinian Studies* XX, 79–96.

Sai, K. (2006) American occupation of the Hawaiian state: A century unchecked. Paper presented at the Dialogue under Occupation conference, Northeastern Illinois University, Chicago, IL.

Said, E. (1978) *Orientalism.* London: Routledge & Kegan Paul.

Said, E. (1993) *Culture and Imperialism.* New York: Knopf, Inc.

Said, E. (1997) *Orientalism: Western Conceptions of the Orient.* New York: Pantheon.

Said, E. (2000) *Out of Place: A Memoir.* New York: Vintage.

Said, E. (2001) Propaganda and war. *Al-Ahram Weekly.* On WWW at: http://www.mediamonitors.net/edward37.html. Accessed 27.12.08.

Said, E. (2009) Edward Said: On Orientalism. On WWW at http://www.mediaed.org/cgi-bin/commerce.cgi?preadd=action&key=403-P-&template=PDGCommTemplates/HTN/Item_Preview.html. Retrieved on December 2009.

Salaita, S. (2005) Ethnic identity and imperative patriotism: Arab Americans before and after 9/11. *College Literature* 32, 146–168.

Salameh, N. and Zak, M. (2006) *Media and the Conflict: Two Articles on a Project Partnership.* Unpublished manuscript. Submitted to the EU Partnership for Peace program.

Samhan, H. (1999) Not quite white: Race classification and the Arab-American experience. In M. Suleiman (ed.) *Arabs in America: Building a New Future* (pp. 209–226). Philadelphia: Temple University Press.

Sarroub, L.K. (2001) The sojourner experience of Yemeni American high school students: An ethnographic portrait. *Harvard Educational Review* 71, 37–49.

Scannell, P. (1991) Introduction: The relevance of talk. In P. Scannell (ed.) *Broadcast Talk* (pp. 1–13). London: Sage Publications, Ltd.

Schaller, M. and Conway, L.G. III (2001) From cognition to culture: The origins of stereotypes that really matter. In G.B. Moskowitz (ed.) *Cognitive Social Psychology: The Princeton Symposium on the Legacy and Future of Social Cognition* (pp. 163–176). Mahwah, NJ: Lawrence Erlbaum Associates.

Schechter, D. (2003) *Media Wars: News at Time of Terror.* New York: Roman and Littlefield Publishers.

Schein, E.H. (1982) What to observe in a group. In L. Porter and B. Mohr (eds) *Reading Book for Human Relations Training* (pp. 68–71). Bethel, ME: NTL Institute Publications.

Scheurich, J. (1993) Toward a white discourse on white racism. *Educational Researcher* 22, 5–10.

Schjerve, R.R. (1989) The political language of Futurism and its relationship to Italian. In R. Wodak (ed.) *Language, Power, and Ideology: Studies in Political Discourse* (pp. 3–73). Amsterdam: John Benjamins Publishing.

Schneider, D.J. (2005) *The Psychology of Stereotyping.* New York: Guilford Press.

Schwartz, M. (2008) Special power. *The Magazine for Marketing Strategies.* On WWW at: http://www.btobonline.com/apps/pbcs.dll/article?AID=/20080505/FREE/16268957/1151/ISSUENEWS#seenit. Accessed 12.01.09.

Searle, J.R. (1969) *Speech Acts: An Essay in the Philosophy of Language.* Cambridge: Cambridge University Press.

Segev, M. and Fine, Z. (2007) *People and Settlements.* Tel Aviv: The Centre for Educational Technologies.

Seikaly, Z.A. (2001) At risk of prejudice: The Arab American community. *Social Education* 65, 349–351.

Shaheen, J. (1988) The media image of Arabs. *Newsweek* 126, 48–52.

Shaheen, J. (2000) Hollywood's Muslim Arabs. *The Muslim World* 90, 22–38.

Shaheen, J. (2001) *Reel Bad Arabs: How Hollywood Vilifies a People.* Northampton, MA: Olive Branch Press.

Shaheen, J. (2008) *Guilty: Hollywood's Verdict on Arabs after 9/11.* Northampton, MA: Olive Branch Press.

Shenhav, Y. (2003) *Jews–Arabs: Nationality, Religion and Ethnicity.* Tel Aviv: Am Oved (Hebrew).

Shenhav, Y. (2006) *The Arab Jews: A Postcolonial Reading of Nationalism, Religion, and Ethnicity.* Palo Alto, CA: Stanford University Press.

Sherif, M., Harvey, O.J., White, B.J., Hood, W.R. and Sherif, C.W. (1961) *Intergroup Conflict and Cooperation: The Robber's Cave Experiment.* Norman, OK: University of Oklahoma Press.

Shiffer, V. (1999) The Haredi educational system: Allocation, regulation and control. *The Floersheimer Institute for Policy Studies* 4, 1–50.

Shohamy, E. (2008) At what cost? Methods of language revival and protection: Examples from Hebrew. In K.A. King, N. Schilling-Estes, L. Fogle, J.J. Lou and B. Soukup (eds) *Sustaining Linguistic Diversity: Endangered and Minority Language Varieties* (pp. 205–219). Washington, DC: Georgetown University Press.

Sibii, R. and Napoleone A.R. (2009, March) Dialogue about occupation: An ideological analysis of DUO II discourse. Paper presented at the Dialogue Under Occupation III Conference, Bogota, Colombia.

Silberstein, S., Doyle, A., Eastman, C. and Watkins, E. (1998) Talking peace, waging war: Mining the language of leadership. In J. O'Mealy and L. Lyons (eds) *The Language of Leadership (Literary Studies East and West 15)*. Honolulu, HI: University of Hawaìi East-West Center.

Smith, L.T. (2006) Choosing the margins: The role of research in indigenous struggles for social justice. In N.K. Denzin and M.D. Giardina (eds) *Qualitative Inquiry and the Conservative Challenge* (pp. 151–174). Walnut Creek, CA: Left Coast.

Smooha, S. (1997) Ethnic democracy: Israel as an archetype. *Israel Studies* 2, 198–241.

Smooha, S. (2001) *The Model of Ethnic Democracy*. Flensburg, Germany: European Centre for Minority Issues.

Smooha, S. (2005) *Index of Arab-Jewish Relations in Israel 2004*. Haifa, Israel: The Jewish-Arab Center, the University of Haifa.

Solórzano, D.G. and Yosso, T.J. (2009) Critical race methodology: Counterstorytelling as an analytical framework for educational research. In E. Taylor, D. Gillborn and F. Ladson-Billings (eds) *Foundations of Critical Race Theory* (pp. 131–147). New York: Routledge.

Spolsky, B. and Shohamy, E. (1999) Language in Israeli society and education. *International Journal of the Sociology of Language* 137, 93–114.

Statistical Abstract of Palestine (1943) *Statistical Abstract of Palestine* (7th edn) (No. 11 of 1944). Jerusalem: Department of Statistics.

Steele, C.M. and Aronson, J. (1995) Stereotype threat and the intellectual test performance of African Americans. *Journal of Personality and Social Psychology* 69, 797–811.

Suleiman, R. (2004) Planned encounters between Jewish and Palestinian Israelis: A social–psychological perspective. *Journal of Social Issues* 60, 323–337.

Suleiman, Y. (2004) *A War of Words: Language and Conflict in the Middle East*. Cambridge: Cambridge University Press.

Tahir, J.M. (1985) An assessment of Palestinian human resources: Higher education and manpower. *Journal of Palestinian Studies* 14, 32–36.

Tajfel, H. (1968) Cognitive aspects of prejudice. *Journal of Social Issues* 25, 79–98.

Tajfel, H. (1978) *The Social Psychology of Minorities*. New York: Minority Rights Group.

Tajfel, H. (1981) *Human Groups and Social Categories*. Cambridge: Cambridge University Press.

Thompson, J.B. (1987) Language and ideology: A framework for analysis. *The Sociological Review* 35, 516–535.

Tibawi, A.L. (1956) *Arab Education in Mandatory Palestine*. London: Luzac & Company, Ltd.

Tibawi, A.L. (1961) *British Interests in Palestine: 1800–1901*. Oxford: Oxford University Press.

Touqan, F. (1970) On WWW at http://www.aklaam.net/forum/showthread.php?t=15913 (in Arabic). Accessed 04.05.11.

Tracy, K. (2001) Discourse analysis in communication. In D. Schiffrin, D. Tannen and H. Hamilton (eds) *The Handbook of Discourse Analysis* (pp. 725–749). Malden, MA: Blackwell Publishing, Ltd.

Tucker, J.B. (2003) Strategies for countering terrorism: Lessons from the Israeli experience. *Journal of Homeland Security*. On WWW at http//www.homelandsecurity.org. Accessed 15.1.09.

Tuckman, B. (1965) Developmental sequence in small groups. *Psychological Bulletin* 63, 384–399. On WWW at http://findarticles.com/p/articles/mi_qa3954/is_200104/ai_n8943663. Accessed 10.11.08.

United Nations (2006, February) *Humanitarian Update; Occupied Palestinian Territory (Jerusalem)*. On WWW at http://www.unicef.org/oPt/index. Accessed 20.3.11.

United Nations (2006, April) *Office for the Coordination of Humanitarian Affairs; Occupied Palestinian Territory (Jerusalem)*. On WWW at www.ochaopt.org. Accessed 20.3.11.

United Nations (2006, November) *Office for the Coordination of Humanitarian Affairs; Occupied Palestinian Territory (Jerusalem)*. On WWW at www.ochaopt.org. Accessed 20.3.11.

United Nations Report of the Human Rights Council (U.N.R.H.R.C.) (2009) 12th special session, 64th session, supplement no. 53A. On WWW at http://unispal.un.org/UNISPAL.NSF/98edce37e189625b85256c40005da81b/d9ffe810b89c0c5f8525766500518f15?OpenDocument. Accessed January, 2010.

United Nations Development Programme (2009) *Arab Human Development Report 2009: Challenges to Human Security in the Arab Countries*. On WWW at http://hdr.undp.org/en/reports/regionalreports/arabstates/ahdr2009e.pdf. Accessed February, 2010.

UNESCO (2002) Developing education in Palestine: A continuing challenge. *Education: Education News*. On WWW at http://www.unesco.org/education/news_en/131101_palestine.shtml. Accessed January, 2002.

UNRWA (1989) *Department of Education Statistical Yearbook 1989–1990* (Vol. 26).

Vaadya, D., Ulman, H. and Mimoni, Z. (1996) *The Mediterranean Countries for 5th Grade*. Tel Aviv: Maalot Publisher.

Van Dijk, T.A. (1994) Discourse and inequality. *Lenguas Modernas* 21, 19–37.

Van Dijk, T.A. (2001) Critical discourse analysis. In D. Schiffrin, D. Tannen and H.E. Hamilton (eds) *The Handbook of Discourse Analysis* (pp. 352–371). Oxford: Blackwell Publishing.

Van Dijk, T.A. (2003) The discourse-knowledge interface. In G. Weiss and R. Wodak (eds) *Critical Discourse Analysis: Theory and Interdisciplinarity* (pp. 85–109). Hampshire: Palgrave Macmillan Ltd.

Van Leeuwen, T. (1992) The schoolbook as a multimodal text. *International Schulbuch Forschung* 14, 35–58.

Van Leeuwen, T. (1996) The representation of social actors. In C.R. Caldas-Coulthard and M. Coulthard (eds) *Texts and Practices: Readings in Critical Discourse Analysis* (pp. 333–352). London: Routledge.

Van Leeuwen, T. (2000) Visual racism. In M. Reisigl and R. Wodak (eds) *The Semiotics of Racism: Approaches in Critical Discourse Analysis* (pp. 333–352). Vienna: Passagen Verlag.

Van Leeuwen, T. (2001) Semiotics and iconography. In T. Van Leeuwen and C. Jewitt (eds) *2001: Handbook of Visual Analysis* (pp. 92–119). London and New York: Sage Publications.

Van Leeuwen, T. (2008) *Discourse and Practice: New Tools for Discourse Analysis*. Oxford: Oxford University Press.

Van Leeuwen, T. and Kress, G. (1995) Critical layout analysis. In *International Schulbuch Forschung* (Vol. 17) (pp. 25–43). Braunschweig: Zeitschrift des George-Eckert-Instituts.

Vaughan, C. (1995) A comparative discourse analysis of editorials on the Lebanon 1982 crisis. In C. Schaffner and A.L. Wenden (eds) *Language and Peace* (Vol. 6, pp. 61–74). Dartmouth: England.

Vološinov, V.N. (1973) *Marxism and the Philosophy of Language* (L. Matejka and I.R. Titunik, trans.) Cambridge, MA: Harvard University Press.

Vygotsky, L.S. (1978) *Mind in Society: The Development of Higher Psychological Processes.* Cambridge: Harvard University Press.

Wa Thiong'o, N. (2005) *Decolonising the Mind: The Politics of Language in African Literature.* Oxford: James Curry.

Wais, E. (2005) Trained incapacity: Thorstein Veblen and Kenneth Burke. *K.B. Journal* 1. On WWW at http://www.kbjournal.org/node/103. Accessed 29.6.09.

Walls, M. (2010) Framing the Israel/Palestine conflict in Swedish history school textbooks. Unpublished Ph.D. dissertation, University of Gothenburg, Sweden.

Waltzer, M. (1987) *Interpretation and Social Criticism.* Massachusetts: Harvard University Press.

War in Gaza: IDF Begins Ground Incursion (2009, January 4). *Fareed Zakaria GPS* [Television broadcast]. Atlanta, GA: CNN.

Warner, M. (2002) *Publics and Counterpublics.* New York: Zone Books [distributed by MIT Press].

Weaver-Hightower, M.B. (2008) An ecology metaphor for educational policy analysis: A call to complexity. *Educational Researcher* 37, 153–167.

Weber, R.C. and Crocker, J. (1983) Cognitive processes in the revision of stereotypic beliefs. *Journal of Personality and Social Psychology* 45, 961–977.

Weber, R.C. (1982) The group: A cycle from birth to death. In L. Porter and B. Mohr (eds) *Reading Book for Human Relations Training* (pp. 68–71). Arlington, VA: NTL Institute Publications.

Weigand, E. (1999) Dialogue in the grip of the media. In B. Naumann (ed.) *Dialogue Analysis and the Mass Media* (pp. 35–54). Tübingen: Max Niemeyer Verla.

Weinstein, G. (1999) *Learners' Lives as Curriculum: Six Journeys to Immigrant Literacy.* McHenry, IL: Delta Systems.

Wells, G.C. (1999) *Dialogic Inquiry Toward a Sociocultural Practice and Theory of Education.* Cambridge: Cambridge University Press.

Witte, G. (2009). Israel's Attacks on Gaza Deepen Palestinian Rift. *The Washington Post.* Retrieved from http://www.washingtonpost.com/wp-dyn/content/article/2008/12/28/AR2008122800115.html.

Wodak, R. (ed.) (1989) *Language, Power, and Ideology: Studies in Political Discourse.* Amsterdam: John Benjamins Publishing.

Wodak, R. (2002) Discourse and politics: The rhetoric of exclusion. In R. Wodak and A. Pelinka (eds) *The Haider Phenomenon* (pp. 33–60). London/New Jersey: Transaction.

Wodak, R. (2007) Pragmatics and critical discourse analysis: A cross-disciplinary analysis. *Pragmatics and Cognition* 15, 203–225.

Wolfsfeld, G. (1997) *Media and Political Conflict: News from the Middle East.* Cambridge: Cambridge University Press.

Wong, S. (1994) Dialogic approaches to teacher research: Lessening the tension. *TESOL Journal* 4, 11–13.

Wong, S. (2005) *Dialogic Approaches to TESOL: Where the Ginkgo Tree Grows.* New York: Taylor & Francis/Routledge (formerly Lawrence Erlbaum Associates, Inc.).

Wong, S., Berlin, L.N. and Nasser, I. (2008) Dialogue under occupation. *Language Policy* 7, 165–170.

Wong, S. and Motha, S. (2007) Multilingualism in post 9–11 U.S. schools: Implications for engaging empire. *Peace & Change: A Journal of Peace Research* 32 (1), 62–77.

World Bank (2006, September 7) West Bank and Gaza: Education sector analysis: Impressive achievements under harsh conditions and the way forward to consolidate a quality education system (Middle East and North Africa, Human Development Group).

World Bank Report (2006) The Palestinian Fiscal Crisis. On WWW at siteresources. worldbank.org/INTWESTBANKGAZA/.../PalestinianFiscalCrisis,Potential Remedies.pdf. Accessed 20.3.11.

Wrong, D.H. (1979) *Power: Its Forms, Bases, and Uses.* Oxford: Blackwell.

Yiftachel, O. (2006) *Ethnocracy: Land and Identity: Politics in Israel/Palestine.* Philadelphia: University of Pennsylvania Press.

Yona, Y. (2005) *In Virtue of Difference: The Multicultural Project in Israel.* Jerusalem: The Van-Leer Institute in Jerusalem and Ha-kibbutz Ha-Meuhad Publishers.

Yu, H. (2005). Edward Said, dispeller of delusions. *Amerasia Journal* 31, 67–70.

Yusuf, M.D. (1979) The potential impact of Palestinian education on a Palestinian state. *Journal of Palestinian Studies* 8 (4), 70–93.

Zizek, S. (1989) *Violence.* New York: Picador.

Zak, M. (2006) The role of language in situations of conflict. In D. Avnon (ed.) *Civic Tongue in Israel* (pp. 161–181). Jerusalem: Magnes Press (In Hebrew).

Zinn, H. (2001) *People's History of the United States 1492–Present.* New York: Harper Publishers Inc.

Zogby, J. (1998) The politics of exclusion. *Civil Rights Journal* 3, 42–48.

Zogby, J. (2010) *Arab Voices: What they are Saying to Us, and Why it Matters.* New York: Palgrave Macmillan.

Zreik, R. (2003) The Palestinian question: Themes of justice and power. *Journal of Palestinian Studies* 32, 39–49.

Index

For Product Safety Concerns and Information please contact our EU Authorised Representative:

Easy Access System Europe

Mustamäe tee 50

10621 Tallinn

Estonia

gpsr.requests@easproject.com